The Challenge of Authenticity
African Culture and Faith Commitment

Published by
Adonis & Abbey Publishers Ltd
P.O. Box 43418
London
SE11 4XZ
http://www.adonis-abbey.com

First Edition, January 2004

Copyright © Jacob Kofi Hevi

British Library Cataloguing-in-Publication Data
A catalogue record for this book is available from the British Library

ISBN 0-9545037-5-9

The moral right of the author has been asserted

All rights reserved. No part of this book may be reproduced, stored in a retrieval system or transmitted at any time or by any means without the prior permission of the publisher

Cover Design   Ifeanyi Adibe

Printed and bound in Great Britain by Lightning Source UK Ltd.

The Challenge of Authenticity
African Culture and Faith Commitment

By Dr. Jacob Kofi Hevi

Other Books by Adonis & Abbey include:

Broken Dreams (Fiction/Town Crier Series 1)
By Jideofor Adibe

Wooden Gongs and Drumbeats
 African Folktales, Proverbs and Idioms
(Fiction/Town Crier Series 2)
By Dahi Chris Onuchukwu

The Making of the Africa-Nation
Pan-Africanism and the African Renaissance
(politics/political economy/history)
Edited by Mammo Muchie

Nigeria and the Politics of Unreason
A Study of the Obasanjo Regime
(Politics/Political Economy
By Victor E. Dike

Table of Contents

Dedication — vii
Forward — viii
Acknowledgements — ix
General Introduction — xi

Reflection 1
The Call as Challenge of Authenticity — 23

Reflection II
Society Today as Challenge of Authenticity — 40

Reflection III
The Church Today as Challenge of Authenticity — 54

Reflection IV
Vocational Response as Challenge of Authenticity — 69

Reflection V
Pastoral Vocation as Challenge of Authenticity — 82

Reflection VI
Meaning of Prayer as Challenge of Authenticity — 98

Reflection VII
Praying as Challenge of Authenticity — 104

Reflection VIII
Faith as Challenge of Authenticity — 117

Reflection IX
Hope as Challenge of Authenticity — 135

Reflection X
Celibate Love as Challenge of Authenticity   165

Reflection XI
Fruits of Love as Challenge of Authenticity   184

General Conclusions   231

Suggested Further Reading   233

Index   235

DEDICATION

This book is dedicated to all who participated in the retreats, which constitute much of the material.

Foreword

The response to the Word of God demands the readiness to be at its service. But this service is not simply allowing oneself to be an instrument, but actively being the agent putting the word into action in the world. This means creatively activating the Spirit of God, the Spirit of the Word, within the culture, in the World, in individuals and in peoples at any time and place. This means the challenge to break through limiting structures of body and mind, and getting to the heart of persons, whatever be their stations in life. These structures may differ from place to place and from time to time. Thus every time or place has its peculiar challenges. So our contemporary African society also has its peculiar challenges, in relation to the indigenous African culture. For the Christian faith, the challenge is to activate the best within the indigenous culture of every people as integral part of universal human heritage. This book suggests how the challenges to faith commitment in general, and in an African socio-cultural context in particular could be converted into opportunities to make faith commitment a truly self-fulfilling vocation that will in turn create authentic discipleship.

Each reflection addresses an aspect of this challenge and recommends ways how one could convert it into opportunities for self-fulfilment.

November 2003

Acknowledgments

Many have contributed to the realisation of this book, among whom I would like to thank:

In the first place, Mr. Erich Hofmann, who has invested a lot of material resources and energy in the realisation of this book in particular, and my research in general. The final text is due to his expeditious and painstaking corrections and suggestions. I am grateful also to his wife, Mrs Erika Hofmann for her concern and generous hospitality. Without their support my research would have been impossible. May God continue to bless them.

Dr. Margaret Marquart for her material and spiritual support in a great way. May God continue to grant her abundant graces: good health and peace

The Seminarians of St. Peter's Regional Seminary, Cape Coast, Ghana, who invited me for the first retreat, and continued to encourage the publication of the series of reflections contained in this book.

The Sisters of the Infant Jesus, Cape Coast, especially the then Superior, Rev. Sister Agnes Cudjoe, S. I. J., who invited me to give the same reflections in an adapted form.

My Bishop, The Rt. Rev. Francis Lodonu of Ho (formerly Keta-Ho) Diocese, who appointed me to lecture at St. Peter's Regional Seminary.

My parents, the Late Joseph Hevi and Mary Kitsi, who had been a source of encouragement and love.

My brother, Vincent Yawovi Hevi, who, apart from his brotherly devotion, has contributed to the preparation of the manuscript. I am grateful to him and his wife for their constant encouragement.

Rev. Professor Andreas Resch, C.Ss.R. who has sustained his interest in my research.

Rev. Father Wynnand Amewowo for taking time to read through the manuscript and making useful suggestions.

Rev. Dr. Apollinaris Anyomi, for devoted brotherly services and for reading through the manuscript and making useful suggestions.

The Staff St. Peter's Regional Seminary, for their support in various ways during my lectureship there.

The Sisters of the Cross (Kreuzschwestern), especially the Province Superior, Rev. Sister Superior Theresia, consecutive House Superiors of "Liebfrauenhof", Voels, especially Rev. Sister Elisabeth Lan, and others, Verena Maria and Barbara, as well as fellow Sisters who provided me a home for several years, as my "family outside home". Without their material and spiritual support my research would have been impossible.

Rev. Father Clemens Ahiatrogah who offered me free board and lodging in Germany and remained my trusted brother. Special thanks also to his cousin, Cyriaque Sena Akakpo, for his invaluable assistance.

Mr. Kwame Assiamah, a computer specialist, who offered his time and resources generously for the preparation of this manuscript. I am also grateful to him, his wife and children for their hospitality.

Dr. Michael Oertl, the founder of the Minorities Association of Austria and Radiation Protection Specialist, who has supported me generously, both materially and spiritually.

Mr. Rupert Lechle, who has been a selfless source of support, both materially and spiritually, and also, together with his wife and children, provided much valued hospitality during my years in Austria.

General Introduction

Some years ago, 1982, to be exact, the Spiritual Director-to-be of St. Peter's Regional Seminary, in Cape Coast, Ghana, approached me to ask whether I could lead that year's retreat for candidates due for ordination as deacons and priests or pastors. In such matters I always felt, as I still feel today, insufficiently qualified. On the other hand, as a Christian, I knew, in spiritual matters, the Holy Spirit could always supplement one's limitations. So, though I had a human excuse, I could not get any Christian excuse to give. I felt this could be my vocation too, a call from God to re-examine my own life in the light of my vocation. "So, here I am. I shall let the Holy Spirit do the work while I remain a faithful instrument."

It was at that point that the ideas expressed in these reflections were born, or rather were given the grounds for birth.

Christian commitment within any human culture demands creatively activating the Spirit of God, the Spirit of the Word, within the culture, in the world, in individuals and in peoples at any time and place. In the process of activating the Spirit of God within the culture, the Christian faith should activate the best within the indigenous culture of its practitioners, parishioners and sympathisers.

Every human culture poses its peculiar challenges to the Christian faith in one form or another. The theme of this book is that the best elements of a typical indigenous African culture are openness, sincerity of spirit, spontaneity, in a word, authenticity. This is far different from superficial emotionalism, which foreign scholars and some of their African followers claim it to be. It is interesting to note that the same thing was said about the first Christians after the Pentecost event. Those who could not comprehend the new spirit of authenticity and joy thought they were drunk.

Thus the indigenous African spirit of authenticity poses a radical challenge to Christian faith commitment in the indigenous African community in relation to its various tenets and principles. This is because indigenous African authenticity demands that one practices what one claims to believe in, otherwise, dire consequences may follow. Thus the practice of the tenets and principles of indigenous African culture poses a challenge to the observance of similar tenets and principles of the Christian faith.

The Theme

How have I come by the theme for the series of reflections found in this book?

It is germane to acknowledge that the incipient ideas were given the impulse by the late Professor Bernard Häring, C.Ss.R., my academic and spiritual counsellor. He had been a deep admirer of indigenous African values and was the supervisor of my PhD dissertation, which was on: Indigenous Leadership Among Ewes of South-eastern Ghana as Moral Responsibility - Implications for Evangelisation, presented to Academia Alfonsiana, in Rome, 1980

This dissertation was a reflective commentary on the cardinal Christian virtues of Faith, Hope and Love, in the context of indigenous African Values.

I believe it will help readers understand the series of reflections better if I give some clarifications of how I came about the title of this book.

As I prepared to meet the first group of those to participate in the series of reflections, I chose as the theme: "The ministry and Self-fulfilment." This was because the group consisted of seminarians at St. Peter's Seminary, preparing for ordinations to the deaconate and the priesthood in the Catholic Church. But I later had a second thought about this because the group also included those who would still come back to complete their studies. I felt it would not be fair to limit our meditations to the Ministry in the field. After some debate in my own thoughts, I came to the word "Vocation", which, I thought, covered both formative and ministerial years of the apostolate. In the discussion with the group later about vocation, we realised that "vocation" could also refer to non-ecclesiastical choice of life. So we decided to qualify vocation with "pastoral", since "pastoral" refers, at least by convention, to specifically Christian leadership function. Thus we decided to devote two talks to vocational response, and vocation itself as self-fulfilment. The expression "self-fulfilment" is to indicate the fact that faith or vocation is not to be accepted and experienced as something externally imposed, without the involvement of the individual, especially as regards one's purpose in life. But rather the faith or vocation is to be experienced and expressed as the fulfilment of one's own purpose in life. Thus these meditations were to help candidates reflect on how they can find personal fulfilment in training or in the field of the apostolate.

Another development of the theme occurred when I had to give the same retreat to a group of priests already doing diverse forms of pastoral work. In this case I had to leave out aspects of the theme relating to training towards the apostolate. The theme however remained more or less Pastoral Vocation and Personal Fulfilment.

The theme was further developed when I had to give the same retreat to the Religious Sisters and Brothers. Since this group consisted of novices and those who had already taken their solemn vows, the theme reverted to the one meant for Seminarians. But the expression: "pastoral" did not fit well in this context, at least at that time, in the 1980s. So the topic came to be: Vocation and Personal Fulfilment, leaving out the qualifying expression: "pastoral".

Another development of the theme was necessary when I had to give the same retreat to the faithful, namely those who were not trained to perform any special functions as ecclesiastical officials, traditionally referred to as the laity.

This original idea was to stimulate reflection on how Christian vocation, like that of Deacons and Priests, especially in the Catholic Church, could be accepted by those concerned, as personally fulfilling.

The series of reflections and their implications for the Christian vocation sensitised the participants to the challenges of the indigenous African culture, as regards making the Christian faith meaningful for personal development, whatever be one's station in life.

For the preparation of the manuscript for this book the theme and the content underwent further transformation. The impulse came from an incident while teaching at St. Peter's Regional Seminary in Ghana. A missionary journalist, on a visit, had posed the question: "What is the greatest moral challenge of the Church in Africa?" I responded without hesitation: " Authenticity"

He appeared shocked, unbelieving. I thought he was shocked by the straightforward way I responded, without mincing words. But his second question, or rather retort, explained his surprise. He immediately remarked rather disappointingly: "But I had thought immorality and AIDS were the greatest problems facing Africa."
My response to that remark was: "I know why you are here; and I know what you mean. You want a Moral Theologian to confirm your stereotypes about African culture. But I am sorry, I have no time." He understood what I meant and left my room immediately in confusion.

My personal experience as a seminarian, later as a Catholic Priest and researcher in Europe had perhaps informed my instantaneous answer to the missionary journalist. I have read and heard so often such stereotyped questions as: "So in Africa you do not have morality?" "So you Africans have only emotions!" Some even theorise that the heat in Africa makes Africans or black people emotional.

However, in Africa, the questions are different. One is constantly confronted by such questions as: "After being anointed, are you allowed to eat food prepared by a woman?" "Can you also heal the sick by laying on of hands?" Often after ordination or profession the first counsel the family gives to the new priest or religious is: "Our son (or daughter), we are a simple family. Please keep to all your promises so that you do not disgrace the family." Some add: "If you cannot keep to the rules, resign in time, so that you do not bring any misfortune upon the family."

In fact this type of searching remark is not put to Catholic clerics or the religious only. In various forms and in various contexts, the same type of searching questions or remarks are often put to any person claiming any religious belief. I am sure that other ministers of religion, be they Christians, African Indigenous Religious believers, Hindus or Muslims would confirm this. For instance at the first Service for a new pastor of the Presbyterian Church sometime ago, a rather young pastor-colleague gave a brotherly counsel to the newly commissioned pastor:

My brother Pastor, if during the time of your commission you had thought you could behave like any other Christian in your congregation, then you have been deceiving yourself. Take this from me today, from this moment onwards, everybody will be watching your steps to see whether you truly believe and live according to what you preach.

He went on to add a personal experience. He said that at one time, some in his congregation were suspicious of his association with a certain lady in the church who was not his wife. Then he overheard someone remark behind his back: "For that Pastor, I cannot take the holy food from his hands. He is not worthy of the Gospel he preaches."

Personally I have always found these questions or remarks more challenging than embarrassing. This is because those who watch the servants of the Gospel closely do not necessarily expect that priests or pastors must be super-humans, capable of overcoming any temptation. The reality is far from this. Africans are usually more considerate than that and are often willing to make room for the fact that their pastors are also human beings, with human weaknesses.

This is borne out by another remark I overheard one day on a "mummy truck". As the truck was passing by a cemetery, a woman fellow traveller remarked: "Look at that grave there. That is the grave of one of our pastors. He committed suicide because he could not bear being accused of embezzling church money." Another woman added with a sigh: "They have been preaching to us to accept our weaknesses. But see what he has done to himself!"

On another occasion I was at a farewell Mass of a Catholic Parish Priest who was being transferred to another Parish. As usual, at the end of the Holy Mass, the parishioners came forward to thank him with gifts and shower him with praises for his hard work.

When it came to the turn of the priest to thank the parishes for their gifts and kind words, he surprised them by rejecting the gifts and the praises. His argument was that the gifts and praises were not out of sincere hearts because he knew that many among them were peddling rumours and serious false allegations against him. According to him, no one had confronted him personally. So he had had no opportunity to defend himself. After the Holy Mass the elderly members of the parish followed him to the parish house. In a very sad manner the leader of the group begged him to sit down so that the matter could be discussed. The Priest protested but the group managed to convince him to sit down. Probably what made him sit down finally was the remark of the eldest member in the group: "But Father, are you not the one who had been telling us to be patient in tribulation?"

He went on: "Our Lord Himself was falsely accused and eventually executed on false allegations. Why have you yourself been so impatient and angry, just after celebrating the sacrament of reconciliation and self-giving love?"

After a long discussion the parish priest agreed he had not, on that occasion, been a good example of one of his most famous homiletic themes.

Once more it is not a matter of simply being "holy" or not. It is rather a matter of being truthful to one's own counsel: turning the other cheek?

I had a similar experience at one of my out-stations when I was working in the parish. At this station I had conflicts with the catechist. Then he started spreading rumours. So I called a meeting of the "Church committee", and confronted the catechist about the rumours. He did not deny them, but he said he had been tempted to spread the rumours because others in the community had become very critical of his ways on account of my remarks.

Instead of accepting his apology patiently, I scolded him at length. Before I became aware of my own reaction some of those present were in tears. After I had stopped my scolding, the head

Christian stood up and said: "Oh, Father, so you can also be so angry!" Another said: "Father, remember what you have been telling us, that everyone should accept offences from others as his or her own cross." Then another added: "Father, we apologise for what the catechist has done. Do not let the sun go down with your anger". I understood at once that I had not been faithful to what I had been preaching.

What our people expect of their pastors is truthfulness, faithfulness, in a word authenticity.

The above incidents inspired the title of this book: The Challenge of Authenticity. This demand for authenticity is not reserved for religious leaders alone. It is a socio-cultural value embedded in African culture. In fact any one who openly confesses a belief in any principle is regarded as a living expression of that principle. If one's life does not sincerely conform to that principle, in other words, if one's life does not authentically express that principle in word or deed, others will openly remind him or her:

If you are an elderly person in the village and you become impatient with others, especially with the young ones, you may hear others remark: "Ametsitsi de doa dzi" This is an Ewe expression, meaning literally: "An elderly needs be patient" Or often people remind you through a proverb: "Devi megbleago de ata ta wotsoa he kpane o" This is an Ewe proverb meaning: "If a child soils your thigh you should not scrape it with a knife."

For those claiming to belong to a religious group, as ordinary members or leaders, the remark is variously:

"Are you not a Christian?"

Or, "Are you not a Moslem?"

Or "Are you not a Yewe believer" Or, "Are you not a Yewe Priest?"

Or "Are you not a Voodoo (Vudu) believer!" Or, "Are you not a Voodoo (Vudu) Priest?"

In my village, any Christian who openly hates a person is banned from receiving communion until he or she reconciles.

For this reason, I have chosen to put the response to the Word of God, the Gospel, in the particular context of indigenous African culture, a society with its demand for authenticity, or in a theological sense, faithfulness, with its peculiar challenges.

These thoughts are therefore to open the hearts and minds of those called to witness to the Word of God in a special way to the challenges as well as the opportunities, which make the meeting of these challenges a truly self-fulfilling vocation.

This is to challenge ourselves to view and experience our vocation, our response to the call of the Word of God, not as the loss of self-fulfilment to a foreign structure of the church, diocese, parish or community but an active participation in the fulfilment of the Spirit at work in individuals and relationships.

This means, as a prophetic endeavour, that the limiting structures need not be seen as obstructing self-fulfilment or authenticity, but should rather be seen as challenges and opportunities for self-fulfilment, to be what you are, to be authentic.

In this sense self-fulfilment is not being comfortable with the Word of God in time and place, but rather being at the service of the Word in time and place. This may demand going beyond the earthly meaning of human self-realisation to the ultimate self-realisation as spiritual experience. This is the challenge to meet the demands of the Spirit at any time or place.

To put it symbolically, I would say that just as overcoming obstacles or hurdles is sometimes a mark of good sportsmanship so also the overcoming of spiritual hurdles a mark of good spiritual self-fulfilment. To carry the metaphor further, just as one often hears remarks about an athlete or footballer: "this is true sportsmanship", one should also be able to remark of a Christian: "this is indeed a true Christian faith", "he/she is a sincere believer in Jesus Christ", "he/she is a true Christian", or "he/she is an authentic Christian."

The spiritual reflections in this book are meant to lead me and others to meet the challenges to the experience of the faith and ministry, in the light of the indigenous African culture, as self-fulfilment, a witness to authenticity. Theologically expressed, a witness to faithfulness to the Gospel of Jesus Christ. These reflections, as the name implies, should not just be read, but are thoughts to be reflected upon. That is, instead of the division into parts or chapters, I deem it more appropriate to divide the book into series of Reflections. Thus each reflection begins and ends with an appropriate biblical quotation.

For the same reason of keeping the spirit of retreat, I decided to eschew references, notes or citations. This is to avoid distracting the reader. Hopefully this will help the reader concentrate on the thoughts expressed and reflect along with the author.

Thus as text to be reflected upon as thoughts being delivered orally during a retreat, with the response or reaction of the audience in mind, the style remains basically oral narration. Some sentences are intentionally short, just a word or phrase. These are for emphasis. Others are long in order not to interrupt the train of reflection. So also some sentences are rhetorical questions, meant to stimulate a corresponding answer from those being addressed.

However the first two reflections are a little bit more formal and analytical as a sort of introduction to the study of vocation, meant for seminarians or other students requiring some analytical insight.

For the rest I wish and pray that the Spirit Himself make up for what is lacking, and guide the reader through the following pages.

The Plan of the Book

This book is made up of a General Introduction, eleven Reflections and a general Conclusion.

The Reflections deal with various tenets of the Christian faith and their implications.. The core tenets are: faith, hope and love.

The first Reflection deals with The Call as Challenge of Authenticity. This is a reflection on the challenge posed by indigenous beliefs relating to the radical nature of the call of the deity, which results in a radical transformation of the person called through possession, into a sort of a living image of the deity, in speech and behaviour, which has important implications for the devotee.

The second reflection situates the call as discipleship in the contemporary society, namely: Society Today as Challenge of Authenticity. This is a reflection on the challenge posed by indigenous African belief that social-moral evils are offences against the communal bond of solidarity, therefore, in a sense, a sacrilege, with dire consequences for the individual and society. Thus this second reflection is on how the African society today, with its political, social and economic crises, poses a challenge of credibility to the Christian claim of being the promoter of justice, peace and love and as the prophetic voice of the society.

The third reflection is on The Church Today as a Challenge of Authenticity. This deals with the challenge of beliefs relating to indigenous religious communities such as those of Vudu (Voodoo) or Yewe cults, which are also applied to the Christian churches or ecclesial communities in respect of structures and strict codes of conduct for leaders and members.

The fourth reflection intensifies the reflection on the church, dwelling on the sacral role of the church, performed by specifically chosen members. Thus the reflection moves on to Vocational Response as Challenge of Authenticity. This is a reflection on the challenge of authenticity of the response to the call of God as participation in the total self-giving sacrifice of Jesus Christ, in the context of the indigenous concept of the consecration of a human being to a spirit or cult, such as Yewe or Vudu (Voodoo).

The fifth reflection further develops the reflection on choice and response into the challenge the socio-political problems of the contemporary society and the church pose to the sacral function itself, namely, Pastoral Vocation as Challenge of Authenticity. This is a reflection on the challenge posed by indigenous African culture, which still identifies the functions of a religious official, mainly, with priestly or cultic function, or at least a spiritual function.

The sixth reflection further develops the reflection on the sacral function of religious officials to what actually this sacral function means to the people, with respect to an important aspect of this sacral function, namely, the Meaning of Prayer as Challenge of Authenticity. This is a reflection on the challenge posed by the fact that in the indigenous culture prayer and sacrifice remain the important media of contact with the supernatural (spiritual).

The seventh reflection intensifies the reflection on the meaning of the cultic function as reflection on the act itself, namely, Praying as Challenge of Authenticity. This is a reflection on the challenge posed by the specifically indigenous mode of praying as one of the dimensions of life, which demonstrates typically indigenous African authenticity through spontaneity.

The eighth reflection moves from the reflection on the sacral function of religion to the specific pillars of the Christian belief, namely, faith, hope and love. Thus this eighth reflection begins with Faith as Challenge of Authenticity. This is a reflection on the challenges posed by indigenous African religious beliefs such as commitment to external acts of cult and certain moral norms, the disregard of which could have dire consequences.

The ninth reflection moves logically to an important element of faith, namely, Hope As Challenge of Authenticity. This is a reflection on the indigenous commitment to hope through the sincerity of spirit expressed in such spontaneous outbursts of enthusiasm as music and dance, as a challenge to the claim that Christianity is a religion of hope of the resurrection.

The tenth and eleventh reflections naturally move the reflections on to love, the most dynamic and practical dimension of the Christian faith with deep socio-ethical connotation. Thus the tenth reflection is on love, especially as expressed in the Catholic Church, as an element of the spirituality of those performing special functions in the church, namely, Celibate Love as Challenge Of Authenticity. This is a reflection on the challenges posed by the similar commitment of indigenous devotees, as a sign of total consecration to the deity, the disregard of which incurs dire consequences. This looks at the challenges of celibate love as the authentic spirit of inner freedom to consecrate one's total life to self-giving love for all, at all times.

The eleventh reflection concludes with Fruits of Love as Challenge of Authenticity. This is a reflection on the implications of the indigenous community as a mystical (spiritual) communion, making an offence against individuals, such as hatred, jealousy, rudeness, and destructive words an offence against the spirit of the individual and the spirit of the communal solidarity, in a sense a sacrilege. This is a challenge to prove the authenticity of the Christian communal solidarity as a covenant of love, based on the fruits of love stated in 1Cor.13: 4-7.

Reflection I

The Call as Challenge of Authenticity

Opening Verse: Rom. 8: 28-30

We know that in all things God works for good with those who love him, those whom he has called according to his purpose. Those whom God had already chosen he also sets apart to become like his Son, so that the Son would be the first among many brothers. And so those whom God set apart he called; and those he called, he put right with himself, and he shared his glory with them.

    Before anything else, let us find out the meaning of the theme for this first reflection.

    What is the "Call"? In the ordinary, superficial sense, the word: "call" is a simple word people use to describe how an individual draws the attention of the others. For instance one could say: "The mother calls her child." The expression can also describe a polite way one person gets into communication with another. For instance one could say: "He called Kodzo at the office."

    The word: "call" can also be used in a technical sense to describe how someone is officially commissioned, or recognised, to perform certain professional duties. For instance one could say: "Mr. Mensah is called to the bar".

    But the word can be used in a deeper sense to describe how an individual is motivated towards a particular way of life or profession, or the way of life or profession itself. For instance one could say: "He feels a call to be a carpenter". Or "It is a woman's call to be a mother". Thus in a dynamic sense the "call" refers to both the "the motivation", the "being drawn" to a particular way of life or profession, as well as the positive reaction, the acceptance, or answer to the motivation or the experience of being drawn towards the particular way of life or profession. Thus it would be right both to say: "Kofi has a call to be a fitter", and "Fitting is Kofi's call."

Normally, in the latter, technical sense the term used for the "call" derives directly from its Latin root verb: "vocare", meaning, "to call", and the noun: "vocatio", meaning a "call". From this Latin noun is derived the technical term for the call: "vocation". Vocation is defined by the Concise English Dictionary, as: "A call, or sense of fitness for, and obligation to follow a particular career" (1988: 2055: S.V. "vocation").

In a religious sense the expression is deeper and more dynamic than the ordinary or technical usage. As the same dictionary defines it, in a religious or spiritual sense "vocation" is: "a divine call or spiritual injunction, or guidance to undertake a duty, an occupation etc."

In the ordinary, technical or religious (spiritual) sense a "call" involves, directly or indirectly, three important elements, often culturally specific. These are identity, relationship and errand-duty.

A call as Identity

To call someone is to acknowledge his or her identity, status or function in the society. This is usually in accordance with the socio-cultural norm or custom, often referred to as etiquette. In its ordinary, simple form, to call a person is to grant the person an identity, in other words, a name. This name distinguishes one person from another, and makes the person you call understand that he or she is the one you are calling. In a general sense, to call is to address another person by name. In some indigenous African cultures the basic identity is the birthday name. For instance a mother may call the son: "Kofi", "Komla" or "Afua" etc. When the relationship between the person calling and the person being called is unequal, or when the person being called has acquired extra elements of identity, in the context of the family relationship, status or function in the community, cultural convention, or etiquette, demands that this "extra" element of identity be acknowledged. In indigenous African culture, generally, a call must acknowledge the type of family relationship as prefix to birthday or surname. For instance to address a brother or sister, you must prefix "Novi-" (an expression in Ewe in West Africa) or "Onua-" (an expression in Akan, also in West Africa). Thus, for instance, if you want to call your brother or sister, you need to address him or her: "Novi-Kofi" or "Novi-Afua". Further, custom demands that you distinguish a younger from an elder sister or brother with the appropriate prefix.

In the same way, to call a member of your family you need to address the person by a family or kinship relational title, usually alone or as prefix, such as "Father" or "Grandfather", "Mother" or "Grandmother", "Uncle", "Aunt" etc. In the same way cultural convention demands that to call a person with special status in the society you need to address the person by his or her title, alone or as prefix. So for instance to call a King you need to address him by: "Fia" or "Togbe" in Ewe or "Ohene" or "Nana" in Akan. Of course this is only a general presupposition. Within every culture there are instances of confusion, since more than one person may bear the same name or title. As it is often said in Ghana, there is "Mensah" in every office. But culture has devised various combinations of names and titles to distinguish one person from another. This is a way in which culture grants each individual his or her own uniqueness.

Thus a simple "call" already identifies an individual, who, by the virtue of the "call", is no longer simply part of a mass. The call grants each an individual existence. A call makes you out of the crowd. This demands that you also, in your turn, react to this identity. This leads to the second element: relationship.

A Call as Relationship

In a sense every call is an offer of relationship, which the person being called needs to acknowledge in turn. Unless you ignore the offer of relationship by not reacting at all to the call, by reacting to it in one way or another, you establish a relationship, either positive or negative. However by reacting, especially positively, by answering or responding to the call, you acknowledge communication between you and the person calling. As long as you choose to respond, you cannot, as it were, go on your own way anymore. Thus a simple call stimulates some movement within you, which influences your attitude. You could no longer behave as if you were not concerned. You need to turn and look at the person calling, or even retrace your steps to meet him or her. In a sense, whether you accept it or not, the person who calls "gets in your way", if not "in your life", as it is often said. Sometimes a simple call, even a telephone call, may demand that you reorder your priorities altogether. This leads to the third element, errand-duty.

A Call as Errand-duty

A call implies an errand-duty. A call implies a new responsibility, duty or function. Your primary reaction to a call implies already the need to perform an act, a function. For instance to answer your mother's call implies you have to run to her, and listen to her as she tells you why she has called you. The reason for such a "call" is often to send you on an errand, or to perform one or the other duty or function. You can refuse to go on the errand. But then you know you have to face the consequences of your refusal. Thus, however simple the nature of the call, a call is always potent with consequences in one way or another. As long as you hear the call, you cannot remain indifferent. You need an inner reaction accordingly. In a sense every reaction to a call, however simple, involves a form of commitment to the "errand-duty" involved. In fact to ignore a call is in itself a reaction, which has consequences in one way or the other.

All these elements of a call: identity, relationship and errand-duty are involved in a more intense way in a "call" in the religious or spiritual sense of a "vocation". By the call the divinity or spirit grants and acknowledges your identity. The call grants you uniqueness. By the call you are made aware that you have an individual identity, no longer just a human being among human beings. You have a name. This elicits a reaction, an answer, and a response. Just as the call grants you an identity and makes you a unique person, you also need to react accordingly with a unique response, a personal answer. This is logical. If you accept a call as a personal address to you, then you are also requested to give a personal answer to the call accordingly.

This personal response begins a relationship between you and the one who calls. In the religious or spiritual sense, a call is an invitation to enter a relationship. For instance, even in an ordinary sense, if your mother calls and you answer, it means you acknowledge that she is your mother, and that she is right to call you. So also, in a deeper sense, when you react to a divine call, it implies you acknowledge that the divinity has the right to call you, to demand your attention. This relationship begins your new direction in life. You have to find out why the divinity is calling you. Thus the relationship leads to your errand-duty.

As the dictionary defines it, and as cited earlier, vocation, in a religious or spiritual sense, means "divine call or spiritual injunction or guidance to undertake a duty, occupation etc.". Just as any call, a divine call is always a call to action, to undertake an errand for the deity. Up to this day, many are called by God to be at the service of His Word. Just as any call, a divine call often means turning around to listen to why you are called, and be given your errand-duty, which often means a new direction in life. This new direction in life is often irresistible. Some do ignore the call or refuse the errand-duty. But they suffer the consequences for ignoring or refusing to react to the call. For instance, Jonah refused to go to preach conversion in Nineveh. But for this refusal he landed in the belly of a whale. In the long run, he had to go all the same, anyway. If you accept the call you have to accept guidance too. You receive direction for what one would term your new errand-duty.
Depending on the context a call involves all these three elements: identity, relationship and errand-duty, with degrees of drama.

In the experience and reaction or response to the call of the Word as Christians, the authenticity depends on how far we sincerely, innerly, experience the three elements of the call, and how far this inner experience is truly actualised in our attitude and behaviour. This is the challenge posed by our indigenous culture.

In the indigenous African culture, at least generally, all the three elements are involved in the call in a most dramatic way.

The transformation of identity

In the indigenous African religion those called may be at first normal people: farmers, housewives, traders, teachers or any other person. The call may take several forms. It may be sudden and dramatic. Someone may be going about his or her normal daily work, then at the work place a sudden force seizes him or her, throwing him or her onto the ground. The person begins to behave "abnormally", running around or speaking a strange language.

Often the spirit, which seizes the person, be it the Vudu (Voodoo), Yewe or ancestor, so the people believe, guides him or her to an official of that religious group who identifies the condition of the person as a sign of a call, a possession by one or the other spirit or ancestor. After initial rituals to calm down the person the family is informed. Then begins the initiation rites. From that time onwards the individual's personality takes on a radical transformation, even physically. In a sense, the candidate takes on the living image of the spirit, which the people believe acts and speaks through the candidate. It is often said that the one possessed "speaks the spirit". Thus the call (possession) transforms the individual into a sort of a living image of the spirit, in speech and behaviour, as if the deity or spirit itself were speaking or acting through the one called. The person may fall into a deep trance, make strange movements or prophesy. For those versed in such matters, the speech and behaviour indicate the identity of the spirit, which the candidate now takes on. Thus from observation the indigenous religious experts can discern the exact spirit possessing the person. They can even make out the name, if the possessed does not reveal it, which often happens. For as the image of the spirit, the possessed may speak out the words of the spirit in the first person: "I, the spirit so and so, or the ancestor so and so..."

According to the belief of the people, at least some indigenous African peoples in West Africa, the Almighty God is so calm that He does not normally seize people in such a violent way. The Almighty God rather calls individuals in a most silent way. It may be in a dream, or through any other non-dramatic sign. In fact those who are called by the Almighty God are very few since He does not need any function performed for Him unlike those called by the spirits or ancestors directly, such as offering sacrifices.

In any case the spirits may also call a candidate in less dramatic ways than the one just described. This may take several forms. A person may suddenly feel indisposed. Sometimes he or she may struggle to go about his or her normal duty. But the condition may remain unchanged. The relatives or the person in whom the candidate confides may advise that he or she seek help from a religious official. This official is often also a diviner (others call such a person variously: fortune-teller_or soothsayer). The expert may recognise at once that the condition of the candidate is a sign of a call from one spirit or the other. Thus, though less dramatic, the candidate in this hypothetical situation also goes through the same transformation.

The dramatic transformation of identity also involves external appearance. The candidate may be made to be bare-chested, there could be marks on his/her body, the hair could be shaven and he or she may have to wear special cowry beads and white clothes.

Whatever the case may be the indigenous people believe that such a call cannot be ignored without dire consequences. However if the person or the family feels strongly against the supernatural call and the respective rituals for initiation, the person may request to be set free through a ritual pacification of the spirit. Or if the person is, for instance, a Christian, he or she can be set free through exorcism.

But if the person accepts the call then he or she has to abide by the moral code of behaviour. Thus Africans believe that if the call and response are authentic, then dire consequences will follow if the one called (possessed) ignores the demands of the spirit.

Some may dismiss spirit possession, or such a supernatural call, as charlatanism. Others may claim the candidates may be under drugs. Or still others may give rational reasons, such as hypnotism, or simply unrestrained emotional outburst of pent-up feelings.

However one may want to interpret the fact remains that the indigenous people concerned believe in such a supernatural call. They believe in the transformation of identity. They also believe dire consequences follow the disregard of the call. For the latter they have lots of proofs from personal experiences, the experiences of others and the history of certain families, lineages or whole communities.

Thus rational arguments notwithstanding, the indigenous people still have these beliefs. These beliefs are part of the indigenous culture. The important fact is that as long as the Christian faith is situated in this indigenous society, with this indigenous culture, the indigenous people, including indigenous Christians, judge the authenticity of the Christian faith according to the indigenous background of these beliefs.

This indigenous belief is the great challenge of authenticity for the Christian, who believes to have been, or is regarded as called by God or Our Lord Jesus Christ.

Do Christians also truly undergo and experience the transformation of identity? Does the person converting from indigenous religion to Christianity experience such transformation? Do the baptised truly experience being born anew? Do those confirmed experience being filled and strengthened by the Holy Spirit? Do confirmed Christians truly experience the possession of the Spirit of God or the Spirit of Christ?

In the crowded business of daily life, are you aware that God or Christ is calling you at all?

Do you listen to the promptings of the Spirit?

Are you aware of the Spirit of God possessing you?

As a Christian, what is the name with which God or Christ calls you? Do you pay attention to the call at all?

If the Almighty calls you "son" or "daughter", what does that mean?

Or are you a Christian without being aware of being called at all to be "devotee" of the Almighty God?

It may be that you just happen to be a Christian. May be your grandparents were Christians, so also your parents. Your parents in turn just had you baptised by the pastor or parish priest or deacon. So for you your Christian faith is simply a matter of "inheritance". It involves no personal call, no personal commitment.

But can that faith stand the challenge of any test in life? Can this "non-committed" and "non-committing" faith face the challenge of authenticity?

If you are a Christian without any personal call, this is the time to reflect, listen and act accordingly.

There are too many problems in life to leave such an important life experience as your Christian faith simply to "chance". It is true that it is not everyone that must be "possessed" by the Spirit and get into trance in a dramatic way, like the prospective devotee of Vudu (Voodoo) we discussed above, or like St. Paul, who is struck to fall from his horse. But I believe, even if you have been baptised as a baby, at an early stage of your development, you require some form of an experience of a divine call. This needs moments of reflection- listening with your mind and your heart.

This is an important challenge of authenticity of faith as a call.

This is important for our reflections on prophetic vocation, prayer and meditation, as we shall see later.

Let us now consider specifically the divine calling to be pastors, religious ministers or ministers of the divine Word. Do seminarians truly experience a call to train for the ministry? Do Novices truly experience the call from God or Christ to undergo transformation to become religious? Do Christians have true inner experience of the call of God?

The Christian may not be expected to have a dramatic experience of the divine call as the indigenous candidates. But the challenge of whether the Christian call is authentic or not remains valid.

It is a challenge for the Christian to demonstrate inner conviction of the call and response in their behaviour, for the confirmation of the call and response as being authentic.

Relationship-Discipleship

From what I have already stated in the introduction above, in the theological or Christian religious sense, vocation refers to active response to the call of God, in the service of the Word of God or in training for this service.

For those who are still to train in response to this call of God, vocation is simply a continuous self-examination in the light of one's call. This means physical, psychological and spiritual orientation towards more and more conformity with the demands of this call. As we shall see later in our reflection on the response to pastoral vocation, training involves continuous discernment. This demands making out opportunities. These opportunities are signs, which constitute divine call in various situations. All these attitudes should make you decide here and now, from the depths of your heart. Active experience of the call is to experience the power of the Spirit as guidance, to integrate all your experiences, failures and successes, sadness and joy, into your striving for the clear goal before you.

All along the important prerequisite for finding fulfilment in your life, at each stage of your formation, or the development of your spiritual life thereafter, is being true to yourself, to be authentic in your response.

In this test of authenticity, the only true "lie-detector" is the heart. The challenge of authenticity is a matter of self-examination, the examination of the heart.

The indigenous belief is a great challenge of authenticity for the Christian, who believes he or she is called, or is regarded as called by God.

Let us now come to the second part of our theme. We have already seen that a call demands a reaction, one way or the other. How do we, or can we find self-fulfilment in training or in the field of ministry? How do we face the challenge of authenticity in training for the ministry? How can we experience our training as reaction to the call of God?

As psychologists would say, personal fulfilment is simply the realisation of oneself, one's purpose in life as a person. Some personality psychologists would argue that self-realisation is auto-determination. This means to be free to determine oneself, to become what one innately desires to become. That is, one's aim in life has to conform to one's inner aspirations. In a word, psychological health is the resolution of the conflict between what one wants to become and what one actually is. Therefore a healthy personality is being true to the inner self. And being true to the inner self, when manifested in one's behaviour, is being true to oneself, therefore being authentic. It is the realisation of oneself as an individual, yet in the community. It is the purpose of one's existence for which one makes a choice at a particular moment, but to be realised later through whatever one does.

In a related sense, personal fulfilment also means the growth of the personality to its fullness. Therefore one of our objectives in these meditations will be to reflect on whatever we are doing, or going to do, as those being called or are already called to minister to the Word of God to others. The challenge of authenticity is to find out whether we actually fulfil our purpose of existence, and how we can make our life fulfil this purpose. It is a reflection on how we can make the response to the divine call (vocation or the daily living out of this call) contribute to the fullness of our personality, with dignity and freedom. Facing the challenge of authenticity in this sense is to continue examining our struggle to become better Christians. This means in effect striving to become more and more human, in the image of God, in the image of the Son, who became like us "in everything, except sin." It is a spiritual journey towards becoming fully mature; with the fullness of Christ himself, who was an authentic human, and an authentic divine being (Eph. 4:13).

Teacher - Pupil Relationship

What if the call involves a teacher – pupil relationship? This will require our reflecting on the role of formal formation in our confrontation of the challenge of authenticity

As we have already seen, a call demands a reaction. It demands a turning around to face the person calling. It means running to the person calling for guidance. This guidance embodies the errand-duty to be performed and a relationship between the person calling and the person called. Since the person receiving the call needs instruction for the errand-duty, the relationship has a pattern. It is a relationship between the teacher and the pupil, the master and the disciple. It is true that those concerned believe that the deity or the spirit calling the individual gives direct instructions. That is also the belief of indigenous African religion. But it is understandable that the deity, the spirit, or the ancestor himself or herself cannot be directly involved in the earthly affairs of prospective devotees. Accordingly this role of a teacher or instructor is often delegated to an earthly spiritual master.

In every religion this relationship exists in one form or another. In certain religions, and in certain cases, the relationship is loose, less formal; in others the relationship is strictly formal.

As we have already seen, among indigenous African religions, especially such organised ones as the Yewe and Vudu, (Voodoo) candidates are taken out of normal society and put into an enclosure. In this seclusion of the enclosure, freed from earthly cares, candidates undergo instructions with strict moral code of behaviour.

We may not claim to know about everything that goes on within those fences or walls. But we can have some idea by observation. At least one thing is clear. Those who come from time to time out of the enclosure for one reason or another observe strict moral code of behaviour. Once more it is clear that the instructions that go on behind those fences or walls transform the identity of those called or possessed into something new, a new personality. May we dare to say, they even become new, "moral persons". Or, at least, that is the belief of the indigenous people who observe them. They become the living image of the One who calls them. It is true there are cases of abuse. It is also true there are cases of selfish spiritual masters who exploit devotees. But from observation they are true to their own call. According to their own religious belief, they are authentic. The indigenous spiritual masters impart something more than knowledge. They impart a way of life. That is the challenge to our Christian call. That is the challenge to the Christian formation of those called. That is the challenge of authenticity.

How do institutions for formal formation of Christian churches face this challenge? How do we sincerely assess the formation of those called by God in our Christian churches?

In Africa, given the conditions of pastoral work, and the meagre means at their disposal, many energetic young men and women offer selfless devotion to the apostolate among our people. The Lord says: "You would know them by their fruits". Therefore it has to be acknowledged that rectors, novice mistresses or novice masters, lecturers, formators, administrators, as well as those under formation are offering their best, going to great lengths in making sacrifices. Certainly judged by the fruits, one could confirm that the best is being offered behind those walls of seminaries, convents and other formation centres.

However, especially in relation to the challenge of authenticity posed by the indigenous African culture and the political, social, and economic situations on the ground, those of us concerned need to admit that something does not fit well, and something ought to be done.

If it is admitted that the Christian vocation is in crisis in other societies, and as long as we now live in a global village, we have to learn from the experiences of other societies, and do some stocktaking before the situation breaks upon us too. The history of the church in societies in crisis now needs be our lesson.

It is in this spirit of sincerity that we need to make the following reflections:

Well. We have to admit that our vocation is in crisis. We have to admit that the call and the formal formation of those called face a crisis of authenticity.

Why?

As many who leave (these include those leaving the church or the Christian faith), or stay often say (quoting an ex-priest theologian): "I was just arrogant, opinionated talking machine". This implies he had been simply a manipulated ecclesiastical robot.

In this case, this personal and journalistic assessment of the situation can be regarded also as the thoughts of, not only seminarians, who were participating in the original retreats, but also in the case of anyone reading this book, a Christian in a general sense. Or this self-examination is also for any one, even non-Christians concerned with the way the Christian call affects our indigenous African society. Then by our commitment to the life and faith of the Disciples of the Lord Jesus Christ, we are all in effect heirs of the Pentecost event. Accordingly, crisis in clerical or religious vocation is necessarily also a crisis in the Christian vocation in general.

This is obvious from the statement of the "ex-Priest": For, how could an "arrogant, opinionated talking machine" communicate the Word of love of a Saviour, who suffered the most humiliating death in his time on earth. How could an "arrogant opinionated talking machine" take on the identity of the saviour accepting the most humiliating death on the cross? Can such a person communicate the message of this cross effectively without communicating his or her own "arrogance" to those whom he or she has to serve with this Word?

In short, putting this self-examination in the context of our reflection, how is our faith commitment a commitment to authenticity? Faith commitment is not simply being a "talking machine", but the word you deliver has to be your authentic self, your inmost being, being what you are yourself within your inmost heart.

We know formal formation is to give candidates formal guidance. This formal guidance is to clarify the call, to sharpen the reaction to the call, to promote the relationship between God who calls and the candidate receiving the call, and of course to clarify and give the impulse towards the errand-duty

Every lecturer makes the effort to make lectures as "normal" as possible. Every course given is meant to provide the knowledge in preparation for life. Lecturers in the seminary especially strive to impress upon seminarians that their studies are to prepare them for their ministry. So the courses are for their reflection, rather than purely as academic exercises. However, often classroom teaching remains an intellectual exercise rather than spiritual formation. Although knowledge is meant to prepare students for life, the desire to get the "stuff" for passing examinations does not leave enough room for reflection.

For instance students, or rather seminarians, who were in my class at St. Peter's Regional Seminary, in Cape Coast, Ghana, in the eighties, would still remember our course on vocation or vows. Now that I can reflect on those lectures, I have to ask myself searching questions. Were the courses on vocation or the Christian call actually an impulse for reflection on the vocation or the call of God? Or they remained "the stuff for examination"?

Did I impart a way of life, or simply knowledge, maybe simply "interesting ideas" about vocation and vows?

I hope those former students who happen to read this book would do their own spiritual stocktaking as they reflect on the thoughts expressed in this book.

These reflections would therefore be a more relaxed internalisation of important points touched upon in class.

It is a common experience that a community in crisis reflects the crisis of the pastor's vocation (although admittedly not in every case).

For those still going to be in training, the question is: "How can I find fulfilment by being true to myself, by being authentic, in a life ruled by the will of others, members of staff, Parish Priests, Bishops etc.?

How can I find fulfilment in rules imposed on me?
For fellow Christians the question is similar. How can I find fulfilment by commitment to authenticity in my faith as a Christian, when the Spirit seems to speak with divergent, sometimes even contradicting, tongues? The Pope says one thing. The following minute the Bishop or Bishops say another. And still further the Parish Priest interprets the same word differently. Not to mention the catechist or teacher who has to communicate it finally to the individual faithful?

The challenging question is: If my faith is, or rather should be, commitment to authenticity, what then is the authentic faith today?

It is my hope, after reading through this book, or rather after sharing in the reflections so far, that those who have doubts whether they are truly called or not will at least re-examine themselves. For those already certain of their call, I hope this meditation will further strengthen their confidence in themselves and their resolve still to strive further.

May the Lord send down His Spirit upon you, to enlighten you through these reflections so that you may find fulfilment in your choice of life, a commitment to authenticity, a life of faithfulness.

Let us end this first reflection with 1 Tim. 3: 1-9.

The saying is sure: If any person aspires to the office of bishop, he desires a noble task. Now a bishop must be above reproach, the husband of one wife, temperate, sensible, dignified, hospitable, an apt teacher, no drunkard, not violent, but gentle, not quarrelsome, and no lover of money.
He must manage his own household well, keeping his children submissive and respectful in every way; for if a man does not know how to manage his own household, how can he care for

God's church. He must not be a recent convert, or he may be puffed up with conceit and fall into the condemnation of the devil; moreover he must be well thought of by outsiders, or he may fall into reproach and the snare of the devil.
Deacons likewise must be serious, not double-tongued, not addicted to too much wine, not greedy for gain; they must hold the mystery of the faith with a clear conscience.

Now, after reflecting on the Christian call, or vocation, as commitment to authenticity, which is rather personal, our next reflection will put this vocation in the context of the society, with its challenges.

Reflection II

Society Today as Challenge of Authenticity

Introductory Verse: Rom. 1: 18-23, 28-32

For the wrath of God is revealed from heaven against all ungodliness and wickedness of men, who by their wickedness suppress the truth. For what can be known about God is plain to them, because God has shown it to them. Ever since the creation of the world his invisible nature, namely, his eternal power and deity has been clearly perceived in the things that have been made. So they are without excuse; for although they knew God they did not honour him as God or give thanks to him, but they became futile in their thinking and their senseless minds were darkened. Claiming to be wise, they became fools, and exchanged the glory of the immortal God for images resembling mortal man or birds or animals or reptiles ...
And since they did not see fit to acknowledge God, God gave them up to a base mind and to improper conduct. They were filled with all manner of wickedness, evil, covetousness, malice. Full of envy, murder, strife, deceit, malignity, they are gossipers, slanderers, haters of God, insolent, haughty, boastful, inventors of evil, disobedient to parents, foolish, faithless, heartless, ruthless. Though they know God's decree that those who do such things deserve to die, they not only do them but also approve those who practice them.

In the first reflection above, we reflected on the call. We reflected on what a divine call or vocation implies, in relation to personal fulfilment through commitment to authenticity. In my opinion, before you can find personal fulfilment in a situation, you have to know the situation, in order to be aware of the forces at work, opposing pressures - intellectual, political, spiritual etc. in the society in general and in the Church or Christian communities in particular. In this second reflection we shall reflect on the society as the context of our Christian call.

Many readers might have heard about, or dealt with social problems as students, teachers, social workers or counsellors. Social problems are common to every society. But to be faithful to our topic, or rather, our theme as explained in our introduction, we shall dwell more on situations in traditional African societies.

Thus our second reflection is on the theme: Society Today as Challenge of authenticity. The crucial question is: How can we find fulfilment in it, or in spite of it, through authenticity of faith commitment?

Indigenous Africans believe social and moral evils are offences against the communal bond of solidarity, therefore, in a sense, a sacrilege. Accordingly the indigenous Africans, in general, believe social and moral evils have dire consequences for individuals and society.

As an elder once put it:
You school people do not want to get children any more. So you talk of family planning and abortion. Why are you then complaining of hunger in Africa? Do you not know that mother earth is also planning her family and aborting her children?

The African society today, with its political, social and economic crises, has made fellow citizens hopeless and faithless. This situation poses a challenge of credibility to the Christian claim to justice, peace and love, especially as the prophetic voice of the society.

What then is our Christian call, our Christian vocation in this crisis society? How do we face the challenge of authenticity within this society in crisis?

As we have already seen in our introduction and first reflection above, in the indigenous African religion a call from the deity or spirit is a radical transformation of the person called. This radical transformation involves moral transformation, which entails also attitudes towards the community or society. This is because, as it is often said, in the indigenous African culture, life is integral existence. Life is not divided into separate compartments. Religion is at the service of society and the individual, so also society and the individual are at the service of religion.

For instance in a typical indigenous African community, when there are social problems such as hunger, disease, violence, theft and deviance, the people turn to religion. Sometimes a member of the community may get into trance and reveal that social evils are caused by immorality within the society resulting from laxity in the observance of the moral code of the spirit or spirits as well as that of the ancestors. Then follows a call to repentance, and ritual cleansing of the community, then by sacrificial offer for the moral lapses.

Often the person getting into trance reveals the divine injunction as a call for repentance and avoidance of certain social evils, which may have become especially rampant in the society. Following this injunction certain rituals are organised by which certain social evils are said to be under ban. These evils may include abortion, stealing, sometimes even adultery and incest. During such a ritual the penalty for each offence is also stated. This ritual is then communicated to the assembly of the whole community. Since the people believe the breaking of the ban on any of the "banned" offences causes misfortune, not only for the culprit, but the whole society, every individual is on the watch out to report such lapses, to forestall any calamity.

Just as religion concerns itself with social affairs, so does the society and its members also concern themselves with religious affairs. Sometimes a particular spirit or its devotees are believed to indulge in antisocial practices. In such an instance the priest or priestess is put under ban and the shrine set on fire.

Against this indigenous religious background, it is understandable that even Christians turn to God or Christ in times of social crisis. This explains the reason why intentions for which the faithful, especially in the Catholic Church offer stipends for Holy Masses include mostly the solution of personal and social problems such as bareness, hunger, poverty and other misfortunes or catastrophes.

This is because, somehow, though those offering the stipends are Christians, they still believe that the problems result from offences against God.

This indigenous belief is a great challenge of authenticity for the Christian who believes that he or she is called or is regarded as called by God to follow Christ as the prophetic voice or the conscience of the society.

But what type of society does God call us to serve as the living conscience and prophetic voice?

This brings us to a reflection on the actual African society today, in 2003.

What is our African society today in relation to personal fulfilment through commitment to authenticity?

How do you live today to find fulfilment in your life as a Christian? How do you find satisfaction in your life in being true to yourself in this society?

Since politics affects all aspects of human life, let us begin with the political situation. Let us find out how the political situation in Africa affects our view of authenticity and personal fulfilment.

When you turn on the radio or television, you hear nothing but the same type of saddening news - threats of war (even nuclear war or "weapons of mass destruction"), invasion and threats of invasion, condemnations and vetoes at the United Nations. We have had Argentina on the Falklands Island and counter invasion by Britain. Now it is an Arab on suicide bombing trip in Israel, another day it is Israeli planes bombarding Palestinian homes.

We have had Iran against Iraq (or vice versa); then Iraq invading Kuwait.

Now the news replays itself in form. One day it is a coalition against Iraq I, then a coalition against Iraq II.

It seems the news items never change in form, but maybe, only in content. The types and forms of the news items seem to survive the decades, if not the centuries, of international meetings, conferences and agreements on justice and peace. Every country or every political leader seems to have "moral grounds" for "breaking the agreement." It may be in the "name of God" or "in the name of Allah", or even "in the name of Jesus Christ."

You begin to ask yourself: Is it really worthwhile? Are you really true to yourself to continue preaching about the love of enemies, justice and peace, when those who send missionaries to evangelise us are themselves the ones perpetuating or conniving at these atrocities?

You begin to question your choice of religious affiliation, or the choice of your vocation. Sometimes you are really at a loss to find the right answers when your friends question your reasons for becoming a Christian. This is because the friends or relatives, who may never have been Christians or have "left the church" and become "born-again" indigenous African religious believers, imply you are only tools for others for their political and economic motives against African interests.

Coming to our own society, African society, it seems that a sort of "domino theory" is at work. One time it is civil war and humanitarian invasion in Somalia, another time it is Uganda, then Sierra Leone, Liberia, Congo, Sudan and so on and so forth. Even as I write there may be one or more countries "joining the line" or waiting for their turn. For the gory news from Rwanda, one can only hope it does not repeat itself anywhere anymore.

Almost each country in Africa has its story of human catastrophes to tell. Almost everyone commenting on social and moral problems in Africa bemoans political corruption. The problem in this case is that it is often the corrupt political leaders that also shout the loudest against corruption and vow to "eradicate" it from the society. So in the long run it seems no one admits to being the culprit. Everyone seems to be, or claims to be, the victim or a vehement critic of "the system". Who then is to convert and stop being corrupt, or being corrupted by, the others? Is it the system? If so, then our social problems have become the academic problem of sociologists. Who or what is responsible? Is it the agent or the structure (or vice versa)?

This is the challenge for Christian leaders as well as for other leaders in the society. It is a challenge to examine our call to discipleship, our role, our faith, our conscience.

Remember that at baptism you have been anointed a king, a prophet, and a priest. Corruption is a call to you and me to put our faith into action as the prophetic voices of the society.

To be a prophetic voice in the face of corruption is a great challenge. As it is said, you cannot "sit on the fence" and complain about corruption. It is exactly because there is corruption that you are a Christian, you are called as a prophetic voice. You have no excuse that "I cannot do anything about it". Who should do something about it?

As I have already remarked, prophecy does not belong only to the Jewish religion in the past. In the indigenous religion, ordinary people are possessed to warn the people against social evils. If there are social evils in the society today, you are called by God (by Christ) to proclaim conversion, and warn the people, be they great or small, of dire consequences.

We may not believe that God or Christ could strike any person dead or cause hunger because of social evils like corruption. God or Christ is known to be too merciful for that.

But sincerely, as African Christians, do we not already have dire consequences of corruption in Africa today?

How come the civil wars? Where do the weapons come from? Is there no corruption involved?

What about hunger, disease, death and abject poverty? Have all these nothing to do with social evils caused by someone?

If you demand money as condition for free services, or extra as condition for paid services, what are you doing?

If our indigenous religion demands integral existence, should we continue giving excuses for our weaknesses, by claiming to divide our lives into exclusive compartments? "I am not a pastor, I am a politician." If you are a Christian, do you cease being a Christian when you become a politician?

If you are Christian, do you cease being a Christian when you become a lawyer, a businessman or a doctor?

If you are elected to a political office, is that not your call, your vocation, your challenge of authenticity to become a prophetic voice among politicians?

If you are a lawyer, are you not called by your Christian faith as a prophetic voice to defend the truth, to defend the defenceless, to defend those who suffer from injustice?

If you are a businessman, is that not your prophetic call to uphold justice in the distribution of goods of the earth?

One may ask: What about the specifically political problem or problems?

The story is the same. Almost every African country has similar political problems. One time it is a civilian rule, another time it is a military rule. Then there is military rule I, military rule II etc. Then follows a political novelty. A democratic election ushers in a "civilian government." The political faces may remain the same but now the military has civilian clothes. Then follow in succession first republic, second republic, third republic etc.

Another problem, or rather novelty is that almost every country has the same "political agenda" or is it rather "economic agenda". This involves a continuous production of ideological terms: structural adjustment, development partners, foreign experts, donor conferences, foreign investors, poverty reduction focus, commitment to producing wealth, but then tighten your belts.

One day Ghana is the African masterpiece of booming free market system, another day one of the poorest of the poor countries.

We are incessantly told: "The donor meeting is a success!"

But when will the receiving nations hold their own meetings?

In the countryside, farmers cry over production of food surplus without buyers! In the cities the government begs for food for the hungry population, from "external sources"!

While the have-nots must tighten their belts, of course our politicians, the haves and their foreign friends, jubilate and celebrate democracy!

Walk along the streets, roads and paths in the cities, towns and villages and watch the faces of those passing by. There is hopelessness. There is faithlessness. Some of our youth have lost their trust in their fellow men. It seems to be even worse than that. To lose trust in your fellow men would be normal. But some have lost trust not only in their fellow men but also in God and Christ.

One day in a bus, some young men were discussing the politics of the day. In the heat of the lamentations one young man remarked:

"For me, even if Christ comes to stand for the Presidency, I would not trust him with my vote!"

But a friend was quick to reprimand him. .

"No. For this you are going too far!"

So hopeless and faithless have our people become. Cynicism! Sarcasm! Or both!

The body to which you belong, the church, you are told, has failed in its task of being for the poor. Your fellow students, stuffed with Marxist slogans, or now better put, since Communism has been "defeated" in the "struggle for Africa" anyway, socialist or radical slogans, tell you, you are wasting your time in belonging to a Christian church, or going in for a "religious profession." You are ignorant, you are immature. Then you begin to ask yourself: Is there any personal fulfilment or commitment to authenticity, in studying a chain of "-ologies" when the future of your own people is at stake? Is it not true what your fellow ex-seminarians or ex-Christians tell you, that you are being brainwashed?

Are you not rather called by God to go into the villages to help with literacy, conscientisation, human rights, primary healthcare etc. during the holidays, instead of giving catechism classes, which do not seem to have any impact?

What is your personal fulfilment in committing yourself to authenticity as a seminarian, a new minister of Christ, or simply a believer in Christ, when things seem to fall apart around you?

Can you be true to yourself in this society today?

Can the Christian faith, your faith, be authentic in our society today?

Coming to the socio-economic situation, the society seems to proclaim and promote personal fulfilment diametrically opposed to the choice you and I have made or are making. Certainly, we are now in the century of the great Gods EROS and MAMMON. No religious fanatic has been as artful, or rather resourceful, and aggressive as the proselytisers of these great gods of our time. This ranges from captivating pictures to hypnotising "smoochy sounds". Their resourcefulness seems limitless. Now they even talk of magnetic arousal perfume and printing ink -all in the name of "maturity," "liberation," "freedom," "enlightenment," "human rights", "self-fulfilment," "self-realisation," probably also "freedom of worship" and, in fact, "being authentic" and "personal fulfilment." A seminarian or a Christian who struggles to be authentic has always to wear some kind of spiritual bullet proof in this world of sexoramas, live shows, adult bookshops, peep-ins and the latest modes. The pious Christian or cleric cannot avoid the psychoactive bombardment even after Mass or Service on Sundays.

Indeed, "the children of this world are more astute in dealing with their own kind than are children of light" (Lk.16: 8). There seems to be nowhere to hide. As I have often said, even to be blind, deaf and dumb is not foolproof. Unless you lose your sense of touch too - and, in that condition, you cannot talk of being authentic or enjoying personal fulfilment, because a human being without any senses is as good as dead.

Thus, gradually, by confusing what is desired with what is desirable, the fulfilment of the senses of pleasure is taken as the fulfilment of the whole person - therefore personal fulfilment. To succumb to such a tempting environment is regarded as being true to yourself, therefore being authentic. That is seen as being feminine or being manly. The contemporary concept of personal fulfilment seems to fit St. Paul's adage: "The meat for the belly, the belly for the meat" (1 Cor. 6:13). Eat and drink, tomorrow you die! "Decadence" is no longer part of the vocabulary of the modern person.

For the young African, or of African origin, in a special way, being authentic, as personal fulfilment, has become a matter of competition for the young man or young woman, competition for the latest sound system, the latest car, a mansion, the most presentable girl friend or boy friend. No effort is too much to get these things.

The luxury automobile has also become a status symbol. To get it, it is easy these days. Start a project for the "poor" in your village. Collect or even fabricate the most disgusting picture of "black" poverty. Thus you are on your way to becoming a wealthy "beggar-benefactor", a manager of a "poverty reduction project". Then you can have anything you desire.

So gradually, however subtle, our ideas of authenticity and personal fulfilment are also influenced by these material values. Those training for the ministry are also tempted to acquire these material things. The longing for them seems to occupy much of our prayer and meditation times.

Yes, the pressure is mounting. Despite our spiritual readings on the beauty and depth of the Marian obedience, despite our daily meditations on the sermons of St. Augustine, on the poverty of St. Francis, despite our yearly retreats, pilgrimages and charitable deeds, we are not spared the crushing effects of this society's radio-psychic bombardments. We are also tempted to aspire after the nice cars, the latest sound systems in order to keep the standard high. Even in these hard times, we find it embarrassing when there is a visitor and the refrigerator is not working, and there is no beer, not to mention whisky for the most favoured visitors. Religious poverty, celibacy or asceticism seems out of place, even contrary to personal fulfilment. According to the social norms of our time, to find fulfilment in authenticity seems to mean to flow with the tide of the material world and its standards.

With this concept of fulfilment and being authentic in the society today, where then lies Christian piety?

Are you still true to yourself; are you authentic in our society today if you struggle to be pious, to pray regularly, to go to confession, to be at the holy Mass or prayer service regularly, to be at the service of others, to be devoted to justice and peace?

Does anyone trust anyone in our society today? Is piety not mere hypocrisy? Is it not being untrue, only pretending and therefore being non-authentic?
Is Christian vocation still valid, still possible in our society today?

Can you be truly committed to your vocation, to your faith, even to yourself in our society today?

The human being today, as it were, is caught in a centrifugal force, where he or she is made to tear himself or herself from the centre of his or her being. We Christians, or those of us who still claim any spiritual relationship with a divinity, are also caught up with this centrifugal force of our society. This force threatens to tear us away from our spiritual core, our humanity, dignity and freedom. Thus we are losing our inner sense of direction. Instead of being directed from within, from the spiritual core, people are letting themselves to be directed by the external world, or external society. People, including the Seminarian, the pastor and other Christians are pressured to conform to the external worldly standard rather than what they can achieve according to their inner convictions and capacities. Thus growth or personal fulfilment, which is essentially becoming what you are, according to your inner capacity, is now changed into having and grabbing from the external world. We are all walking the tightrope of the world's judgments, always pretending, or rather acting out what the world says we are. And since we cannot become what we are not made to become, we often fail the standards of this world. We - the seminarians, the religious and ministers of the Word of God have more chances of frustration than the others because the more we are forced to compete with the others; the more we are left alone with our guilty consciences. Our experiments goad us on. Let me taste it only once, only today, only this month, only these holidays, but once tasted, the experience generates more desire.

Then for our function as spiritual leaders, our typical African society presents its own indigenous problems beyond spirit possession, witchcraft, mystical powers (juju) or magic, which are common in any society today, even if other societies choose to term the belief in such forces or spirits as esotericism or occultism. Most often, we fall into either of the two extreme positions. We either deny their existence altogether, thus unable to help those who come to us for help, with the excuse that it is all psychological, or we fall prey to them ourselves. Your own relatives may tell you, you have headache, you have stomach ache, or you are involved in an accident because this or that person is jealous of your being a Seminarian, a pastor, or simply a successful Christian. Many a time, you tend to believe it. And it actually happens when you begin to believe in this that you also correspondingly begin to doubt your own belief in your own spiritual strength. Therefore you also doubt whether you can commit yourself to authenticity of the Christian faith and find any personal fulfilment in your Christian vocation.

In other societies a pastor may avoid confronting the power of spirits and other forces at work in the society. Or some may simply avoid the problem and refer such cases to counselling offices.

Even in such societies pastors after a while also begin to realise they have to face the reality or lose their parishioners to other religious movements, including to indigenous African religions such as Vudu (Voodoo) and Yewe, or one or the other Asian religions such as Hinduism and Buddhism. So other societies are facing up to the challenge of these beliefs. Christians of all denominations are beginning to question whether all the cases of evil spirits could be explained away.

But the challenge in a typical indigenous African society is really serious. You cannot run away from the truth. You are challenged to commit yourself to authenticity. This is because in the indigenous religious context, a lie, untruthfulness, is supposed to incur disaster. The religious leader is especially expected to commit himself or herself to the tenets of his or her belief. If he or she is regarded as failing to live up to these tenets, it is believed the ancestors or the spirits can strike him or her with illness or even death, if he or she is not cleansed in time. The same principle is being applied to the Christian leader and to a lesser degree, to the Christian believer.

While doing pastoral work, I was challenged several times to answer yes or no to this question: "Do you have the power to drive out evil spirits or not?"

The challenge of authenticity in the indigenous African society is made more pressing on account of the status of the religious leader in the society. The society regards the pastor so high that you actually feel disappointed in yourself when you are not able to live up to the expectations of "Father", "Pastor", "Man of God" or "Christian." Many a time, you feel either flattered or disappointed when, as a Seminarian, a Novice, or even a teacher, a Head Christian (Church President), a catechist, or even an ordinary Christian, people tend to desire your company only to be whispering at your back, counting your falls (and your faults).

In certain communities, irrespective of whether urban or rural, this typically African commitment to authenticity is indefatigably striven after. In these communities the ordinary faithful strive after Christian perfection, even beyond the demands of Church law or rules.

In my village (or town, whatever one may regard it), any Christian openly hating the other, as I noted earlier, is banned from receiving communion by the faithful themselves. In one case a woman, who liked taking others to court instead of having matters settled by the elders of her Church, was also suspended.

The least misstep against the tenets of the Gospel incurs the remark:

"Are you not a Pastor?"

"Are you not a Christian?"

As one old man explained to me, and as I had already mentioned above, if you profess the belief in a spirit or commit yourself to a mystical power or force, you are bound, at the risk of your life, to observe all the tenets of the religious group, tabus (taboos), regulations, rules etc. Otherwise you risk, not only your own life, but also the life of your family, lineage, community or nation.

That is why in a typical indigenous African community, no death, sickness or misfortune is regarded as mere incident or accident. Every such occurrence is investigated, the (supposed) cause identified and pacification sacrifices offered in the form of indigenous rituals or Christian liturgy.

Thus in our typical indigenous African society the demand for authenticity is almost absolute. It demands faithfulness, honesty, probity and moral courage, but also humility, the willingness to accept one's weakness and submit to forgiveness and reconciliation.

Despite these crises, let us not lose hope. Let us continue to trust in the power of the Spirit of God working in us, in the world and also in our typically indigenous African society today. "With God, nothing is impossible". Let us say: With God everything is possible (cf. Luk. 2: 37).

Well, this is the challenge of authenticity and personal fulfilment posed by our society today. This is the situation in which we are to realise our personal fulfilment as trainees or workers in the Apostolate, or simply as followers of the Word of God.

To complicate matters, we are faced with difficulties regarding our vocation, not only in the political society, but also in the ecclesiastical society, the Church. This will be our theme for the next meditation.

Our Lord Jesus Christ himself faced the same type of social problems in his time. He is our consolation:

Let us encourage ourselves with His words:
I have told you all this so that you may find peace in me. In the world you will have trouble, but be brave: I have conquered the world" (Jn.16: 33)

With him we shall conquer the world too!

This is our faith. This is our hope.

Let us close this reflection with Philippians 4. 8:
Finally, brothers (and sisters), whatever is true, whatever is honourable, whatever is just, whatever is pure, whatever is lovely, whatever is gracious, if there is any excellence, if there is anything worthy of praise, think about these things.

Reflection III

The Church Today as Challenge of Authenticity

Introductory Verse: 1 Tim. 6:3-10

If anyone teaches otherwise and does not agree with the sound words of Our Lord Jesus Christ and the teaching, which accords with godliness, he is puffed up with conceit, he knows nothing; he has a morbid craving for controversy and for disputing about words, which produce envy, dissension, slander, base suspicions, and wrangling among men who are depraved in mind and bereft of the truth, imagining that godliness is a means of gain. There is great gain in godliness with contentment, for we brought nothing into the world, and we cannot take anything out of the world; but if we have food and clothing, with these we shall be content. But those who desire to be rich fall into temptation, into a snare, into many senseless and hurtful desires that plunge men into ruin and destruction. For the love of money is the root of all evils; it is through this craving that some have wandered away from the faith and pierced their hearts with many pangs.

In our last meditation, we dwelt on society today as the context within which we are called upon to commit ourselves to authenticity as personal fulfilment. As we remarked, our society today has, and promotes a type of authenticity and personal fulfilment diametrically opposed to true Christian vocation-especially our pastoral vocation. Though we may not say the situation in the Church is also diametrically opposed to authenticity and personal fulfilment in pastoral vocation, it is no less challenging, if not discouraging.

Indigenous religious communities such as Vudu (Voodoo) or Yewe cults have, generally, respective structures and strict codes of conduct for leaders and members. However no one is required to be a sort of permanent member apart from those called (possessed) by the spirit as devotees - priests and priestesses. These devotees are the only ones, who undergo initiation rites. So also structural details are often under absolute secrecy, and known to the devotees alone. On account of this absolute secrecy of the indigenous cults, anyone interested in the details of their organisation has to be initiated as a de facto devotee. The person who obtains the secrets as de facto devotee is in turn under oath, even under the pain of death, never to reveal them to any "lay", non-initiated, person. It is believed that the revelation of the secrets of the cult incurs dire consequences for the one who reveals them, including even death.

For the others, who are not initiated devotees, the services of the devotees are available if one makes a request. These services are often outside the strict enclosure. Thus in a strict sense only initiated devotees could identify, and could be identified, with the cult, the group and its structure.

With this at the background, all baptised Christians could be regarded as "devotees" by virtue of their baptism. This is because Christians themselves regard baptism as initiation. Thus it is understandable that indigenous Africans identify Christians with the institution called the church and its structure. For the indigenous Africans, therefore, any scandals affecting the church as an institution has repercussions on the image of individual Christians, even if they are not officially designated part of the official structure.

This fact that the Christian is often identified with the institution, the Church, which he or she belongs to, has implications for the Christian.

This is a serious challenge for those who consider themselves as simply "lay" people, to be concerned with the image of the institution they belong to as their church. As a Christian of any denomination or ecclesial communion, you are challenged by the indigenous African authenticity to be co-responsible for the image of your church as a whole. For our indigenous people, the authenticity of the church implies the authenticity of your own faith, and vice versa. You can no longer remain so-called "passive" church member. You are challenged to be actively involved. For our indigenous culture you cannot continue excusing yourself with such arguments as: "I am only a lay person", "I am only a church member", "it is the responsibility of the parish priest", "it is the pastor's responsibility" or "the presbyters must see to that". You are challenged to accept the problems of your church as your problem. You are challenged to do something about them. For if the church as an institution appears to be unfaithful to its tenets, therefore putting its authenticity into doubt in the society, then the authenticity of your own faith is at stake.

This challenge to be responsible for your church implies another important challenge, the challenge of secrecy. As we have seen above, keeping the secrets of one's cultic group is an absolute norm in the indigenous culture. Thus, as far as the indigenous culture is concerned, it is not only the officials of religion who have to be discreet about what they say, such as the rule of confessional secrecy of the clergy of the Catholic Church. The faithful also have the responsibility for the secrets of the church as an institution.

It is true, the responsibility for internal "secrets", matters relating to important and delicate decisions, "sub secreto", as it is put in the Catholic Church, or the weaknesses of leaders or officials as well as ordinary members, are entrusted first and foremost to those in authority. In the indigenous cultural context, it is demeaning and destructive if a parish priest or a pastor blurts out secrets of other church officials or ordinary members, the so-called "laity". It is a great challenge, especially for Christian leaders to "hold their tongue", when talking in public. Such "loose talks" by people with spiritual authority destroy the credibility of the church as an institution entrusted with important and delicate matters of the institution itself, and those of other, ordinary "lay" members. This is a great challenge of responsibility for church leaders, or rather Christian leaders. A parish priest or a pastor said to have "okro mouth", as Ghanaians would put it, loses respect, not only in the church but also in the indigenous society. It is a matter of personal honour. To ignore this challenge of secrecy, or discretion may not incur dire consequences as in the indigenous religious cults. All the same it destroys the trust ordinary people repose in leaders; it poisons relationships and the whole atmosphere of trust. More importantly, it destroys the credibility of the pastor's role as a counsellor, and spiritual mentor. Such a "careless" attitude of church leaders toward delicate matters of importance creates a sad situation of dilemma. In such cases members of the church are forced to keep pent-up moral and spiritual problems to themselves until they explode. This is also one of the reasons why members switch to other religious movements. This mistrust in the missionary churches has forced some members to become clandestine members of indigenous cults, or to have a sort of divided spiritual allegiance, a syncretistic relationship, which destroys or at least weakens the authenticity of the faith, which demands being faithful to the call to be a Christian.

This challenge of the indigenous religious observance of secrecy needs sincere self-examination by leaders.

As an indigenous proverb puts it: "The monkey says, if they laugh at me, they are also laughing at the one carrying me."

This is food for thought for religious leaders, as well as any type of leader in the indigenous society.

In the same way, and as I have already stated earlier, ordinary members of the church, the so-called "laity", are co-responsible for the sacred, and therefore for the secret character of the Church. Reciprocal respect challenges you too as a member to respect the sacredness and secrecy of the Church, leaders and fellow Christians. The secrecy of decisions on delicate matters concerning the character, especially weaknesses of leaders is also entrusted to you as a member of the church. Loose talks that tarnish the image, not only of the leaders but also of the church, as an institution to which you also belong must be avoided.

This is not to condone the weaknesses of leaders. We Christians have the responsibility for "brotherly" or "sisterly" correction. Careless talk about such matters hardens weaknesses rather than help to correct them. Moreover when such talks get back to the leader, parish priest or pastor, it destroys his or her zeal for the community as a whole, and discourages free relationship with other members. If the leader is forced to keep problems to himself for fear that some members of the congregation or parish may leak them to the public, this could gradually destroy the leader psychologically, if not spiritually.

As another indigenous wise saying has it: "The duck says it is soiling the coop for the owner, it forgets that it is soiling its own bed."

This is also food for thought for the Christian faithful.

To say "we are the church" is a challenge to our concept of the church as community that includes others and us.

We have to realise that it is this religious respect for secrecy that has saved our indigenous society and culture from destruction by external forces all these centuries, if not millennia. As I have already mentioned, for our indigenous culture, what is secret is also sacred, and what is sacred must remain secret.

This brings us to the reflection on the popularisation, or even commercialisation of our indigenous religion and our sacred institutions. This is sometimes borrowed from other cultures as modernity or civilisation.

It is a great challenge to us as indigenous African Christians. Our faith teaches us that the Almighty God is the Creator and the Father of all creation. He has sent His only son, our Lord Jesus Christ, to save humankind, the world, and in fact all creation, and to present all finally to the Father. This means by the virtue of the assumption of physical nature, as a divine being, He also fulfils the mission of sacralising creation. As Christians, are we not to continue this mission of sacralising creation?

Is it not a reversal of our mission, the reversal of the process of sacralisation, if we either give up our responsibility for the sacralisation of created universe, by condoning desacralisation, or even actively supporting or indulging in the desacralisation of sacred things, by putting them on the "open market" as commercial entity saleable objects?

If we regard the Church as a "sacred" institution, including, not only the physical structure, but also the organisation as a whole, does our indigenous cultural attitude towards sacred organisations not pose a challenge to us to have an attitude of respect, or even awe, towards all that constitutes being a church, the structure, the community and persons, including you yourself?

As baptised Christians we have to realise that it is not only religious officials who are "sacred" by virtue of anointing as part of ordination or commissioning ritual, but each Christian, like you and I, is also "sacred" by virtue of anointing during baptism and confirmation.

"Do you not know that you are God's temple and that God's Spirit dwells in you?" (1 Cor 3: 16).

This challenge of our indigenous culture gives a new dimension to our being Christians, the "devotees" of the Almighty God, adopted sons and daughters in His divine son, our Lord Jesus Christ.

This challenge gives a radical meaning to the passage in the letter of the St. Peter:

But you are a chosen people, a royal priesthood, a holy nation, a people belonging to God, that you may declare the praises of him who called you out of darkness into his wonderful light (I Pet 2: 9).

This challenge has spiritual as well as moral implications for our attitude towards the church, the community, other members, fellow human beings, ourselves, our relationships and in fact all creation.

For instance, what does the sacred bond of marriage imply for the relationship between husband and wife? What does the sacredness of life imply for the relationship between child and parent? We shall deal with these questions in more detail in Reflection XI, which is on Fruits of Love as challenge of Authenticity, in relation to community as communion.

The challenge is for the African Christian to demonstrate the authenticity of the church and its moral code of behaviour as sacred, through inner conviction, which will issue in his or her behaviour.

A related challenge, as a consequence of the sacredness of the church, is for the church leaders to prove that the church is truly universal, which could identify the spiritual needs of its African members, and not a foreign institution, imposed on the people.

If the presupposition in the introduction is accepted, that is, that the Christian faith is to redeem the best in every cultural expression of humankind, then the sacred character of religious institutions, persons and relationships is one of the best elements in the indigenous African culture, which the Christian churches need to cherish, through respectful attitude towards them. For instance what should be our attitude, as Christian churches or individual Christians towards such sacred institutions as kingship or chieftaincy, the throne, the stool or the skin?

It is a serious challenge for Christian churches as sacred institutions to reflect on this matter. The ambivalence of the churches on this matter puts the authenticity of the faith of indigenous African Christians at stake, if they happen to become kings, queens, chiefs or elders.

Likewise, in the indigenous religion, there are certain days declared as sacred to the guardian spirit. People abstain from going to the farm. It is true many stay home for fear of dire consequences. We Christians may not fear dire consequences if we go to farm on Sunday. But apart from the Sabbath injunction, does it not make sense, with the background of our indigenous cultural attitude to the sacredness of nature and life, to offer a day in a week to reflect on the sacredness of nature and the sacredness of our own life, which is not a machine?

The challenge is to live out the Christian faith as relevant, and not superfluous or antagonistic to the indigenous African culture.

Many times our frustration in the apostolate stems from the fact that we have or we are given the impression that as soon as we are ordained, our ideas about the church will radically change. But most often to the contrary, ideas remain, the situation remains just as it may have been when you asked that Father to enter the Seminary. There is no assurance that at ordination things will radically change.

In the case of other members of the Christian churches, you may have wonderful expectations when you request from that Father or Pastor to convert from the indigenous African religion to become a "baptised" Christian. But when you become aware of certain scandals as an "insider", then begins your own challenge of the authenticity of your faith.

The Church remains divine but functions through human beings. To be frank, you may remain a "faithful Christian" in one or the other church or congregation for a long time but you may find out that your concept of the Church, of theology, of pastoral life or being a Christian has not changed much since the time you decided to become a Christian.

Miracles are hard to come by these days. So it may be disappointing to expect your Church to change in your favour. The Holy Spirit may never be "on strike", as the late Professor Bernard Häring used to say, but human beings can also refuse to acknowledge the work of the Holy Spirit since they have free will and reason through which the Holy Spirit has to work. So we have to face the challenge of the state of affairs in our Christian Churches or congregations too.

Is the Church today inclined to accept the fact that the seminarian, the village pastor or ordinary faithful also needs to derive personal fulfilment through commitment to authenticity from his or her training, apostolate, or Christian living?

Theology seems most confusing today. Who decides what a pastor has to believe in, teach and practice? Who decides what the faithful have to believe or live?

For instance the "Decree on the Training for the Priesthood", in the Roman Catholic Church, "Optatem Totius" of Vatican II, article I, gives the responsibility to Episcopal Conferences to institute major Seminaries. But article 16 of the same document decrees that theological studies are under the direction of the Magisterium. This may sound very simple, but in practice, it is not so simple. Theology seems most confusing as it affects our whole vocation, our whole Christian life. The Seminarian - especially the "unfortunate" one who cares to read extra, not only Karl Rahner but also Hans Küng, or may be also the rebel priest, is being bombarded from two extreme theological ideological points of view, ultra-conservative and ultra-progressive.

Other religious denominations or congregations may have similar situations as far as theology is concerned, be it Anglican, Methodist, Presbyterian or Baptist.

Just like our contemporary political party alliances, unwilling as we may be, we Christians are being pressurised or rather tempted to belong to one or the other party, the conservative or the progressive. Almost every so-called traditional Christian denomination has got its "traditional" and "reformed" partitions.

In the Roman Catholic Church, for the ultra-conservative, the Second Vatican Council does not seem to have taken place at all. Even granted it has, they view it as mostly the work of the devil. For this theology, faith is simply the intellectual acceptance of articles of faith according to "tradition". Your behaviour does not matter much. They still regard the Canon Laws on habit and on the enclosure as articles of faith. For this theology, the benediction, the rosary, the novenas, pilgrimages etc. are the only valid devotions. Anything more or less is from the devil. For this theology the seminarian, the Priest or the faithful can find personal fulfilment only through commitment to authenticity of the tradition, in obeying the rules, in observing the rubrics of the Latin text. For the Seminarian, he has no choice but to read only books by authors who follow the "tradition". Authenticity means for this group orthodoxy in the sense of "traditional" teaching before the Second Vatican Council.

For them, to commit yourself to authenticity is to commit yourself to orthodoxy. For the Priest, these ultra-conservatives believe that being authentic or personal fulfilment lies only in saying daily masses, administering sacraments in the strict Tridentine Latin formula, saying your office and conducting your novenas. All other (protestant or even "communist") innovations lead to perdition. "Vernacular" masses (in the indigenous language), singing and dancing, spontaneous prayers, yoga meditations, laying on of hands over the sick, charismatic movements, ecumenical services and so on and so forth are all seen as coming from, and leading to the devil. They also believe that to talk politics in favour of the poor or to leave the sacristy for social work is to renounce the faith and become an atheist. Your place in society, conservatives say, is the sacristy. Let not the lay people interfere. Your personality is your cassock.

From the ultra-progressive side, Vatican III does not go far enough and has already been overtaken by events. There needs be no fixed creed or prayer formulae, no identifiable Church or special ministerial office, no sacraments except perhaps baptism, no formal Eucharistic Celebration, but only communal banquets with any type of food, with the presiding celebrant chosen at random. According to this theology or pastoral theology, the "married priest" is already an anachronism since there is no need for special spiritual functionaries. They believe that to be authentic you must be fully human; you must enjoy full personal fulfilment and have as many experiences as possible. They also believe that fasting, meditation, and prayers are for those who have time. For them, to commit yourself to authenticity, to find personal fulfilment, you must be consumed in social work. They also believe that you should strive to realise your intellectual, social or even economic ambitions. Don't limit yourself to pious preaching, they will tell you. "Take the gun and fight the capitalists beside the poor." They also believe that celibacy is a crazy old man's idiosyncrasy and that its observance is a symptom of a psychological hang-up. They see it as not a matter of conscience but of immature fixation. After all you are still young; enjoy your youth! Let the Pope and the Vatican see to themselves!

These extreme theologies (or may we say ideologies?) confuse and frustrate as they affect your training and your ministry, your Christian life.

As a seminarian, as a person training for the ministry, may be you also find the seminary staff divided, giving conflicting directions. At one end, the academic staff may stress intellectual training, while at another end, as one Seminarian once remarked, there could be spiritual "intoxication" to the detriment of moderate and integral intellectual formation. All are forced to become ascetic.

While your spiritual director tells you to spend more time praying, the Rector tells you to improve upon your studies. Which way do you go? How do you live an authentic life and find self-fulfilment in rules imposed on you from above? How do you find spiritual fulfilment when problems with friends, problems with relatives, problems with studies, etc. seem to tear you apart? How do you find personal fulfilment in being authentic, being true to yourself, by the help of people you cannot confide in?

I once saw a cartoon in a newspaper in Ghana. In a big church, a mouse was caught in a trap. The caption was: "And they say they are Christians!" Inside the church are brothers and sisters full of "love" for one another. But as soon as each one comes outside, in the family, in the community, in the society and at the workplace, in the real world, there is enmity, hatred and rumours of hatred.

Would Vudu (Voodoo) or Yewe devotees behave towards one another that way just after leaving the shrine? This is a challenging question for reflection.

What about the unity of Christians?

In the various churches or congregations there are prayers, novenas, workshops and seminars for Christian unity. There are ecumenical movements, common prayers and other common activities. But Christianity remains divided: Roman Catholic, Anglican, Orthodox, Presbyterian etc. On our continent Africa, I guess there are thousands of denominations, with new congregations springing up almost every day. There are open conflicts, even open hatred and, sometimes, violent clashes. Till today only few denominations can share a meal at the holy table together.

As indigenous Africans, we know there are differences between Vudu (Voodoo) and Yewe devotees. There are still other various indigenous religious groups all around Africa, South of the Sahara. Almost every community has its guardian spirit. But we hardly notice any open conflicts, let alone violent clashes.

According to our indigenous African culture the greatest sign of unity is sharing a meal together. To refuse to share a meal with your fellow human being is sometimes interpreted as a declaration of open hatred or distrust. In certain communities such a refusal will incur dire consequences. So those who refuse to share a meal are often asked to pay for ritual reconciliation.

With this indigenous cultural background, how can we sincerely explain this as indigenous African Christians? We are all children of the same Father. But we do not, or are forbidden to share in a meal together. In fact we are initiated "devotees" of the same spirit. But we do not, or are forbidden to share in the same sacrificial meal together. Is it without any consequence if each eats alone? As indigenous Africans are we comfortable in claiming that our Christian faith is built on love, forgiveness and reconciliation when we cannot share a meal together at the Lord's Table? What message do we send to our indigenous religious devotees, whom we are eager to convert and "win for Christ", the Saviour of all mankind?

The divisions among Christian churches are indeed a scandal, the more so for us, indigenous Africans. This is a challenge for reflection. This is a challenge of authenticity for all Christian churches, denominations or congregations.

Even as an "ordinary Christian" how do you find personal fulfilment in your Church, which is often full of hide-and-seek characters, priests, pastors, Bishops, Church officials, about whom you hear so many scandalous rumours? These days, before you begin to digest one scandal, another one explodes. Even if the news is about people far away, you begin to wonder whether your indigenous African churches are safe. Sometimes sitting before the television, when foreign channels broadcast certain scandals about your church in countries far away from Africa, it becomes a real challenge to be able to look your neighbour in the face, if he or she happens to belong to another church or another religion.

As a Roman Catholic, you may take your parish priest as a model of piety. But the next moment you hear he is a married priest. If you belong to another denomination, your situation is the same.

You may take your pastor as a model of Christian piety. But the next moment you hear he has left the church or is having an illicit affair with a member of the church.

As Christians in our time, can we find any trustworthy models of our Christian faith in our churches or ecclesial communities? For the newly ordained, the confusion about what actually a pastor or priest is, is most challenging. Which camp will you belong to? With the conservative or the progressive? Which party contributes to authenticity and personal fulfilment?

If you join one or the other, you don't overcome your frustration. You only increase it. You may have won freedom but your conscience decides. You know, we are in the age of hyper mobility! Can you endure being an independent candidate in this divided and dividing Church? Can you be authentic; can you find fulfilment in being the odd man (or woman) out? Are you, as a human being, not entitled to at least a certain degree of intimacy and certainty? Can you be yourself and bear the name of a hypocrite, a proud man, a proud woman, a pretender, the holy angel?

In this confused atmosphere, can you commit yourself to authenticity demanded by our indigenous African culture, being yourself in the Church today, which you as an African need to regard as sacred?

These are the challenges of authenticity in our churches or ecclesial communities today! These are hard facts. I don't mean to discourage readers who are thinking about entering the seminary to train for the ministry, or those thinking of converting to the Christian faith. But as I have said, miracles do not occur often these days. You better know what you are getting into and prepare for it.

This state of affairs of our Christian churches or denominations is certainly a challenge of authenticity. Our Lord counsels us:
"Beware of false prophets who come to you disguised as sheep but underneath are ravenous wolves. You will be able to tell them by their fruits... I repeat, you will be able to tell them by their fruits"
(Mt. 7:15-16).

You can take your own stand if you are aware of the prevailing opinions and life styles, and you have the courage to take a stand on the principle that contributes to your personal development in your commitment to authenticity. You have to be you. He has to be him. She has to be her. I have to be me.

This is the world you are being trained for. This is the world in which you are called to witness to the word of God. This is the society in which you are called upon to witness to Christ, to witness to justice, peace and love. This is the Church in which you are going to work in, the church in which you are working in; this is the Church of Christ you are committing yourself to. This is the Church to which you belong and are called upon to support or rather realise as the instrument of love and reconciliation. This is the Church you are to hold sacred. This is the institution in which you are called upon to commit yourself to authenticity of faith.

This is your church. This is your congregation. This is your challenge as a Christian. If it is not authentic as a sacred institution, it is your challenge to make it sacred. After all you are the church. It is sacred because it is the work of the Spirit of God. The challenge is, in spite of everything, to accept to remain an authentic instrument, a humble servant.

Remember the assurance of the Lord: Mat. 16: 18-19

The church is built on a rock, and the gates of the underworld can never hold out against it. You can trust in that. It has been vindicated for more or less two millennia.

In our next reflection we shall meditate on how we can derive personal fulfilment from this situation, through our commitment to authenticity in our response to the call of God, as seminarians, as newly ordained or commissioned pastors, or as faithful flock. This is the Church in which we are to commit ourselves to authenticity in our vocational response and vocation itself. For the meantime, let us reflect on St. Paul's counsel (Eph. 5: 1-20):

Therefore be imitators of God, as beloved children. And walk in love, as Christ loved us and gave himself up for fragrant offering, a sacrifice and us to God. But fornication and all impurity or covetousness must not even be named among you, as is fitting among Saints. Let there be no filthiness, nor silly talk, nor levity, which are not fitting; but instead let there be thanksgiving. Be sure of this, that no fornicator, or impure person, or one who is covetous (that is, an idolater) has any inheritance in the kingdom of Christ, and of God. Let no one deceive you with empty words, for it is because of these things that the wrath of God comes upon the children of disobedience, for once you were darkness, but now you are light in the Lord; walk as children of light, offer the fruit (the fruit of light is found in all that is good and right and true), and try to learn what is pleasing to the Lord. Take no part in the untruthful works of darkness, but instead expose them. For it is a shame even to speak of the things that they do in secret; but when anything is exposed by the light it becomes visible, for anything that becomes visible is light. Therefore it is said:

"Awake, O sleeper, and arise from the dead, And Christ shall give you light."

Look carefully then how you walk, not as unwise men but as wise, making the most of the time, because the days are evil. Therefore do not be foolish, but understand what the will of the Lord is. And do not get drunk with wine, for that is debauchery; but be filled with the Spirit; addressing one another in psalms and hymns and spiritual songs, singing and making melody to the Lord with all your heart, always and for every thing giving thanks in the name of our Lord Jesus Christ to God the Father.

Reflection IV

Vocational Response as Challenge of Authenticity

Introductory Verse: Mt. 16:26.

"What, then will a man gain if he 'wins' the whole world and ruins his life "?

As we have already seen in the first reflection, a "call" implies identity, a relationship and errand-duty. A positive response implies the acceptance of the identity, which, in turn, implies a special relationship, and this relationship leads to the acceptance of the errand-duty. Thus in this fourth reflection we shall be reflecting on the response to divine call, the relationship that ensues and the respective errand-duty.

Our positive response to the call of God in His son Our Lord Jesus Christ means we accept a new identity, our new status as adopted sons and daughters of the Almighty God, whom we can now call: "Father". This already poses a challenge since it opens to us a limitless cultural and spiritual horizon, with respective responsibilities, but also opportunities. We can no longer go on living simply as "indigenous Africans" but as brothers and sisters of all humankind. Using our "cultural language" we shall say we have been initiated into the divine family, out-doored with the new name: "Christian". Like in indigenous religion, we also have "marks", even a "seal", but with a difference. The marks of our new identity are invisible; they are spiritual. However we do not enter the new "family" empty-handed. We bring along the best in our culture, to increase the spiritual heritage of the family.

With this new identity the relationship is now a matter of course. We become disciples of the divine teacher, our Lord Jesus Christ, through the Holy Spirit.

He teaches us why the Father has called. We are to participate in the total self-giving sacrifice of Jesus Christ, the Son. Which means we are also to offer and consecrate ourselves with the Son. This is our challenge. For, as we know, for us the authenticity of out belief demands more than simply keeping the teachings. We are also to follow the moral code of behaviour.

This is a challenge in the context of the indigenous concept of the consecration of a human being to a spirit or cult, like Vudu (Voodoo), Yewe or some other spirit. According to the indigenous belief, apart from physical signs such as marks on the body and cowry beads round the neck and the wrists, the consecrated devotee is considered no longer for worldly pursuits or worldly honours.

The challenge is how far is the sacrifice of our worldly life, ambitions and wealth as consecrated people of God authentic in the light of Our Lord's own words: "What then will a man gain if he 'wins' the whole world and ruins his life?" (Mt.16: 26). This statement sounds simple, without the ulterior exegetical meaning or meanings, which biblical scholars may attribute to it. But let us pair it with another statement reported by another Evangelist, this time John, and also attributed to Jesus Christ: "Yes, God loved the world so much that he gave his only Son" (John.3: 16). These two statements taken together bring the radical meaning of the first statement (Mt. 16: 26) to the fore.

One could have the feeling of some irony, when considering these two passages at a first glance. The first statement implies it is not worth the trouble to sacrifice one's life for the world. But the second statement implies God himself gave his only son for the world. What happened to the life of this Son of God? I mean the earthly life of this Son of God?

We know, in human terms, the life of this only son of God was ruined, at a prime age, the age of a university student or young professional, the age of a seminarian or devotee-apprentice, at the age of the full flowering of life. His companions deserted him, just as you are deserted when you responded to God's call. Or when you strove towards being faithful to your call. When you indefatigably stuck to the truth.

"You don't mean it!" His utmost friend, Peter, might have thought! He did not expect that he, the Master, was going to be treated that badly in the true sense of the word. Authenticity! True to his word! Or they had not understood what he had been telling them!

He was tortured and crucified. So in human terms, our Lord Jesus Christ "ruins" his life as he "wins" the world. As he puts it in his farewell address to his friends: "I have conquered the world" (John. 16:33). That is the irony. That is the human irony, or even a divine irony. "What then will a man gain if he wins the whole world and ruins his life?" (Mt.16: 26).

Just like the innocent passers-by who mocked at Him on the cross, we could also, in our human ignorance, utter in our Lord's own words: "What then will a man gain if he 'conquers' the whole world and ruins his life"- on the cross? Oh, a poor radical! But, brothers and sisters, if we were to say that, if we were unable to read behind the literal meaning of the words: "wins" and "life," then we would be unable to give any plausible response to today's society's perception of authenticity and personal fulfilment. We would have had to go along with the thinking of the society. We would have had to go along with the thinking of the world. We would have had to admit we have "ruined" our lives by entering the Seminary, by applying for ordination, by taking our vows, by going about preaching the Gospel, by demonstrating for justice and peace, in short, by trying to prove to the world that Christian virtues are still worth keeping and striving after instead of flowing with the tide of the world, with the trend of the society, with the latest fashions.

If the word "wins" and "life" has no ulterior meaning, then our life is a ruin, the spiritual life we claim to live and share would only be a façade of a ruined life, a façade behind which there are only remains of burnt-out life, ash and charcoal, or as psychologists may put it, only a substitute for a life ruined, a sublimation of unfulfilled purpose of life. In that case, if that is true of us, our vocational response, our choice of life, our ministry, in fact our whole life would then be at worst a mistake, at best a symptom of frustrated personal fulfilment.

But we learn that pastoral vocation can fulfil our lives. We learn and believe that our Christian faith can fulfil our lives, our utmost desires. We learn that our response to the call of God in a special sense will fulfil our aspirations for spiritual heights -if we are authentic and if we are faithful to the vocation.

This is the crux of the matter. In indigenous African culture, in the indigenous African religion, to offer your own son as a mighty king is a really serious matter. In our indigenous culture to consecrate your beloved child to a spirit or deity is a serious matter. Then it is a life really offered.

Therefore if we proclaim to our people, to indigenous Africans, that the Almighty has offered His own, and only son, for the salvation of all human beings, it is something really serious. The seriousness of this belief in our indigenous African culture challenges us to be serious about it. We are challenged to mean what we say, to be authentic.

So then if we tell our indigenous African brothers and sisters that vocational response is participation in this ultimate sacrificial offer of the Son of the Almighty, then for our people, it is something most sacred, it is something tremendous. In the context of our indigenous African culture then, vocational response is a true consecration to the Almighty, being set apart for the Almighty alone. With this realisation of the tremendous meaning of vocational response in the indigenous African culture, we can no longer be light-hearted about it. We can no longer joke with it. That is the tremendous challenge of authenticity.

Look at those consecrated to the deity, to Voodoo or Yewe. As soon as they enter their seclusion, you can no longer consider them in the external world. They are marked out. They no longer speak the language of ordinary human beings in the world. They have physical marks of their being consecrated. They may have cowry beads round the ankles, the arms and wrists, the neck, and sometimes woven into the hair. These indigenous devotees may move about, go to the market or to the farm. But they no longer consort with fellow human beings in the worldly sense. They are set apart. They are truly sacred. At least, we would grant that they truly believe their "vocational response" has radically changed them into a true offer to the deity or spirit. They are aware, or at least they believe, dire consequences would befall them and society if they disregard the rules, the code of conduct demanded by their consecration to the deity or spirit. They know they are "sacred". You cannot engage them in ordinary conversation. You cannot ask their hand in marriage, if they are women. You cannot ask them to marry you, if they are men.

We can grant they are not simply "credulous", not knowing what they are and what they are doing. We can grant they are not charlatans. We can grant they are not pretending when they speak their "sacred" language. We can grant they are not pretending when they dance according to sacred rhythms. We can grant they are truly in a trance when they are in a trance, truly out of this world. It is true. There may be cases of "artificial trance" induced by substances, or "natural" hypnotic tricks. But we can grant the "deceit" is not all the time, and not in all cases. In short we can grant they are self-conscious that they are set apart for a sacred way of life, for sacred acts. They are cultic personalities. They have been offered; or rather they have offered themselves, their worldly existence, to the deity or spirit.

As a Christian, does your vocational response affect you also in such a radical way? Do you believe within your heart you have been offered, consecrated, or rather that you have offered, consecrated, yourself with the Son of God?

If we have not yet confronted ourselves with the authenticity of Christian vocational response in this way, this is the time we better think up. Christian vocational response has to be meaningful, for our own self-fulfilment, for the church, for the faith, for the world and, especially, for our people, the indigenous Africans.

Otherwise, it would mean our Lord himself, the great Apostles, Peter and Paul and others, the great doctors of the Church, Thomas

Aquinas, the ascetics, St. Francis of Assisi, the great Christians of our time, Pope John XXIII, and others like Martin Luther King and hundreds, or thousands or even millions of others who give their lives for the truth, for the world, for the cross, by saying "NO!" to existing social systems, political systems, religious systems, or even ecclesiastical systems, have all made a mistake!

Well, you have doubts. So does your seemingly satisfied and successful colleague has his or her own doubts. So also your fellow Christian, who goes to church at least on Sundays and feast days has his or her own doubts. So also do I have my own doubts. But have you thought about the ministry, about your vocation, your faith this way?

Is it not possible, in fact even certain, that our faith, our pastoral vocation, which does not conform to the world, the society, still has meaning, if not for you and me, at least for others? Sometimes to experience the Christian vocational response as a real challenge of authenticity, which affects the depths of our being, we have to personalise our reflection.

If my vocation, my ministry, my faith has meaning for fellow human beings, as something really challenging to my physical, intellectual and spiritual energy, sometimes almost to the limit, is it not then authentic, a true participation in the self-offer of the Son of God? There is the offer of sleepless nights, headaches, frustrations, depressions, loneliness and humiliations, which I readily accept as a challenge. If I go through all these consciously for the sake of those who ask for my prayers, those who request my holy Masses, those who ask just for my presence in times of sorrow, or even material help, am I not living out my response to the call of God? As a seminarian or novice, if my life is meaningful to those I teach catechism, to those I give spiritual talk, to those I visit in the surrounding villages in rain or sunshine, day or night, during the holidays or on pastoral assignment, is my vocational response not then meaningful, therefore authentic?

Do I, do you, have to gauge your usefulness by the standards of the world, the world, which you deny yourself by deciding to follow the Son of God, who sacrificed himself on the cross? Do I, do you, have to go by the praises of the authorities or even of the people you serve?

If my training or ministry has meaning for the young catechumen, for the sick who find consolation, if not a cure in my laying on of hands, if my ministry has meaning for troubled married couple, or the troubled youth, who find consolation in my willingness to listen to them, should I not find fulfilment in this life of mine, provided I am sincere, committed to authenticity?

If my vocation has meaning for all these fellow human beings, then does it not follow that my response to the call to train for the ministry serves a purpose, or rather gives meaning to my existence? Am I not then sacrificing my life, my world, in being for others? By allowing those in authority to release their own tension on me as my cross, for the sake of all to whom I am going to be of service to in the future, am I not then meeting the challenge of authenticity? Are all these not part of the "package" of the self-consecration, the consecration of my worldly existence? Do all these not amount to my losing my earthly life with the Son of God, in order to find it in eternal life? Am I not, in fact, being my brother's keeper by bearing the moods of those, who for reasons known only to God, lose their nerves, their temper on me?

Am I sure I don't have also my moods, which trouble my parents, my friends, the faithful and the staff? Do I not give trouble to others myself by my temper, my confusion, my nervousness, even as slight a thing as illegible handwriting, lack of attention, rude remarks, even if unconsciously? If others have to bear all these as their call to be of service, am I not also responding to the call of God to be of service- to bear the weaknesses of others without grumbling, the weaknesses of those in authority and fellow Christians as my Christian vocation- a response to the divine call to consecrate my life, in one or the other ministry? Are all these not part of the training in authenticity. Being true to myself!

If I accept the political situation, the economic situation as my Christian vocation, to do something, to deny myself something, are the hardships not training me to meet different situations and persons, and serve them without being turned off by their human weaknesses, with patient endurance? With all the faults of those in authority over us, can the golden rule not work in their favour too? "So, always treat others as you would like them to treat you" (Mt. 7:12).

If each time I say yes, I accept suffering for the sake of the word of God, is it not then the fulfilment of my vocation, a response to my call, a self-sacrificing, a self-offering call? Is that not losing my life for the world?

If you are always to accept and grumble about situations in the Seminary, in the novitiate, in the Church, in the country, and in the world, without doing anything about them, are the situations not a call from God to use your own talents to help to solve problems responsibly, without bitterness. Instead of complaining about conflicts, is it not a call from God to suggest solutions through the appropriate medium? If it does not work, is it not your responsibility, your call to make it work? Will it not be personally fulfilling if you make it work? Is the situation of conflict not a challenge to make your vocational response authentic, as participation in the sacrifice of the Lamb of God for our reconciliation?

Now, if all these difficulties help you to use your reason, to use your talent for problem solving, does your life as a seminarian, your life as a novice, your life as a pastor, your life as being a religious, your life as a community leader or Christian faithful not serve a purpose? If the purpose of a rational being, of any human being, is to use his or her intelligence and talents to solve daily problems of life, does a problem-solving Christian not fulfil his or her purpose for existence as a human being?

Is the life of a seminarian or novice, a pastor or Christian faithful not personally fulfilling, if after his or her training, he or she can breathe a sigh and say with pride, with a true Christian pride, I have made it at last, in spite of difficulties? I have met the challenge of authenticity.

Now, if life in the Seminary and life in the ministry or society serves the purpose for which you have been created as a problem-solving being, for which you exist, does it not mean that it fulfils your reason for being, and makes you become what you are made to become, a human being, different, unique, yet able to be because of, and for others - the sick, the distressed married couple, the youth, whom you help find meaning in their lives, thus making your own life meaningful and fulfilling? Are all these not meeting the challenge of authenticity?

Whether you realise it or not, your patient endurance and courage to question and change what has to change inspires your friends and others. More than that, because you treat these people as persons, different and unique, because you do not pray for or help them in any way for money or self-gratification, you also become more and more a person who can help other persons, having learnt by experience the hard way. It is the realisation that you are at the service of others in what should be your commitment to authenticity, your personal fulfilment, so that you can also say with confidence: "I have kept the faith. All there is to come now is the crown of righteousness reserved for me" (2 Tim 4: 7-8). As a seminarian, as the one training for the ministry, will it not be personally fulfilling if you can say that from the depths of your heart at your First Mass or commissioning ceremony?

Now, we have seen that without the world's pleasures, without wealth, we can still find personal fulfilment in our lives, in our vocation, in our ministry, in our Christian faith, by committing ourselves to authenticity, by being faithful followers of Jesus Christ. Therefore we have an answer to offer the society today, a society, which places all value on sensual pleasures and material goods. Indeed we have to answer because we cannot leave such an all-important fact as the purpose and meaning of our choice of life to chance.

How do we answer the world, today's society?

Let us now go back to our Lord's statements, or rather warning: "What then will a man gain if he 'wins' the whole world and 'ruins' his 'life'?" (Mat.16: 26), and " 'yes' God loved the world so much that he gave his only Son" (John.3: 16).

The meaning of the words "wins" and "life" explains a Christian's right relationship with the world- the society today, even the Church today, and therefore gives the answer to the world's perception of authenticity and personal fulfilment.

What do the words "wins" and "life" mean?

The meaning is what the Son of God is sent to do. That is: "so that through him the world might be saved." (John 3: 17). Therefore, the paradox is cleared. Our Lord does not warn his disciples of "ruining" their lives by "winning" the world, and then, ironically, "ruins" his own life by "winning" the world. No! Our Lord came to "save" the world, for its own sake. At least, that is what we, those who accept his word, believe.

He did not come to "win", to "possess" the world, using the world for his own gratification. "The Son of man" came to save the world for its own good. He came to make it conducive to the well being of human beings. So, our first Christian answer to today's society, the world of today, is that the human being is created, not to "possess," that is "win" the world, but to "save" the world from its materiality. Therefore, personal fulfilment does not lie in possessing or enjoying worldly material values, but in saving the world from these very material values by gradually imprinting spiritual values on it through human-spiritual existence.

Our personal fulfilment lies in commitment to authenticity of faith in saving the world, the society, and the church from political, economic and moral confusion, thus saving ourselves. We are called to save, not to possess, or enjoy. That means society or the church today needs saving. And it is this need of saving which validates our vocation, the spiritualization of human society.

This world of falsity, this world of insincerity, this world and society full of false prophets, this world of self-deceit, this world of non-authenticity, it is this world, which is a challenge to us to be sincere, to be true to ourselves, to be in a word, authentic. This fact of "spiritual" existence brings us to the meaning of "life." What is life? Or, to put it more concretely, what life do men and women, or Christians need to preserve?

We have to find out this also because the verse just before the verse we are considering, i.e., Mt.16: 25, states: "For anyone who wants to save his 'life' will lose it: but anyone who loses his life for my sake will find it." Which life has to be "lost" and which life will be "found?"

Even without the expert, scholarly analysis, one, as a "lay person", can understand that the life that can, or even has to be lost is not the same as that which will be found. The life, which will be found, therefore, must have more value. That is explained later in the same verse- namely, the life for the sake of Christ. This life is not material, physical or even just biological existence. This life is the life, which has value and meaning independent of or in spite of the material world and its pleasures or possessions. Life is not having but becoming.

As our Lord counsels, according to Luke.12: 15: "Watch, and be on your guard against avarice of any kind, for a man's life is not made secure by what he owns, even when he has more than he needs."

If you have had to counsel a drug addict, whose life has been destroyed; if you have had to counsel a wayward girl, who has to take drugs to avoid committing suicide; if you realise some rich people have to take drugs, who have ruined their lives and marriages because they have always had more than enough, then we have to accept the truth that there is no authentic personal fulfilment in sensual pleasures or the possession of material goods.

So then, do we have a Christian answer to today's world's or society's conception of authenticity or personal fulfilment? Yes. We have. We can answer that human life is not valued according to worldly possessions because a human being is not to possess but to save the world. Your life is not valued by the number of degrees you have, by your university scholarship, by the type of car or house you own. Even psychologists will tell you that the desire for these things is, in fact, not self-fulfilling desire but a symptom of frustrated self-fulfilment. An authentic response to a call, the life that is personally fulfilling, is the life that has meaning, in fulfilling its purpose of "saving" the world from its materiality and inordinate ambitions, which only prevent personal fulfilment.

So you find fulfilment not in competing in the eagerness to possess, but in saving the world, today's society from this eagerness, this greed to possess. This saving life, which is valid irrespective of material existence, is truly eternal. What makes us consider the martyrs and other saints, as people already achieving personal fulfilment is that they are still living among us even when their possessions, even their mortal remains, are non-existent.

Le us heed our Lord's warning:
Do not store up treasures for yourselves on earth where moths and woodworms destroy them and thieves can break in and steal. But, store up treasures in heaven where neither moths nor woodworms destroy them and thieves cannot break in and steal. For, where your treasure is there will your heart be also" (Mt.6: 19-21).

Let us say where your heart is there you will find personal fulfilment. If your heart is in becoming a parish priest or pastor, it is only in responding to this pastoral vocation that you can find your life fulfilling.

Now, apart from the fact that personal fulfilment is not having or enjoying, but in becoming what you can become because of what you are created to become, it is also a fact that true growth or maturation is not letting yourself free to continue experiencing, or rather testing all possible human situations. Even the most worldly psychologist realises that every human being has to set himself or herself an ultimate value of life, an ideal, towards which the person has to be guided from infancy to make him or her better able to develop true human values in the future.

So also, if spiritual values are worth cultivating, baptism in a particular religious faith, or a vocation, like pastoral vocation, can be a means of self-guidance towards the final acquisition of these spiritual values. Thus, even if you have entered the Seminary as a boy of 15, 14 or even 12, you are not thereby prevented from maturing. This early decision can foster your willingness and zeal towards later fulfilment of the Christian values and virtues acquired through the ministry. Since one is always free to continue training for the ministry or not, and since any human being is capable of changing for the better by his or her own free will, a vocation can still become a personal fulfilment. Never mind the funny and flimsy nature of your first attraction into the seminary; it is God's call, whether it is the attraction of the cassock, the car, or Father's toffee. God calls by the most unlikely signs. Provided you now willingly accept this first step, every other step, every endurance of suffering, suffering from personal weakness, suffering from authorities, suffering from friends, relatives and your own people, it is all a step in the progressive response to your pastoral vocation as your aim, your goal in life - therefore, personal fulfilment.

Every hardship, every negative pressure from political or economic situation of today's society should not be a discouragement but rather an opportunity to make your response personally fulfilling. If the world is corrupt and needing salvation, then your pastoral vocation, a vocation to participate in our Lord's salvation of the world from corruption, has valid reason of being meaningful in the world, therefore, personally fulfilling. Let us still remember St. Paul's words: "This may be a wicked age, but your lives should redeem it" (Eph.5: 16).

Thus we have seen that we can derive personal fulfilment from our response to pastoral vocation. Therefore, vocational response can truly be personal fulfilment.

In the next meditations, we shall meditate on Pastoral Vocation as Challenge of Authenticity.

Let us close this meditation with 2 Pt.1: 12:

Brothers, you have been called and chosen, work all the harder to justify it. If you do all these things, there is no danger that you will ever fall away. In this way, you will be granted admittance into the eternal kingdom of our Lord and Saviour Jesus Christ.

Reflection V

Pastoral Vocation as Challenge of Authenticity

Introductory Verse: 1 Pt.2: 4-10

Come to him, to that living stone, rejected by men but in God's sight chosen and precious; and like living stones be yourselves built into a spiritual house, to be a holy priesthood, to offer spiritual sacrifices acceptable to God through Jesus Christ. For it stands in scriptures:
"Behold, I am laying in Zion a stone, a cornerstone chosen and precious, and he who believes in him will not be put to shame." To you therefore who believe, he is precious, but for those who do not believe,
"The very stone which the builders rejected has become the head of the corner," and "a stone that will make men stumble, a rock that will make them fall," for they stumble because they disobey the word, as they were destined to do.
But you are a chosen race, a royal priesthood, a holy nation, God's own people, that you may declare the wonderful deeds of him who called you out of darkness into his marvellous light, Once you were not people but now you are God's people, once you had not received mercy, but now you have received mercy.

In our last reflection, we reflected on how to make the response to pastoral vocation a personal fulfilment through commitment to authenticity, in, or in spite of today's society and today's church. Now we shall meditate on making the pastoral vocation itself commitment to authenticity, which assures personal fulfilment.

How do we make or shall we be able to make the pastoral work a true personal fulfilment through commitment to authenticity?

In the indigenous culture a priest is a cultic figure. In a general sense our indigenous people regard a priest or pastor as a person who offers sacrifices. Thus our people regard the pastor as first and foremost a cultic figure or at least a spiritual leader. The Pastor or Parish Priest is supposed to offer gifts to God on behalf of the people. Especially in the Catholic Church, as it is explained to them, the Eucharistic sacrifice is regarded as a true sacrifice of the body and blood of Christ, in the forms of bread and wine. Since the people do not usually bring the offered goods themselves they are satisfied that they bring the goods indirectly in two ways. In one way, they have the opportunity to offer money for their intentions. In another way, which seems to be peculiar to African Catholics, they bring offering to the altar themselves, mostly money, but also other material goods such as food and drink.

Following the logic of offerings for sacrifice in the indigenous culture, some say they do not need to ask the parish priest or pastor to account for monies collected during the Eucharistic celebration, which they regard as sacrifice anyway. Their argument is that what is given is just like an offering brought to indigenous priests or priestesses for sacrifice. Since these indigenous priests or priestesses are not supposed to account for the offering brought for sacrifice, they do not see the reason why the parish priest should be made to account for collections during holy Mass or Prayer or other religious services.

Apart from material sacrifices, the people also regard prayers as a form of sacrifice, or at least as part of the sacrificial rite or ritual. Thus other pastors whose denominations do not have such elaborate liturgical celebrations or ritual as the Holy Mass in the Roman Catholic Church, are supposed to offer prayers for the faithful or congregation.

As cultic figures, priests and pastors of any denomination are regarded, according to the indigenous logic, as those exclusively for spiritual services. These days, whenever a new pastor or parish priest (pastor) is announced, the first question is: Can he (she) offer healing prayers?

In normal circumstances the indigenous Africans put the greatest value on the spiritual services, not on the socio-economic services. Thus, with their indigenous cultural backgrounds, indigenous African Christians regard the religious leaders as "spiritual" leaders, "men of God", as they are fond of calling them. For the faithful, that is the identity of a religious leader, a pastor, parish priest or any officially commissioned religious official.

Therefore what they regard as the responsibilities of the religious leader are in one way or another spiritual: praying for them, listening to their confessions or problems, visiting them at home, at the workplace (even at the office), but especially at the sick-bed. If they can afford it, the people would be willing to offer anything to support their religious leaders, to keep them busy exclusively with spiritual matters.

However, certain developments in the Christian churches or denominations, especially those with direct link to Western missionary activity, threaten the authenticity of the role of a religious leader as first and foremost a spiritual leader. This is the challenge of authenticity. Who is an authentic religious leader? Or rather what makes a religious leader a true religious leader, therefore an authentic religious leader?

The authenticity of this status in the society is a great challenge in two senses. The first is the sense of superfluity resulting from adjustments in church leadership structure, mostly with foreign influence. The second is being overburdened, especially with the socio-economic crisis in Africa.

Let us reflect on the first point, the sense of superfluity.

Although it sounds contradictory, it is a fact that the scarcity of ordained priests or pastors in certain societies threatens their specific role to become superfluous. As we have seen in the last reflection, to enjoy personal fulfilment is to commit oneself to authenticity, to fulfil one's purpose of existence. That is, to be of service to fellow human beings, and in saving human society from material enslavement.

The question now is, if all Christians are the "new Israel", the chosen race inheriting the faith of Abraham (Ps.4: 16), what then are the status and the role of traditional Christian priesthood or pastoral ministry?

For those who form part of the traditional clergy, especially in the Catholic Church, one of the causes of frustration in the ministry is the loss of identity, the loss of being a unique person created and chosen or called by the Creator for a special purpose, the loss of being authentically yourself. The question is, with the rise of "lay theologians" and the multiplication of ministries even in the Catholic Church, is there any role left to play by a traditional cleric, pastor, or in the Catholic ecclesiastical language, ministerial priest?

After all, as some say, Vatican II has dismantled the hierarchical structure of the Church into "a people of God" (Constitution on the Church, art.9) who are the messianic people to establish the Kingdom of God, initiated by and in Christ, by delivering creation from its slavery to corruption into the freedom of the glory of the sons (or rather children) of God (Rm. 8: 21).

But if all Christians are a people apart, is there any reason for a specially instituted priesthood? Can every Christian not perform the function of a priest by the virtue of baptism - being incorporated into the chosen race, a royal priesthood, a consecrated nation, a people set apart (1 Pt.2: 9), as we have already seen?

Is a vocation to the ministry of the Word as a special divine call still anything to offer personal fulfilment? Is the office of the pastor, the ministry, or to put it in ecclesiastical language is the ministerial priesthood, an anachronistic hang-up from pre-Vatican II days? Is the ordination something important for personal fulfilment through the commitment to authenticity, a public confirmation and consecration, giving an indelible character to the candidate? Or is the ordination only a sort of general formation after which you can now select a field of specialisation as a lecturer or teacher, a diplomat, a banker, a scientist, etc.? Or is the ordination truly a commission to fulfil your life-long goal of being a pastor, of being part of the holy priesthood, a people set apart, a holy nation?

Should we accept the ultra-conservative stand that the Pastor is a cultic figure- only to sacrifice? Or do we accept the ultra-progressive view that the specialist role of a pastor is now irrelevant?

We are told the ministerial priesthood should be personally fulfilling, if we commit ourselves to authenticity. Accordingly, we have to find out the role of the ordained minister in the post-Vatican II age. To find this out, let us see what Vat II tells us in the Constitution on the Church. In article 10, we read:

Christ the Lord, High Priest, taken from among men (Heb.5: 1-5) "made a kingdom and priests to God his Father" out of this new people. The "baptised" mark that word, the "baptised" not only the ordained by regeneration and anointing of the Holy Spirit, are consecrated into spiritual house and a holy priesthood. Thus, through all those works befitting Christian men (and women) they can offer spiritual sacrifices and proclaim the powers of him who has called them out of darkness into his marvellous light (1 Pt.2: 4-10). Therefore, all the disciples of Christ, persevering in prayer and praising God should present themselves as living sacrifice, holy and pleasing to God (R.12: 1) everywhere on earth they must bear witness to Christ and give an answer to those who seek an account of that hope of eternal life which is in them.

Reading only this passage, one has the impression that the ultra-progressives are right after all. This is because "all the disciples of Christ," not only the apostles, but all the "baptised" followers of Christ are "anointed" and "consecrated" into a spiritual house and a "holy priesthood."

But the passage following this passage "seems," I say, "seems", not to be in favour of that interpretation. This is because it states:

Though they differ from one another in essence and not only in degree, the common priesthood of the faithful and the ministerial or hierarchical priesthood are nonetheless interrelated. Each of them in its own special way is a participation in the one priesthood of Christ.

Can we reconcile these two statements- all are Priests, but some belong to the common priesthood, others to hierarchical priesthood, which is understandably the priesthood of deacons, Priests, Bishops, Cardinals and the Pope?

If we cannot reconcile the two priesthoods then our pastoral vocation is at best superfluous, at worst pretentious. But, as we have said in the last meditation, we cannot let such an important matter as our whole life commitment hang in the air. Our vocation is worthwhile, therefore personally fulfilling through commitment to authenticity; or not worthwhile therefore not personally fulfilling. In that case, our role, I mean the role of ordained priesthood or priests in the society as pastors is either authentic and meaningful, therefore fulfilling, or non-authentic, meaningless, therefore not personally fulfilling.

Accordingly, we have to find out our role in the post Vat. II Catholic Church. Let us make the effort to understand the two passages for our own welfare. I can understand the relationship between the common priesthood and the hierarchical priesthood in a layman's way.

I believe we can understand the common priesthood and the hierarchical priesthood without falling to either of the two extremes- ultra-conservatives and ultra-progressives. In the first place, let us note that Vatican II no longer stresses "hierarchical subordination" but "each in that way which is appropriate to him or her" (Art.11). Thus, even accepting the progressives' concept of functional difference only, we can say the ministerial priesthood, in our context, pastoral vocation, making others aware of their priestly functions, and reconciling them with God by preaching the good news, which gives them the Spirit, enabling them their sanctification, thus consecrating them to God, surpasses the ordinary Christian acts in "degree" and is "essentially different."

Thus, our pastoral vocation is not rendered superfluous by the universal Christian vocation, but rather validates it by making it authentic, meaningful. Our function in the society then is to make others aware of their Christian or religious functions. Our work is to consecrate humankind, the world, to God by spiritualising it, saving it from corruption and decay. That is the authenticity of our ministerial priesthood, the spiritualization of the material sphere of human existence.

I believe our argument thus far holds also for the consecrated life, the life under vows, or the cloistered life, if we may term it so. Accordingly our vocation too has its identity, it is unique. Since our vocation is unique, we have to provide our unique service to our people, to our society, to our nation, to our country, to our continent, in fact to our world. So we have to provide our spiritually hungry world with the spiritual food, the word of God- by preaching and praying.

Others are also called by God to offer themselves by acts of service and prayer. But the hectic daily life consumes a lot of their time. Therefore those specifically called to be pastoral ministers are to make the spiritual service of prayer and other forms of liturgy their special dedication. This preserves the identity of pastoral vocation in confrontation with the challenge of authenticity posed by the sense of superfluity.

Thus, we shall find fulfilment through commitment to authenticity in our pastoral vocation if we are pastors, clerical or religious, not only in the Church (building), but also on the street, on the farm, in the house, in fact wherever we may be. Since our function as pastors is to lead humankind towards the awareness of human's spiritual potentialities, the confusions in the world - political, economic or social, need not frustrate our work as pastors, but rather they need be regarded as opportunities for making our lives meaningful in the service of fellow human beings, provided we commit ourselves to authenticity.

When people are torn away from their centre, from their humanness, dignity and freedom, it is our vocation to redirect the human being back to the inner self, spiritual potentialities, the inner strength to bear suffering, disappointments, fears and doubts. In this sense, in our own struggle to commit ourselves to authenticity we motivate others also to commit themselves to authenticity in their own way of life.

The second challenge threatening the authenticity of pastoral vocation is being misdirected or overburdened. The socio-economic needs in Africa make such a demand on pastors that socio-economic services seem to out-weigh the main spiritual function. It is a dilemma. As we have seen in our reflection on the Society Today, through economic policies, often imposed from outside, families are being deprived of their economic base by certain policies of the government. Thus the churches have to add material services to their already overstretched spiritual resources.

For instance while the people wait for their pastor to pray with, and for them, he or she is busy either organising food, carrying cement for building projects, or even outside on a begging trip for most of the time, for old clothes and funds for "development projects". Even when the pastor or parish priest happens to be present, discussions are more on material welfare than spiritual development. This leads to, not only physical exhaustion, but also, psychological and even spiritual exhaustion. Humanly speaking, it is asking too much to expect the religious leader to maintain his or her patience all the time, and be disposed to reading, prayer and spiritual reflection, even if he or she has any time left at all for such "otherworldly" matters. This wears the pastor down and affects the essential pastoral services.

This is the challenge and dilemma. Would it be pastoral or even Christian to devote time to prayer and meditation when the people are hungry, thirsty and unclad? In the indigenous context the people miss the authentic spiritual services.

I remember at one time, someone asked whether Catholic Priests could also heal a lame person through praying over the person. The priest answered that Catholics did not need such prayers because the church had orthopaedic centres to make limbs for the lame. Then the person retorted: "But lay people too could make such artificial limbs!"

Probably the priest missed what the question actually meant, and therefore he missed the answer too. The retort made it clear that the pastor's role is not material support but spiritual healing.

Any time a new pastor is being installed, the questions the faithful often ask is: Can he pray over people? Can he preach? Can he hear our confessions? They hardly ask whether he can build schools, make wells or donate clothes. This shows once more that for the people, the parish priest or a pastor is first and foremost a spiritual leader. The result is the temptation to compromise the Christian faith or church allegiance.

Deprived of spiritual services in the Christian community, they seek such services in the indigenous religion, often in secret. This syncretistic attitude causes unfaithfulness, compromising the authenticity of the faith, with all the burden of guilty conscience. Or, which is less frustrating, they wander from one indigenous African Christian church or religious movement to another in which pastors, prophets or prophetesses and spiritualists keep strictly to spiritual services.

To uphold the authenticity of pastoral vocation pastors are challenged to practically redefine their Christian pastoral role. This redefinition is both to keep to the specifically spiritual function and at the same time motivate the political leaders concerned to formulate sustainable policies that will cater for the socio-economic needs of the population. This is the prophetic spiritual service, which solves, or at least minimises the problem both ways. This prophetic spiritual service would induce conversion, especially in leaders, which will in turn reduce the pastoral burden of socio-economic services.

This needs sincere reflection, especially in denominations still attached to foreign "donor" churches. If indigenous African Christian movements are capable of supporting their leaders without foreign support, why do main missionary churches still need to be so dependent on foreign support?

Thus, for a pastor, every occasion is an opportunity to realise his (or her) purpose of existence. If there is violence, the pastor is called upon to bring peace. If there is corruption, the pastor is called upon to bring conversion. Where there is exploitation, the pastor is called upon to bring justice. Where there is oppression, the pastor is called upon to promote human dignity.

A pastor cannot tell African politicians how to govern, but the pastor can, and in fact ought to tell politicians how the common man (or woman) is suffering, how the common farmer in the village has not got even a cake of soap to wash his clothes, even for the wife to wash her children.

Or rather the pastor needs to ask searching questions. Why do so many people lack the basic necessity of life while those who are elected, or who elected themselves to cater for these needs live in affluence? Every leader in the society, however high the position, and however mighty he or she may appear needs pastoral, spiritual, care. The mightier the leader is, the greater the challenge of authenticity for the pastor as a prophetic voice.

If there is lack of conscientious leadership in Africa today, the year 2003, do African Christian pastors provide these leaders enough pastoral, spiritual care? The Pastor can make the politician aware that the local clinic is not functioning, or tell the diplomat that the villagers are displaced and homes destroyed because the government has given the land, the livelihood of the people as concession to his or her countrymen or women, who happen to be "foreign investors", as condition for development aid.

The pastor's role is to use every opportunity of meeting a person in authority to motivate the person's inner dignity and freedom in such a way that he or she acquires the sensibility towards the plight of fellow citizens. That is being authentic in the service of the people and the nation, or rather the continent. The pastor needs to make the leader aware of his or her responsibility for providing dignified living conditions for all peoples instead of lording it over them and robbing them of their dignity and freedom.

Let us remember that St. John the Baptist was only an eccentric wanderer in the desert. But he did not keep quiet in order to win favour from the imperial Roman governor or to avoid trouble to himself and his countrymen. He boldly told the imperial representative in plain words that his marriage relationship was immoral, that it was wrong!

It is true he paid for this bold stand with his head on a silver platter. But just as Jesus Christ, whose forerunner he was, for him that was the only way to stand for the truth, to be truthful to him. In effect to accept to pay for being truthful with his life, St. John the Baptist was only being authentic, being true to his vocation as the holy precursor, the forerunner of the Prince of justice and peace. And that is true self-fulfilment.

Can you stand up to your "first world" diplomat in the same way in matters of principle and in matters of justice and moral integrity! If not, if you fear losing the development aid for your projects, are you not then being untruthful, and therefore avoiding being yourself, being authentic and in fact unable to find fulfilment in your vocation as a pastor, as a Christian, as a disciple of Christ?

Let us remember: It was, and it is still comfortable to be a false prophet. It is temporarily secure to play the false prophet, to play to the ego of the powers that be. But that is only temporal. This is because false prophets only keep the powerful blind to the doom all around until it becomes too late! The moment of truth will inevitably break upon the unsuspecting powerful, sweeping the powerful and the false prophets along! The truth often breaks upon the world with devastation beyond control.

History has enough proof of that. The Old Testament has enough of such history. Africa itself has more than enough of such history. Let us not deceive ourselves. By running away from telling the truth as it is, by failing to commit ourselves to authenticity today, we are only prolonging the agony of our people, and postponing the moment of truth for our people. Somehow the truth always refuses to be shelved forever! The truth has to be out one day!

So then the pastor, or let us say the disciple of Christ, is to be, as one spiritual writer, Henri Nouwen would put it in his book, The Wounded Healer, (1972: 36), the articulator of inner events. He or she has to offer fellow human beings creative ways to communicate with the sources of human life. The pastor is to stimulate people at every opportunity to recognise God's work in their own lives and in the lives of others. The Pastor, as primarily a spiritual leader, has to use every opportunity for spiritual dialogue with the person he or she meets, on the street, on the bus, at the office, or even in the drinking bar. You as a pastor, your vocation is to inculcate spiritual and moral principles in every person you happen to meet in order to provide him or her with the spiritual strength, the inner capacity to endure problems and courage to stand his or her ground in honesty and in truth. After all as a pastor your first responsibility is to inform and enlighten by the word of God.

Every meeting with a pastor should generate the experience of conversion, a spiritual rebirth. A meeting with a pastor should be a moment of salvation. We should not deny the politician or the diplomat this opportunity.

Finally, our Lord Jesus Christi should be the model of a pastor. Your meeting with a rich person or a person in authority should result in conversion. When people accuse you of dining with corrupt people, your host should be able to proclaim from the depths of the heart at the end of the meal: "Look, Sir, I am going to give half my property to the poor, and if I have cheated anybody I will pay him back four times the amount." Then you can say proudly, to the hearing of your accusers: "Today salvation has come to this house, because this man (or woman) too is a son (or daughter) of Abraham, for the son of Man has come to seek out and save what was lost" (Lk.19: 9-10).

Every human situation is a fertile ground for the word of God. You are to sow the seed of this word, take care of it, let it grow, and bear fruit in plenty. Thus the uniqueness of the pastoral vocation as spiritual service means also that it has to be at the service of the vocation of fellow Christians, as a call to be prophets to fellow human beings, through the baptismal anointing of chrism. Thus pastors vindicate their unique vocation of making others aware of their own prophetic call as followers of Christ.

Sometimes the Spirit leads us to confront an "impossible character". This is an opportunity to lead him or her to confront his or her authentic self. But in any case you need prepare yourself spiritually, some time for reflection, some time for prayer, for the guidance of the Spirit to inspire you, to guide you on how best you can go about it. For to motivate someone to confront himself or herself, you should have gone through this confrontation yourself, to be strong enough to go through all that it takes to relate with an "impossible character" or an "impossible personality".

In any case, we have first to be humble enough to admit to ourselves that we are also running away from confronting our authentic selves, our inner selves. Then we should have the courage to work through the humiliation of accepting ourselves. It is only then we can acquire the strength for motivating and supporting others to work through theirs.

Thus our reflection so far teaches us that the challenge of the authenticity of pastoral vocation by the threat of superfluity and misdirection is rather an opportunity to strengthen its identity and uniqueness. For the challenge to redefine pastoral vocation as prophetic spiritual service is in itself the rediscovery of its authenticity.

Taking our Lord as model brings us to a practical point.

Probably African Christian religious leaders need search their own hearts first with hard questions as challenge of authenticity. If Christian leaders are called to be prophetic voices in the society, are they faithful to this call, to this vocation?

We all know the loudest and most effective prophetic voice in any society is the life of the prophet itself as living proclamation. The only proof of the authenticity of the pastoral vocation and the authenticity of the word pastors proclaim could be judged only by the way of life of the pastors.

If things do not seem to improve in African societies, in spite of the preaching of pastors, then pastors have to ask themselves whether their own lifestyles match the gospel they preach. This is because the vice, which our Lord was most hard at condemning, is the hypocrisy of religious leaders (Mat 23). Therefore even before we raise our prophetic voices against politicians and diplomats, we have to search our own hearts with sincere and hard questions.

If our indigenous African society is admittedly, materially, if not the poorest of the poor, as some would claim it to be, at least among the poorest, and pastors are to identify themselves with the lives of those whom they serve, then what about the option for the poor? What does the option for the poor mean?

We, indigenous African pastors or pastoral ministers, cannot even talk of "identifying" ourselves with our people. We are part of them. This is an important question especially for those who, by virtue of their vows or solemn promises have proclaimed to God and fellow human beings that they have left everything to follow Christ, in the service of the poor. How true, how authentic are those promises in the lives of those who make them publicly?

This is a matter of making each individual in the society reflect on his or her stewardship. Politicians are to govern, diplomats are to create understanding among peoples, lawyers are to serve the truth in protecting human rights, dignity and freedom; the police are to secure public and individual rights, the army is to defend citizens against aggression, business persons are to distribute goods, scientists are to research to satisfy human needs, teachers are to form new generations of citizens, farmers are to produce food, physicians are to protect health, and preachers are to preach the word of God, in and out of season, pleasant and unpleasant.

At least, politicians, diplomats, administrators and businesspersons have not taken any vows or made any promises publicly that they have left worldly goods in order to follow Christ. Is it not in order, at least humanly speaking, that your life as the prophetic voice itself needs be seen as proof, that it is valid? If we preach that the gospel is not for mere hearing, but for living, do we, who preach this gospel, live it as true at all? Or is it all misunderstanding? Are we, Christian leaders, true prophetic voices by being rich benefactors of our people?

What about our Lord's own words (Luke 22: 25)?

The kings of the Gentiles exercise lordship over them, and those in authority over them are called benefactors (emphasis mine). But not so with you; rather let the greatest among you become as the youngest, and the leader (emphasis mine) as one who serves.

Are we not to be dependent on the people for our material welfare? If the saying is true: "Money is power"? Can we still sincerely be servants of the people if they depend on us for their material welfare? "What about our Lord's advice: Carry no moneybag, no knapsack, no sandals, and greet no one on the road" (Luk 10: 4):

Are our lives as pastors of no consequence to the gospel we proclaim? What about our Lord's statement: "You are the salt of the earth; but if salt has lost its taste, how shall saltiness be restored?" (Mat 5: 13). Can pastors regard their lives as "private" affair?

What about our Lord's injunction: "You are the light of the world!" (Mat 5: 14)?

This need to live out the Gospel as confirmation of its authenticity, especially in the indigenous cultural context, is a great challenge of authenticity.

If the Christian community is striving towards perfection, then the leaders need to lead the way. In this sense our Lord's words to the rich young man needs reflection: "You lack one thing; go, sell what you have and give to the poor, and you will have treasure in heaven; and come, follow me." (Mark 10: 21-22)

As I have already mentioned, indigenous Africans are concrete thinkers. Our indigenous Africans need role models for the gospel as the vindication of its authenticity. Who could be these role models, if not those who proclaim it?

Those who publicly promise to follow Christ need constant reflection, confronting their own lives with the gospel. "This may be a wicked age, but your lives should redeem it" (Eph.5: 16). This is a great challenge of authenticity for pastoral vocation among our people, a challenge to be true to the gospel. That is the way to make this vocation unique and valid. As Christian leaders our intentions need constant purification.

In essence, as a prophetic voice in the society, pastoral vocation is not only unique and necessary, but also most needed in the indigenous African society today - in the Church, at the office, at your work place, in the military barracks, at the police depot, in the society. Let problems not discourage you but rather stimulate your spiritual creativity to convert them into opportunities. Accept them as calls from God in different situations, call to authenticity to which you can respond, and thus find fulfilment in your pastoral or Christian vocation, vocation for building a holy nation, a holy priesthood, a people set apart to offer spiritual sacrifices. That is your joy, the joy of being authentic, being truthful to yourself and others.

Let us now end this meditation with Eph.4: 25, 29-32:

Therefore, putting away falsehood, let every one speak the truth with his neighbour, for we are members, one of another. Let no evil talk come out of your mouths, but only such as is good for edifying, as fits the occasion, that it may impart grace to those who hear. And do not grieve the Holy Spirit of God, in whom you were sealed for the day of redemption. Let all bitterness and wrath and anger and clamour and slander be put away from you, with all malice, and be kind to one another, tender-hearted, forgiving one another, as God in Christ forgives you.

After reflecting on our pastoral vocation it is appropriate to reflect on the most important source of strength for the fulfilment of our pastoral vocation, namely, prayer. Thus our next reflection will be on the Meaning of Prayer as Challenge of authenticity.

Reflection VI

Meaning of Prayer as Challenge of Authenticity

Introductory Verse: Mark.1: 35-39:

And in the morning, a great while before day, he rose and went out to a lonely place and there he prayed, and Simon and those who were with him pursued him, and they found him and said to him, "Every one is searching for you." And he said to them: "Let us go on to the next town, that I may preach there also; for that is why I came out." And he went throughout all Galilee, preaching in their synagogues and casting out demons.

In our previous reflection we meditated on Pastoral Vocation as a Challenge of Authenticity. We realised that Pastoral Vocation could be authentic, unique and relevant as a prophetic spiritual service. We shall devote the following two reflections to prayer and meditation, Reflections VI and VII. Reflection VI is on The Meaning of Prayer as Challenge of Authenticity.

In the indigenous culture, prayer and sacrifice are very important media of communication with the supernatural, the Almighty (God), the guardian spirits and the Ancestors. As we have already seen, among many indigenous African peoples, the Almighty is not the immediate object of cult. But the people pray to him indirectly through other supernatural intermediaries.

Just as with the pastoral vocation itself, the hectic of pastoral life makes pastors lose the authentic meaning of prayer as basically conversation with God. Many Christians struggle to keep to their spiritual exercises and prayers. But in some cases prayer has become simply either a meaningless routine or a dispensable obligation. This challenges the authenticity of Christian pastoral role as means of contact with the supernatural, through prayer and sacrifice. In the indigenous African society, to maintain the true meaning of prayer in the life of a Christian believer is a great challenge.

For those who train for the ministerial priesthood, or go through religious formation in the seminary or novitiate, we learn about prayer formulae and types of meditation and devotion. But can we, actually say we find personal fulfilment in our prayer and meditation? Do we sincerely experience spiritual refreshment in the Holy Mass, the office of the Hours or devotion? Are you satisfied with your spiritual growth? Can you sincerely say you have been able to meditate any day?

Sometimes we make prayers a routine to follow throughout the day, at a fixed time. But for all Christians, especially for pastors, our spiritual life of meditation and prayer should not even be considered an "obligation" (implying an implicit force), but simply a normal aspect of our pastoral vocation, if we mean to experience personal fulfilment in it through commitment to authenticity.

In the first place, prayer is one of the most important spiritual services of a pastor to which the people have a right. Though all Christians are to be in constant communication with God, those who have to struggle to earn their living in the hectic of daily life may not have time themselves. So they expect their pastors to keep "the line of communication" with the divine constantly open through prayer. They expect the pastor to address God on their behalf about their various needs and also express their gratitude, hopes and joys to Him. This requires that prayers be meaningful and relevant to the specific reasons for the prayer. These are so varied that the traditional "prayer-book system" of especially pastors of missionary churches does not seem to be adequate within the indigenous African context.

When one takes note of prayer in the indigenous religion, be it as part of a sacrificial ritual or libation, it has a general structure. First the relevant spirits or ancestors are addressed. These are in turn requested to convey the message to the Almighty. After that follows the relevant intention. At prayer those around register their agreement with varied comments such as: "exactly!" "That is what we mean!" or "more than that!" Sometimes when the prayer is perceived as not adequately expressing the intentions being prayed for, those around complement the words of the officiating leader with various expressions, such as: "Don't forget the children!" "We offer our thanks too!", or "We need peace too!"

It is interesting that even in the missionary churches, as soon as a prayer is being said, the people around add their comments with various acclamations, such as: "Hallelujah!" "Praise the Lord!" or "Amen!" It is true that this type of involvement in prayer may be from the influence of indigenous African Christian churches or congregations. But is it not clear that it is simply the adaptation of the indigenous religious prayer system, which makes the prayer relevant and inspiring?

Sometimes, using a prayer book, the situation becomes awkward. One could feel that the people would have liked to be involved, to make the prayer relevant to themselves and the occasion or intention. But "prayer book" expressions seem to stifle their involvement. They know it is for the pastor to pray for them. But somehow they feel it is their prayer, their communication with the divine, through the pastor. So they wish to communicate their actual feeling, their actual situation, their actual intention to God, not in a general way, but in a specific way, with their joy, sadness, hope, anxiety, bitterness, thanks and praises.

If they are ill for instance, they want, in a sense, to put their indisposition before God. If they are sorrowful, they want to communicate their sorrow. If they are thankful for any grace or gift from God, they want to communicate thanks specifically to God. If they are full of praises, they want to be free to express these to God.

Once more, even in this communication with the divine through prayer, the typical indigenous desire for sincerity of spirit, authenticity of intention comes out clearly. In a sense, in the continuous communication of their response to God's call in prayer, they wish to express their inner freedom as adopted children, by hiding nothing from their Father. From the depths of their hearts they want to express fully how they feel about the graces they have obtained, how they have used them, and what else they look forward to in the future. Is this not a positive prayer attitude which could make Christian prayer more meaningful to our people?

Do our various prayers, with their general formulae, such as those for the Eucharistic celebration, for the sacraments, or even for various occasions such as prayers for the sick, the dying or the dead, as well as burial, actually communicate respective intentions of those concerned to God? If prayer is so general that it does not address the actual state of affairs or intention inadequately, or so cold that it leaves those present also cold, without any actual effect on them, is it still a meaningful communication with God?

This needs reflection and further investigation by theologians, biblical, spiritual, pastoral, liturgical, catechetical and of course cultural experts, in the process of enculturation. This is a continuous reflective striving to make the Christian faith relevant, effective and authentic in the indigenous African cultural context. Given the importance of prayer in the life of the Christian, to make prayer meaningful, self-communication with God is indeed a challenge of authenticity.

In the second place, even if we perform other ministerial functions perfectly, even if we fulfil our "obligations" of celebrating the Eucharist and saying the office of the hours, all would remain dry, hollow. We would feel empty if we cannot foster truly strong life of prayer. Especially, in our indigenous society, our people place so much trust in our spiritual power, that the lack of spiritual confidence in ourselves affects our whole attitude and response to the people.

Thus prayer is one of the most effective elements of our pastoral vocation. So it is one of the most important requirements. But most often there is not enough time devoted to it in the life of a pastoral minister because of constant trekking and other non-spiritual matters, referred to above

There is also a related challenge. If it is accepted that pastoral ministers are to communicate the intentions of the faithful to God, then, given the official liturgical, spiritual and theological formation of pastoral ministers, especially in missionary-related churches, how do we sincerely identify ourselves with the intentions of the indigenous people without compromising our critical perspective, and therefore our authenticity? Or when we are "made" to offer some intentions to God, which, theologically or scientifically, you cannot identify with. Are you then pretending?

In a concrete case, let us say you are invited to drive out the spirit of a deceased husband worrying a woman, or evil forces ruining someone's profession. How do you sincerely communicate these intentions to God? As one of my theological Professors remarked traditional philosophy and theology, even traditional science, are becoming superfluous, if not in fact obsolete even in Western societies. For us, indigenous African Christian leaders, this is a challenge to accept the humility, to go back to the few elders still alive, and retrieve the philosophical and theological wisdom of our indigenous black African heritage in order to be authentic spiritual leaders of our people. To use the topical indigenous African concept, there is an urgent need of "Sankofa" philosophy and "Sankofa" theology. Otherwise we shall have our own indigenous African threat of superfluity, if not irrelevance.

We need to root the faith deep in our people to stand every storm. We need not "impose" the Christian faith, we need only water it to grow, with deep and firm roots, strong stem, wide and thick branches and leaves, and, of course, abundant fruits.

The attitude of our Lord Jesus Christ himself challenges us. His spiritual leadership was rooted in the indigenous culture of his people, clarifying the traditions. That is why his mediation on the people's needs to the heavenly Father through prayer remained truly relevant to the indigenous people of his time, their thinking and way of life.

This is the challenge of authenticity posed by the indigenous African meaning of prayer as communication with the Supernatural. To face this challenge we need inspiration from the Holy Spirit. As our Lord himself teaches us (Mat 6: 7-8):

*And in praying do not heap up **empty** (emphasis mine) phrases*
as the Gentiles do; for they think that they will be heard for their

many words. Do not be like them, for your Father knows what you need before you ask him*

This is why St. Paul says (Rm.8: 26):

The Spirit too comes to help us in our weakness. For, when we cannot choose words in order to pray properly, the Spirit himself expresses our plea in a way that could never be put into words.

We have now reflected on the meaning of prayer and meditation as communication. In our next reflection we shall continue the reflection on prayer and meditation, dwelling on praying and meditating itself.

Concluding verse: Rom 12:1

Brothers, I implore you by God's mercy to offer your very selves to him, a living sacrifice, dedicated and fit for his acceptance, the worship offered by mind and heart.

Reflection VII

Praying as Challenge Of Authenticity

Introductory Verse: Mat 26: 41

"Watch and pray that you may not enter into temptation; the spirit indeed is willing, but the flesh is weak. "

In the previous meditation, we made the effort to understand the meaning of prayer as communication with the divine. That is rather theoretical. Now we are meditating on how to pray various prayers that we have to pray or meditate upon.

One of the dimensions of life, which demonstrates typically indigenous African authenticity through spontaneity, is prayer. Within a moment the person is already in the spiritual world. In this state individuals report spiritual communication with the deity or Ancestors.

As we have seen from the reflection on the call, an important aspect of divine call is a transformation of identity. An important aspect of this transformation is being in trance, being cut loose from the external world, and transported into the spiritual world. This is a challenge to pastors still stuck with prayer books, formulae and techniques, which make praying a dry and sometimes uncommitted exercise. It is a great challenge to the Christian, especially the pastor, to be sincerely, internally and externally, involved in prayer, as spontaneous and authentic exercises.

As we realised in the previous reflection, prayer or meditation implies withdrawal from the external world in order to communicate with one's inner self. To aid this withdrawal, the usual way is to tone down the function of the physical organs and the nerves through fasting or one or the other spiritual "techniques."

Christians practice fasting as the traditional means to tone down the nerves, to tone down the functioning of certain physical senses and reactions, in order to facilitate prayer and meditation. Fasting, as we know, weakens the body and, of course, also the functioning of the physical organs and the nerves. Since there is also the lack of energising sugar or carbohydrates, fasting blunts the functioning of the senses. In this situation of physical debility, all human activity is now centred on the brain, the mind, now fully turned in on itself. Thus, the person can now withdraw peacefully into himself or herself, communicating with his or her inner self where he or she finds God.

Some spiritual masters maintain that fasting purifies the blood of degenerating elements, and thus prolongs life. Whether this is scientifically valid or not, we leave that to biologists or gerontologists. However a practical altruistic function of fasting, especially in lent, is to leave something for others in need, through self-denial.

What is the common posture or body position for praying?

In the Catholic Church, we know about kneeling. But according to some spiritual experts, kneeling is not an ideal posture for a spiritual exercise (unless, of course, as penance). This is because, as they say, kneeling puts pressure on the knees, causing even painful distraction.

Well, what is the best composure then?

To be frank, I do not know much about prayer techniques myself. All I know is that for the full benefit of prayer and meditation, the body should be composed in such a way that the nerves are relaxed, inducing normal blood circulation to or through essential parts and organs of the body, especially the brain, which, in turn, helps to control one's thoughts. These technical composures range from lying on your bed to the Yogic Shirshâsana (the topsy-turvy pose), head on the ground or floor, your palms flat besides the head. In fact, a Yoga expert considers this pose the most beneficial spiritual exercise because then the brain to which all nerves lead enjoys maximum blood allocation (See Rele, V.G. et al. 1958 Yogic Âsanas for Health and Vigour {A Physiological Exposition}, Bombay: D. B. Taraporevala & Sons & Co.). However, we have to be aware that some Catholics reject any Yogic âsana posture as at best non-Christian, at worst satanic.

Concerning other postures, it is said an ordinary way to pray or meditate is to sit straight on a chair, or stool, head upright, back straight so that the spinal cord, the main nervous conduit is well positioned and free, then hands on the thighs inside down or up, depending on the composure giving the maximum comfort and calm. Or you can try the so called "perfect posture", said to be a variation of yogic Padmâsana, sitting straight on the floor or mat, thighs flat on the floor, then gradually bent at the knees, bringing your two feet together in front, ankles resting one beside the other or on the opposite thighs, palms on the knees inside up with the thumbs and pointers touching. For those well advanced, these postures lead to gradual absorption into the spiritual state- a sort of gradual withdrawal from the material world into the spiritual state of existence.

However, especially in the West, some say those who are yet to begin need other aids such as candlelight or pictures as points of contact for concentration. Many a time, we fail in our attempts to meditate because we start at once with meditation on ideas, passages from the Bible or other books, which is for those already advanced in Theology in general, or Biblical Theology, Biblical Commentary, or Spirituality.

As we know from child pedagogy, to train a child to reason you have to start from what a child can see, touch, and feel physically. So the rational of the Western posture or technique is, if we are unable to meditate on ideas or words, why not try the infant way?

Begin from what you can feel and touch to help exercise concentration as basic step towards full withdrawal into the spiritual world. For instance, you can make the effort to concentrate on the dancing flame of lighted candle. You may fail at the first instance, or you may even doze off, but try and try until you are able to concentrate fully on that flame, and be lifted up into the spiritual world. Or a picture of the cross may lead your thoughts way up to heaven. Thus, for those already advanced, an appropriate posture leads to the spiritual state- a sort of gradual withdrawal from the material world into the spiritual state of existence.

We can ask an important question here. Why are those in traditionally acclaimed Christian societies leaving the traditional Western prayer techniques to embrace the "techniques" of other cultures, such as Yoga and Zen? I know a house superior of a religious order, who even wants to do away with chairs and benches from the chapel altogether. Of course, some elderly members of the congregation are against this "pagan" novelty in their spirituality.

Does it mean that Western Christians themselves find their traditional prayer postures inadequate? If so, can the indigenous African culture also offer something?

Apart from those techniques, from my experience with indigenous African retreatants and members of Charismatic movements everywhere - Africa, America or Europe, there is what I could term biblical or may be African way, namely, spontaneity, or even authenticity!

I term this posture the "Biblical Way", because the Old Testament, especially the Psalms mention raising hands or lifting the eyes up to heaven. In the same sense I regard it the "African Way" because when Africans, especially indigenous Ghanaian elders pour libation, they look downwards while pouring the liquid, water, alcohol or mixtures on the earth. But after that they usually raise the calabash, cup, glass or whatever is being used up with the eyes towards the sky.

On account of its spontaneous character, I am reluctant to term it "technique".

What is this spontaneous way of praying?

As soon as the leader announces the time for prayer by individuals within a group, the two hands go up, eyes closed, while standing or sitting. Then individuals begin to pray aloud or in silence. In a short time the person is already in the spiritual world.

In this state individuals report spiritual communication with God or Christ, or the Holy Spirit. This communication takes various forms.

One may be confronted with one's "dirty past" in a dramatic way. For instance the person may see himself or herself covered with filthy mud, or simply appearing very ugly and terrifying. Long-standing worrisome questions may be answered, or instructions given about change in life for the better. Some may be induced to confess or reconcile in public.

This way of prayer by indigenous Africans is also a way of commitment to authenticity. You do not struggle to master any technique, or concentrate on anything physical, but you just let yourself go with the Spirit, being yourself, being spontaneous.

As an African way of praying or meditating, this spontaneous posture for prayer needs investigating and fostering for us indigenous Africans. It is true some regard it as only an uncontrolled trance just as in our indigenous pre-Christian religion. But this latter criticism is unfounded, because whether West European or Asian, prayer postures are carried over from pre-Christian religion and culture. Moreover as I have just remarked, this indigenous African spontaneity is very akin to the biblical attitude of prayer or meditation. For instance Isaiah 38: 14 says: "My eyes are weary from looking upwards..."

Our Lord Jesus Christ himself used the same prayer posture: John 11: 41 says: "And Jesus lifted up his eyes and said, 'Father, I thank you that you have heard me...'"

It is the external expression of the inner sincerity of spirit, the external expression of inner commitment to authenticity. This spontaneous spiritual expression is not only a sign of spiritual health, but also, I believe, psychological health, a sign of self-acceptance in spite of all earthly problems and disappointments. This psychological health is certainly conducive to physical health, and psychosomatic well-being.

It is interesting that unlike in European Christian spirituality, African spirituality has fewer physical elements or tools such as statues, holy pictures, relics, monuments or flags. This unique indigenous African spirituality is most demonstrated during

Corpus Christi processions. In Europe Corpus Christi processions include other physical objects carried alongside the monstrance - figures, pictures, relics, flags etc. But among indigenous Africans there is usually only the monstrance carried during the procession. So also during these processions, unlike in Europe where individual families expose their "holy objects" along the route, among indigenous Africans these "private expositions" are generally non-existent.

What about the indigenous rhythms of the indigenous African drums? I know in certain parts of Europe these indigenous African rhythms are even in University clinics to aid the process of healing. We know indigenous religions use such rhythms to induce the state of trance and other cultic activities. I believe this is also a worthwhile aspect of the indigenous African culture for investigation by Theologians, Liturgists, Biblical scholars, Spiritual experts, Psychologists, Medical scientists and, of course, cultural experts.

However, just as the European or Asian spirituality can degenerate into syncretism, this indigenous "African way" too, can degenerate into uncontrolled trance state. So there is need to control any type of posture for prayer or meditation in order to keep acculturated forms, be they African, Asian, European or American able to maintain Christian identity. In a word, we may say what is important is commitment to authenticity, being true to yourself.

For the rest, I think every individual can cultivate his or her own way of effective prayer and meditation. What is needed is that each one should, as a spiritual leader, develop strong spiritual life in depth as a constant source of energy for himself or herself. As a spiritual master guiding fellow Christians in their response to their call, the pastor, or any Christian spiritual leader, is to develop and maintain effective and deep prayer life, which would truly inspire those whom he or she leads to provide the spiritual dimension of life as a balance to material existence - leading a life that is inspired by inner direction.

True prayer and meditation should help obtain energy for the start of work in the morning, continuously tested and replenished.

Some of us may say we have no time. Certainly no one could say he or she is busier than our Lord Jesus Christ. Let us examine a typically busy day in the life of our Lord:

"In the morning, long before dawn he got up and left the house and went off to a lonely place and prayed there" (Mk.1: 35). Then afterwards "he went all through Galilee, preaching in their synagogues and casting out devils" (Mk.1: 36).

To begin a hectic day, our Lord withdraws from the external world to a lonely place, to be in intimate contact with his inner self as a source of new energy afterwards during the day. This makes his work throughout the day conform to his inner direction- the Will of God, the Father. So also before any important act our Lord prays to the Father to glorify His name through Him- be it healing or raising from the dead.

Before the final act of self-surrender in the garden of Gethsemane, he falls down and prays three times before getting the courage to tell his disciples: "Get up! Let us go!" (Mt.26: 46). It is only prayer and meditation, which can give us strength for our spiritual and temporal worldly tasks.

Effective meditation can save us from many emotional problems- anger, nervousness and other forms of irritation, by toning down our nerves. Even our formal prayers can be personally fulfilling, provided they involve commitment to authenticity, being yourself, and not mere practice of "technique". For instance, when saying, reciting or praying the Psalms you have to be present with your mind, heart and spirit. You need make the prayer your prayer.

What do we do to incorporate the sometimes "irrelevant" aspects of official prayers, the Psalms, the Prophets or other biblical passages? When you meet names like Israel, the king, apply them to yourself, the Christian community, the Church, or the world in general. All nationalistic and political prayers could be given spiritual interpretation or meaning.

So also one can convert "hate" Psalms into a spiritual rejection of evil in the society as "enemies" against whom one has to "fight" with spiritual weapons. Or, as one author suggests, one could convert such "hate" Psalms into prophetic anger against social evils-exploitation, oppression, discrimination, etc., of our time, as a sort of psychological release of tension against perpetrators of these evils. So also our liturgical functions could be reinvigorating if done calmly and meditatively.

Once more let us be inspired by our indigenous attitude towards sacred objects, sacred acts and sacred music, with the concomitant solemn composure. We can in particular note exceptional silence, when and where it is necessary, when moving into the shrine for cultic functions.

Prayer as meeting with the divine, communicating our selves with and to the divine, as we have seen, certainly requires sacred attitude of respect, if not awe. This attitude of respect and quietness induce refreshing experience. You can experience this refreshing energy if for instance you are present with mind and heart at the celebration of the Eucharist. Or if you yourself are the celebrant you can always remain fresh if you pray the Mass attentively- without rushing through. Begin the Mass after composing yourself by meditation with the experience of being connected with God, the spiritual centre of your being. Or even you can imagine yourself in God's presence. Really go into yourself and as it were, beam or radiate your spiritual power over the people. Make the penitential rite an act of true, authentic, reconciliation.

This need for authenticity in the introductory rite of confession, forgiveness and reconciliation is demanded by our indigenous African culture. Our people believe performing or undertaking a ritual without a clean disposition renders the act null and void and could even be fatal for the individual and the community. In this case, commitment to authenticity implies sincerely inducing a clean heart, disposed to celebrating a worthy Eucharist, which is in principle the celebration of reconciliation between God and human beings on the one hand, and between human beings on the other. Especially as the celebrant, your commitment to authenticity implies truly representing Our Lord, offering himself, broken and shared for the salvation of all. In this sense, as the celebrant, you bear the wrongs of the others in the community, which you bring to the altar. You need forgive sincerely yourself from the depths of your heart and pray for the repentance and forgiveness of your faithful. It is spiritually destructive if you are ill disposed before Mass and celebrate with anger in your heart.

In the context of, or rather in response to the indigenous African cultural demand for authenticity, one may ask a fundamental question concerning the validity of a sacrament or a sacramental act. Is it sacramentally worthwhile to celebrate the Eucharist, a sacrament, or rather the sacramental celebration of divine love and mercy in a state of anger, which influences your whole attitude and even the proclamation of the word of God, the homily? Is it worthwhile beginning the Holy Mass if you are not ready to forgive and reconcile?

This is a fundamental question for us as indigenous Africans, who have become the Disciples of Christ. It is true; God or Christ may not strike us down or dead for celebrating the Eucharist with unclean hearts. But this calls for reflection in view of possible and real conflicts in our "Eucharistic Communities", often between the faithful or a section of the faithful and the pastor, or even between the pastors or the faithful themselves.

Our need to commit ourselves to authenticity as indigenous African Christians requires that we rethink the distinction between liceity and validity of sacraments seriously. Can we separate the two characteristics of the effect of the sacraments? Can we accept sacramental celebration when it can be regarded only licit in principle, but not valid? If there is open animosity between the celebrant and the faithful on one hand and between individuals among the faithful on the other, is the sacramental celebration still valid?

This is a challenge for indigenous African Christian Theologians, Canonists, Liturgists and of course Moral Theologians. It is true that the Eucharist itself is the celebration of forgiveness. Therefore we may believe our wrongs are forgiven in the act of celebrating the Eucharist itself. But if throughout the celebration the animosity remains till the end, is it still sacramentally effective?

Of course no human being is worthy before God. But commitment to authenticity requires some degree of credibility, some degree of being worthy, to make a sacramental celebration or even prayer and meditation worthwhile.

If pastors cannot eat together on account of conflicts, could they concelebrate effectively? Is that celebration still "eucharistic"? Is the prayer: "Our Father..." valid if after the words: "Forgive us our trespasses as we forgive those who trespass against us...", your heart still remains rigidly unforgiving? Can you offer true peace when there is violence of hatred in your heart?

Commitment to authenticity in prayer and meditation, or better expressed, prayer and meditation as commitment to authenticity need deep reflection and humble contrition. This commitment to authenticity needs affect also the word of God and its effect on us in the context of prayer and meditation.

At the time of readings, you can gain fulfilment in listening consciously to the readings, mentally selecting good ideas you could apply to your life. If you are delivering the sermon or homily beam your love and spiritual power over the listeners, sincerely wish all well. Then say each prayer meaningfully, together with meaningful gestures.

Before communion, be truly united with the people to share the one body and blood of Christ with them. Avoid making discriminatory remarks about those fit or unfit for communion, since communion itself has a healing and reconciling force. Moreover if there is need for self-examination, the appropriate place is the introductory penitential rite, the kyrie (in the Catholic liturgy). After such a celebration with fully conscious participation with mind, heart and spirit you can be sure to have toned down your nerves, really refreshed with new energy. Such a living participation in a liturgical celebration makes the Pastor's life always light and energetic as it diminishes tiresomeness.

Thus, for continuous strength, the Pastor needs meditation before and after any major activity.

For this kind of prayerful life to be personally fulfilling in the apostolate, the Pastor or any spiritual leader needs share his or her spiritual experiences with the faithful by developing charisms as integral elements of the apostolate, especially the charism of healing. He or she can organise prayer sessions early mornings and evenings. These prayer sessions can actually resuscitate dormant communities. If you have the bent for charismatic life, you can allow the spirit to work in your faithful. They have a right to your prayers as spiritual leader. So give them freely.

The charism of healing is important because as we have already remarked, for indigenous Africans, life is integral existence. Therefore health is bound up with religion. Indigenous African healers, medicine men or medicine women, always include religious acts in their healing art. They often withdraw into the innermost shrine to communicate with the supernatural.

This withdrawal into oneself, into the inner core, is a necessary exercise to overcome being torn apart by the centrifugal forces, which we touched upon in our meditation on society today. For, especially in our technological age, the human being loses himself or herself in the external world, no longer in touch with himself or herself, his or her inner being, which is the source of meaning. So, as it were, the human being is cut from his or her spiritual "supply depot", a ship without an anchor, a sort of psychic dizziness. In this state, life becomes aimless, since the human being loses contact with the spiritual self, we may say his or her soul. Now ruled from outside, the human being becomes just like an unwilling horse drawn away from water. In this situation of the loss of self-control, the human being can make the effort to achieve great things in life but will meet frustrations, doubts and fears.

Moreover life becomes simply mere repetition of activity-rising, studying, working, eating, sleeping, standing and sitting. This is an endless cycle, which does not leave any room for silence, withdrawal into oneself. This creates a spiritual hole, existential vacuum, which has to be filled by conversing with one's inner self about one's potentialities and needs as self-direction for existence. That is why we read Mk1: 35-36: "In the morning, long before dawn he got up and left the house, and went off to a lonely place and prayed". It is only after that, that he received the spiritual direction and strength to continue his work of preaching, healing, etc.

So also when the human being is physically too weak, or the will power too loose, or when overwhelmed by troubles and disappointments, a situation which can lead to self destruction, suicide, the only way to resuscitate oneself is this withdrawal into contact with one's inner being, where the human being can be at home, and at peace with himself or herself. With this inner peace, the human being can control himself or herself and cut himself or herself loose from external attractions. For, sometimes torn between this inner drive and external pressures, it is only this silent withdrawal that can enable the human being to overcome these external pressures, an exercise which can be painful indeed.

This is also clear in our Lord's struggle in the garden of Gethsemane. It is the struggle between inner drive to fulfil his purpose on earth as a saviour, by dying on the cross, and worldly desire to avoid pain. He knows he has come purposely to suffer, die and rise, or be raised, the third day. But when the time comes he displays a most human emotion. As the Evangelist reports "sadness came over him, and great distress" (Mt.26: 39). How hard to leave those worldly attractions - good company, some wine, large following, popularity! After all, he could have escaped. He could have commanded an overpowering heavenly army to defend him. But then he would have lost his purpose of existence and, in fact, the purpose of becoming a human being itself, his authenticity. That would therefore be unfulfilled life. He could free himself from those worldly desires only by one means. That is by withdrawing from the world into himself. As we read, "he fell on his face and prayed" (Mt.26: 39), because "the Spirit is willing, but the flesh is weak" (Mt.26: 4). Then a third time he goes away and prays. It is only then that he gets the courage (humanly speaking) to cry out: "Get up! Let us go!" (Mt 26: 46)

That is the dramatic way a human being can free himself or herself from worldly attractions, to conform to his or her inner life. It is only there that he finds his or her authentic self, the purpose of existence. Without that withdrawal into the intimacy with the inner being, where he meets God the Father, Jesus might have succeeded as a popular prophet, a wonder worker, but not the authentic Jesus Christ, the saviour.

Thus, in order to realise the absolute value of divine mercy in saving humankind in spite of strong external pressures, Jesus Christ has to fall down three times, to communicate with this inner deposit of goodness, which gives him the power to conform to the intrinsic drive towards the realisation of the authentic self, the purpose of existence.

It is through this constant contact with the inner core that the human being discovers his or her intrinsic inner drives to which he or she has to conform as a move towards authenticity, towards self-realisation, thus bringing out what is in him or her. Anyone in constant contact with this inner self also realises his or her inner dignity and freedom. Therefore he or she is no longer easily attracted or possessed by the external material world. He or she no longer fears poverty, embarrassments or any external dishonour.

Thus meditation and prayer, the intimate dialogue with one's inner self, investigating one's ends in particular situations, make the human being enjoy inner personal fulfilment, irrespective of worldly values. As Christians, especially as pastors, we need to develop and have confidence in our spiritual potentialities and spiritual endowments. If we achieve the state of being able to make a true meditative prayer we shall certainly find it fulfilling and rewarding. Our Lord assures us: "I tell you therefore, everything you ask and pray for believe you have it already, and it will be yours" (Mk.11: 25).

We have now reflected on the act of praying. But in principle and from experience prayer is effective only as an act of faith. Therefore it is appropriate that our next reflection is on Faith as Challenge of authenticity

Let us end this reflection with Mt. 7: 7-8.

Ask, and it will be given you; seek, and you will find; knock, and it will be opened to you. For every one who asks, receives; and he who seeks, finds; and to him who knocks, it will be opened.

Reflection VIII

Faith as Challenge Of Authenticity

Introductory Verse: John 10:17-18

For this reason the Father loves me, because I lay down my life, that I may take it again. No one takes it from me, but I lay it down of my own accord. I have power to lay it down, and I have power to take it again, this charge I have received from my Father.

In our previous meditations we gave our Christian answer to today's society's perception of the world, authenticity and personal fulfilment. We found it was not acceptable because a human being is more than matter, life is more than material life, authenticity is more than life without control, and that personal fulfilment is more than material success.

As already mentioned above, the indigenous African religious belief involves commitment to certain beliefs. These beliefs are not necessarily written in a physical book or document. They are not articles of faith to simply commit to memory. Thus it is understandable that the people have what we may term a living faith, or rather a visible faith. This faith or system of beliefs is expressed in external acts of cult and observance of certain moral norms, the disregard of which could have dire consequences. Therefore if Christians are convinced of their Christian faith, then they are challenged to prove its authenticity in the way they commit their lives to this faith, through the visible moral code of behaviour.

There needs be inner commitment to authenticity, in a word, faith unfeigned (1 Tim.15). Thus if we are convinced that our Christian faith is a valid, or even a superior alternative to the belief system of our indigenous African religion then we are challenged to prove its authenticity through our commitment to the moral code of behaviour demanded by the Christian faith.

Thus the challenging question is, as Christians, do we have any concrete alternative to offer the world, to offer our indigenous Africans, to offer today's society, even today's polarized Church?

If we are convinced that there is personal fulfilment through commitment to authenticity in a way of life different from that of the contemporary society, then we have to show it in our lives. For, we can be authentic and achieve personal fulfilment only if we live what we believe in. It is only when we commit ourselves to authenticity that we can have a true personality, an integrated personality, and not dual personality. It is only an integrated personality, one in belief and action that can achieve fulfilment. That is why our Lord counsels: "If your virtue goes no deeper than that of the scribes and Pharisees (in our case, the world and society), you will never get into the kingdom" (Mt.5: 20).

If we know there are human values, spiritual values or virtues, which alone can truly fulfil human aspirations, then we have to demonstrate these values or virtues in our own lives wherever we find ourselves, in the seminary, in the convent, in the institutions, at the workplace, on the street, in the market, at home or even in the laboratory. It is for that reason that the Second Vatican Council calls the Church a sacrament- revealing God's love and true human nature. If then the Church has to be a symbol of values or virtues that people, the world and society need, but do not have, then it falls on you and me, as Christians, and the more so as Pastors, the ministers of the word, to live out the values or virtues in and outside the church.

The Church can serve its purpose, the Church can have meaning, and the Church can fulfil its mission only if it has something to offer the world- to save it from materiality.

But who is the Church?

As we have seen already, the Church is you and I - a Christian, a Seminarian or Novice, a Religious, a Minister of the Word of God, a lawyer, a politician, a businessperson, a soldier, a policeman, a teacher and any person called to follow Christ, living as part, as members of the Church, the disciple of Christ. The Church finds fulfilment only in us- the members. So also we find personal fulfilment only in the Church- fulfilling its mission in our lives through lasting values or virtues. This task has to begin in the seminary, in the novitiate, at home, at school. In this context the seminary has a special role to play. The seminary is the powerhouse from which the spirit living in young blooded apostles should shoot off to embrace the world.

For those readers who do not fall into this group the following reflection is still useful as an element of our Christian faith. Even if one does not make any life commitment through promises such as marriage or oath of office, the vowed state of life affects the life of faith directly or indirectly.

Moreover the state of life of every human being at the age of reason requires making a promise in one form or another. Infants have to agree to conform to certain rules laid down by parents. It is normal to hear a mother say to a child: "Do you promise…? The same happens when a child enters kindergarten, primary school, or university. After studies, even after university formation, there is always a ritual of oath taking at graduation. Every profession demands one or the other form of promise or oath taking - legal, political or scientific career.

Then certain states of life, such as marriage or partnership, require the ritual of promise by those entering the relationship, one to the other. In any form one may consider these promises or oaths as entailing, at least by extended interpretation, explicit or implicit, forms of the three vows or solemn promises in the Catholic Church for clerics and the religious.

Any state of life implies obedience, be it to the partner, employer, head of department or one's doctor. Likewise any state of life implies poverty, using material goods moderately, be it common property of partners, official property of a firm or even doses of medical prescription. In fact frugality is a cardinal value in most families.

So also in a sense any state of life involves chastity, care taken in relationship with the opposite sex, be he or she your co-worker, your secretary, your patient, or even your marriage partner. It could be interesting to dwell further on the application of solemn promises to various states of life. That may be a topic for another book. For now I believe these few connections are sufficient.

Accordingly we shall reflect on how we could live obedience as a sign of faith, poverty as a sign of hope and celibacy as a sign of love. I hope from the implicit connections made above, the following reflection would be of some inspiration to those who do not need to take these vows or make these solemn promises. Moreover since the observance or the living out of these vows or solemn promises affect the relationship of those who make them with others in the Church, community or society, I believe these reflections are useful to all readers.

It is true that some make technical differences between vows taken by the Religious and promises made by the candidates for the priesthood. Some Religious claim priests do not take any vows. But for the indigenous Africans, who look up to you for spiritual leadership, there are no differences between religious vows or clerical promises. Our people hardly differentiate between "Father" and "Brother". Most of the time whether you are out of the novitiate or the Seminary, you are either "Father" or "Sister". And for them you have made public promises to which you have to commit yourself, as commitment to authenticity. I would not want to disturb the flow of our reflection with these technical distinctions. Let us leave that to Canonists and Spiritual Theologians.

Those who might have been preparing for Catholic pastoral ministry or religious life might have learnt, or are still learning, in the Seminary or novitiate, that a vow or solemn promise or still specifically a declaration of liberty, is a response to a specific call to Christian holiness, a gift of the spirit, a charism (Vat. II: Lumen Gentium or The Dogmatic Constitution on the Church, No. 42). Therefore in principle the Church does not give it by herself. So the Church cannot take it away. It is an individual gift to you for building up the people of God.

If you are not yet disposed to the set of three gifts or charisms - obedience, poverty and celibacy, then you are almost too late, although still not too late.

In the seminary or novitiate, the moment you start intensive preparations towards the public proclamation that you in fact have or are sincerely disposed towards the set of gifts, have you had time to reflect on them? Have you had time to reflect on the indigenous African cultural demand for authenticity of commitment to those gifts? Are you fully prepared in the depths of your heart? Are you disposed towards the gifts of obedience, poverty and celibacy? Or do you only wait for "those formalities" to pass, then you can lead your life as you deem it fit?

I should think everyone, alone with God, has to answer for himself or herself. For the meantime, let us find out how authentic commitment to these gifts could help us find fulfilment in our pastoral vocation. Let us begin with obedience as a way of commitment to authenticity of the act of faith, a way of practising true faith.

We know that every Christian community, like any religious community, including the seminary or novitiate, is a community of faith. That is, a community of those who believe in our Lord Jesus Christ. Or to put it more eucharistically, we may say, a communion of those who have become children of God by faith (Gal.3: 26). So in order to be true to yourself, in order to be able to find fulfilment, you have got to have faith, you have got to believe. Otherwise everything becomes empty. Then, without faith, without trust, all your work, all your studies, all your struggles, in fact, all your sufferings become meaningless. You have to make up your mind: You are not a social worker. For our people you are distinct. Even if you happen to be employed, your own colleagues or even your own employer will call you "Father" "Pastor" or "Sister". You cannot run away from it. That title sticks on you wherever you go.

That is why already as a Seminarian, or Novice, a would-be pastor, or a would-be religious, they call you already: "Father", "Pastor" or "Sister". You are not just "Mister!" You are not just "Miss" or "Mrs". This is not to say, anyway, that it is the title, which shows what we are. No! Probably, this title even obscures your true role, probably the reason why our Lord spoke against titles, whatever meaning experts may give to his statement in Mt. 23: 9.

The point is that if you enter the seminary or the novitiate without believing anything, if your philosophy convinces you that there is no God, let alone God's Son called Jesus, but you pretend as if you believe and people trust you because they think, or even believe, you believe, because of which they accept you and your word, then it is unjust, even self-deception. If in fact you don't believe at all, but pretend you believe, and so make others put their spiritual trust in a fake, then you are exploiting the people. In short then, if your vocation is only all a make-up, if your faith entails no commitment to authenticity then you are a living disaster.

This holds also true for the one, who is convinced it is wrong to be a Christian and at the same time be a priest or priestess in the indigenous African religion, and preaches against it publicly but secretly indulges in it himself or herself for personal gain. For, that is not only simply syncretism or "enculturation", but also, in a sense, spiritual or even religious schizophrenia. And that is against the indigenous cultural principle of authenticity. Moreover to proclaim to lead a way of life, which you know, contradicts your inner conviction, which you know contradicts your conscience, is against a cardinal principle of morality. That cannot make you a happy or healthy person, be it in body, mind, heart or spirit. Moreover the indigenous African demand for commitment to authenticity in belief and practice makes such a person unacceptable as a member of the indigenous African religion. Certainly such a person cannot find personal fulfilment in pursuing his or her vocation in the Seminary or novitiate because there is no inner commitment to authenticity

You can find fulfilment in the Seminary or novitiate, and later in the ministry or service only when you truly believe. In short self-fulfilment demands faith unfeigned (1 Tim.15). This is not to imply you must never have doubts. Doubts can even lead to stronger and deeper faith. For doubts are healthy, provided they do not remain permanent anxiety, but are part of human struggle for perfection.

Now, what is this faith? What is this belief, then? Leaving aside the subtle distinction between Fides Quae and Fides Qua for the theologians, we can say faith is more than innumerable articles or propositions kept in memory. Faith is the expressive response of, and to, the Grace of God as a gift of the Spirit. Faith is a gift in two senses. In the first sense faith is in itself a gift of the spirit of God as grace. In the second sense the capacity to respond to this gift of faith is also a gift of grace. No human being is worthy of it, in the sense of reward for one's own work.

Faith is trust, namely trust in the divine Providence and the working of the Spirit. Lastly faith is life. Since life is a struggle, faith is also a struggle. Faith has to be won every day. That is why faith is dynamic. Accordingly, we may regard faith as:
The free gift of faithful trust in the love of God, despite human failures and weaknesses, through the Spirit of Christ as the new principle of existence.

Faith is a gift to the Christian, to the minister, to be shared. It has been freely given and therefore must be freely shared with fellow ministers, fellow Christians, and fellow human beings. This is exactly what we are doing now. The author of this book, or of these reflections, is sharing his faith with readers, be they seminarians, lecturers, novices, novice masters or mistresses, pastors or pastoral ministers, fellow Christians, fellow believers in God, invoked by any name, or fellow human beings.

In this context, in his turn the author will be happy to be at the receiving end of this sharing of faith when readers begin to share their reactions to these reflections with the author. Thus we continuously support one another on this spiritual journey as we support and share nourishment one with the other. So as a reader, you are requested to share these thoughts with whomever you happen to meet.

Faith is most joyful if you can share it without seeking privileges or even recognition. However, in order to give, one must have. No one gives what one does not have. Positively put: You can give only what you have. Thus commitment to authenticity, in the sharing of faith demands constant deepening of our own faith. For those interested in the intellectual deepening of the faith, they can deepen the faith through reading the scriptures, commentaries, encyclicals and other theological tracts. This type of intellectual deepening of the faith is useful, not only for pastors, ministers or teachers, but also for those who wish to bring the knowledge about their faith up to the level of their own formation in other fields of knowledge.

For pastors, ministers or any person involved in religious instruction, this intellectual deepening is important, if not for anything, at least for self-confidence. After all witnessing to the gospel in our ministry is our vocation, our responsibility. That is also expressed by the Second Vatican Council Fathers in their proclamation of the Word of God, the Scriptures, as the "soul" of ecclesiastical studies. For Seminarians or Novices your life of faith as a future Pastor, Religious or Minister, is to transmit this Word as an essential responsibility. The Word should be part of your training and pastoral work later.

In the indigenous African society, technical and practical knowledge of the Bible is required, including particular chapters and verses. Know your Bible well. Otherwise you may be embarrassed by questions "from the floor".

For those of us, who have the responsibility to instruct others, we should be able to prepare our catechism classes, talks, and sermons well, so that after delivering them we can experience a sense of fulfilment. And that fulfilment is possible only if you are innerly committed to authenticity, making the Word part of you. Especially, a sermon or homily should be, as St. Paul puts it, "not plausible words of wisdom but the demonstration of the spirit of power!" (1 Cor.2: 4), and I add, the power working in and through you. In this context, I should think the way you prepare and give your catechism classes, talks or homilies would make you feel anxiety or joy, personal fulfilment or emptiness, even disappointment, after delivery. Especially, if the homily is spiritually poor, either scolding or frightening, you will feel something lacking. But if the homily is rich, with a powerful healing theme you will feel the joy and personal satisfaction.

Accordingly, I think, there are three stages of preparing homilies, always bearing in mind that you are going to impart faith, which saves without strings attached. The first stage is thoroughly negative, mostly denunciations of the laziness of the people, against too little collections, against their sins, etc. I sincerely believe this kind of homily needs reworking because it would imply faith is only negative judgment. The second stage would be a mixture of both negative and positive elements. This is often in the form of condemnations as in the first type, but with the call to penance in order to avoid the anger of God and experience His love.

The above type of sermon or homily, I think, is not bad. This is a typical prophetic homily. After all, our Lord used it too. Remember his denunciations in Matthew's gospel, especially chapter twelve "brood of vipers!" (Verses 34ff.): "white-plastered tombs!" (Mat 23: 27-28) and the like. But such a sermon or homily needs improving upon, depending on the circumstances or the type of congregation or hearers, towards the third stage of completely positive sermon. It is like this:

"Well, fellow Christians, we have been weak in the past but God wants to show us our human nature, so that we may more easily appreciate his redeeming love. You have to change because God wants you to change. God, in fact, gives you his grace provided you are open to this grace and sincerely strive to do his will... "

This latter stage of preparation or kind of sermon speaks straight to the heart. The people will come to you and say: "Father (or Pastor), thank you, your sermon is good today." You will also experience a true sense of fulfilment that your faith is really healing - not only for the people but for yourself too. For, a true homily is not just given, but shared. Your whole attention should be concentrated on the people so that you feel that you are actually going out of yourself to reach into their hearts.

Just as faith is a free gift for sharing so also it is a total trust-confidence in the divine providence and the Spirit of Christ at work in ourselves, our neighbours, our society, and, of course, in our

Church. To experience true personal fulfilment, we have to be confident in our spiritual powers, especially in today's indigenous African society demanding commitment to authenticity

May I share with you a personal experience once more?

One time during my pastoral visits, a young man stood up and said: "Other Churches are laughing at us. They say our Fathers cannot heal because they have no spiritual powers. Tell me, Father, now: 'Do you also have the power to heal or not?' "

I was caught unawares. That was certainly a typical challenge of authenticity in an African cultural context. Were it somewhere else, I could have responded simply: "That is not Catholic!" Or, as a colleague in another cultural context responded to such a question: "That is all from the devil, from Satan, to tempt true Christians". Or still, as a theologian once commented on such a question, "That is not traditional". But in a typical indigenous African context, such answers would be destructive of the faith of well-meaning Christians. Moreover the person asking the question would regard such answers as simply escapist. The question or remark which would follow would be: "But Our Lord Jesus Christ healed people and said the charism of healing would be one of the signs of the authenticity of faith of His followers".

That question was therefore indeed, a challenge of authenticity. The hearers may not regard me as a fake disciple or a fake pastor. This is because, at least since the Second Vatican Council, many indigenous Catholics, literate or illiterate, have had to know the Bible chapter by chapter, verse by verse, and word for word. This is because of the competition among Christian Churches to see who knows the Bible best. To be part of this competition many Catholics have developed some form of attachment to the Word of God. You can see people reading the bible at the most odd places. It could be on the farm, along the road, in the market, in the shop or on the bus. Therefore to avoid answering the question by indulging in academic commentary or exegesis would not work.

So I was challenged to answer. Well, the Holy Spirit works at odd times and in odd ways. Instantaneously I said: "Certainly we all have the gift as Christians. Therefore we Catholic Priest also have the gift. But the faith of the person to be healed is also important". Then I added: "In the final analysis, only God heals. We are only his instruments". That was rather an impromptu answer. But at the end one of them came to my rescue. He explained that just as the Apostles had different gifts, so also Catholic Priests have different gifts. But certainly, every Catholic Priest, according to him, could lay hands on people for healing, but just as Jesus Christ often affirmed, the faith of the sick person also counts.

Then ensued a lengthy discussion on Our Lord's criteria for valid discipleship. In the end I said, anyway, we had such gifts also of course, but in the Catholic Church we need prepare the faithful for it. I guess that was an instinctive escape. I guess many of you, who are pastor-trainees, may have already had similar confrontation of authenticity during your pastoral assignments. Not to be able to answer would be embarrassing indeed!

The question is straightforward. Do we, as Catholics, as Seminarians, as Pastors, have the power to heal or not? Sometimes we explain it off by saying, after all those of other "sects", not "Churches", are only deceiving the people, they use chloroform, etc. We say we have hospitals for the sick, orthopaedic centres, etc. So when people come to us for healing we turn them off. When it is a case of possession, we sometimes even look on hopelessly, or, should I say faithlessly.

This question is a typical question demanding authenticity.

To face the question sincerely, do we say healing is not part of our ministry or we are not confident in our own healing faith? I would say, to find personal fulfilment in the ministry, everyone needs develop his or her spiritual gifts to the full. If you have the charism for healing, I don't think there is any sense in being shy or afraid of failure.

I guess if we, just like the disciples, would also go to Jesus Christ "privately" to ask "Why were we unable to cast it (i.e., devil) out?" Our Lord would answer: "Because you have little faith." If you are already in the Seminary or novitiate, you should continue to discover, test, develop and even use your spiritual gifts. They are not for hoarding; they are for sharing. Our Lord assures us:

*"I tell you solemnly, if your faith were the size of a mustard seed
you could say to this mountain 'move from here to there' and it
would move; nothing would be impossible for you (Mt.17: 20).*

We need have confidence in the Holy Spirit working in ourselves, in our neighbours, in the Church and in the society. Remember what Paul tells us:

*"Proof that you are sons is that God has sent the Spirit of his son
into our hearts, the spirit that cries 'Abba, Father' and it is this
that makes you son, you are not a slave any more" (Gal.4: 6).*

Many a time, we think the spirit is at work only in us, bishops, priests, deacons, seminarians, and the religious etc. and not in the faithful, whom we often refer to as the "laity". We try to manipulate the faithful to do our will sometimes against the Spirit. In the long run we frustrate ourselves because we give our own responsibility, our faith, up to laws and rules. For instance, if there is not enough collection, we do not appeal to their free will in faith but we make laws and rules: "no payment, no burial". So we make them pay, not out of faith, but out of force. We trust in our rules more than the Spirit to generate faith in people. This leads to a cycle of frustration, less people come to Church, more laws, less faith, etc.

We have said faith is confidence; trust in the Spirit at work in the community, the seminary, the novitiate, the church and the society. This brings us to one of the most problematic and sometimes most suspect of vows or solemn promises, because its demand from authority could be devastating, and most un-Christian indeed. This is obedience.

On the positive side obedience in the spiritual sense could be considered as trust in the Spirit at work in our neighbour, in the staff of the seminary, the rector, the novice mistress, the superior, the church president, the Christian mother, the catechist, the bishop and the Pope. However, as any of us may have experienced at one time or another, the fear of obedience is that there is no guarantee that what you obey to do is actually leading to the aim of your agreement to obey.

For those under formation as prospective pastors in the Seminary, many questions about the validity and purposefulness of actual cases of obedience to rules or authority crop up in the mind of the individual, who has to obey. If I don't go to town in the night, shall I gain anything? Is it the will of God that Seminarians should not go to town any time they will? Does my obedience to stay in the seminary at night make me a better Seminarian or a better Deacon? Does my stay in the Seminary not rather make me a hypocrite, filling me with bad thoughts instead of making me chaste?

If I go to Mass every day, do I gain anything? Does my spiritual life become better and stronger at all if I go to Mass, if I don't feel like going? After all, I am a Deacon. After all I am a mature Seminarian. Or still worse there is the fear whether the person who orders has any good intention at all. Is it not just ill will? After all, are we not mature enough to decide for ourselves? Why do the Bishops push us around like small boys during holidays and so forth and so on?

This questioning state of mind could be applicable to other categories of persons who at one time or another have to obey, as part of their Christian vocation. Thus the Novice, the Religious, the parishioner, the student or the pupil could have the same doubting questions when requested to obey. In that state of doubt, there is doubt whether my obedience helps to make me pleasing to God, or helps me achieve the purpose of my life. There is doubt whether authority really has good intentions. In either case, there is no strong reason for obeying.

If you obey that way, if you obey to please the authority, just to avoid punishment or simply to be in the good books of the authority, your obedience is blind obedience. You obey out of weakness. You lose your freedom in obeying. You do not have the courage to say: "I am going to do it because it will lead to the good of the community, the Seminary, the Church, the Society. But rather you obey, as we may say, with a "long face": Unng...." Or you obey just for the sake of obeying: "Well, they say I should do it. So I do it."

This kind of obedience without faith, this type of obedience without trust, this type of obedience without inner commitment to authenticity can lead to desperation. Obedience without reason, blind obedience, obedience to avoid being "sacked", obedience for the sake of obedience leads to the weakening of vocation, the weakening of faith itself.

But is there any reason then to make a solemn promise of obedience? Can we get any encouragement anywhere? Is our obedience not in vain? Or can our Lord himself offer us the model of obedience with full hearts?

Yes, if we consider the sacrificial death of our Lord, it can offer us encouragement to obey. This obedience to the Father to die for humankind is not a blind obedience, but trusting obedience. So we read from John 10: 17-18:

"The Father loves me, because I lay down my life in order to take it up again. No one takes it from me: I lay it down of my own free will, and as it is in my power to lay it down, so it is in my power to take it up again; and this is the command I have been given by my Father."

Has our Lord any assurance that his obedience will be effective? If we mean a "scientific" assurance that after his death humankind would be radically changed to do good, our first meditation tells us "No!" There is still sin and sinful humankind, like you and me. Our Lord does not wait for proof that his obedience would be effective. For, he obeys to die, so Paul puts it, "while we were still sinners" (Rom.5: 8). Not when we showed signs of conversion, making the sacrificial death less risky. For, when we were still helpless, Christ died for the wicked," not on his own, but at the Father's command and at the time God chose (Rm.5: 6).

Thus, our Lord knew, to die for sinful humankind was a risk; to obey the Father for the sake of unreliable humankind was a risk, yet he died the death we celebrate each time in the Eucharist or the Lord's Table. This was not a blind obedience. He admits, he dies according to the command given him (Jn.10: 18). Yet, he says confidently: "I lay down my life... I lay it down of my own free will"

How can a command (Jn.10: 18) become his own free will?" It is because, as he puts it: "The Father loves me, because I lay down my life." Thus the obedience of our Lord to the Father becomes a personal act of courage. So he can say: "I lay down my life...", because he understands and accepts the command as his. So though it is out of obedience, he accepts it in good faith - on trust in the Father. This acceptance of the command gives him the courage to die and to be able to say: " I myself have laid down my own life." He gives his own life in trusting the will of the Father - whose will is one with His - "I and the Father are one" (Jn.10: 30). Thus our Lord Jesus Christ could make the sacrificial death his own choice because he trusts the Father.

This teaches us that we can have personal fulfilment in fulfilling the promise of obedience if we accept it with our free will, trusting the Spirit at work in the Seminary, in the community, in the society, in the Rector, the staff and the Bishop, for the good of all. That means you obey not because you have to obey but because of the good that will come out of your obedience. Trusting the Spirit, you can say: "I am doing it because I am no longer forced to do it." You can say because you accept to do it freely, it becomes your personal act of the will. It is then founded on personal commitment to authenticity of purpose, therefore personal fulfilment. This type of obedience with all its doubts and pains is part of our continuous striving to realise our pastoral vocation as Seminarian, later as a Pastor.

This type of obedience does not take away your freedom, because, in fact, you freely accept doing it. As we know, freedom does not mean being able to act without restraint, but the inner capacity, the inner strength to know and do the good, irrespective of external pressure- physical, psychological or otherwise, therefore self-direction.

With this understanding then, by accepting even a command freely you protect your freedom from outside influence of world attractions and personal weaknesses. You save this freedom for the good of the community in trusting the spirit out of faith. You need the understanding that when you obey you do not obey the Bishop, the Rector, the staff or the President of Students or Seminarians' Representative Council, but the Spirit at work in the community, sharing in the obedience of our Lord to the Father. This is the obedience as a sign of faith, unflinching trust as a lifelong sacrifice.

However, following our Lord's example, we have to be aware of a radical difference between obeying a divine authority, the heavenly Father himself, and obeying a human authority, even if by faith, that authority stands for God's will. Our Lord himself warns his disciples against the abuse of authority. He also warns those who would have to obey that they would have to choose between obeying God and obeying a fellow human being, even if the human being stands in the name of God.

That is the real drama of obedience. To have to obey, when you are convinced the authority does not stand for the will of God. In such a situation the same principle applies. If you obey an order, which your faith, your conscience tells you does not stand for the will of God, or even radically stands against the will of God, this is also unfaithfulness. That is against the authenticity of faith. For, history has shown that easy obedience to avoid the pain of punishment, also leads to the temptation of those in authority, making it too easy for them go against the will of God. This type of blind obedience, be it in the church or the army, has been the cause of the greatest human catastrophes in history. The argument: "I am only taking orders," is not an act of faith. That is an act of timidity, the lack of faith.

If, however, you can stand on your feet, come what may, as an act of faith: "I refuse to obey because I am in conscience convinced the order is evil, it is against the will of God". But then you have to add: "I accept the consequences". That then is the ultimate act of freedom, accepting the challenge of authenticity of your faith. That is martyrdom! Whether in the church or state, history shows that such internal martyrdoms have saved nations, institutions and organisations from backsliding. In fact such internal martyrdoms truly stand the challenge of authenticity. That is in fact the ultimate act of obedience in faith, or rather obedience to the faith: "Take up your cross and follow me", and you will know the truth, and the truth will set you free!" (John 8:32) As we read from Heb.5: 7-9:
"During his lifetime on earth he offered up prayer and aloud and
in silent tears, to the one who had power to save him out of death,
and he submitted so humbly that his prayer was heard. Although

he was son, he learnt to obey through suffering; but having been made perfect, he became for all who obey him the source of eternal salvation."

By this trusting obedience in faith, he became a source of salvation. This faith in Jesus Christ as Saviour is also faith in obedience as means of salvation, conforming your will with the salvific will of God, who alone knows what is good for me, for you, for others and for the Church.

Thus in obeying to do what we sincerely believe is the will of God, we are doing what is good for us. For, just as all people were made sinners as a result of the disobedience of one man, so says St. Paul: "in the same way they will be put right with God as the result of the obedience of one man" (Rm.5: 19).

It is often said that when Priests and Bishops hear a talk about obedience they look down. When they hear about humility, they look up. But this obedience is not only one-way. For, if we believe the spirit is at work in the community, then we have to obey, the Bishop, the Moderator, the Pastor or Parish Priest, but also the catechist and the ordinary faithful at times, because the spirit speaks through them too.

That is why in obeying his Father in Heaven our Lord has to obey human beings on earth, his parents at Nazareth. For those who think they have power to have him put to death or save his life, our Lord maintains: "You would have no power over me, unless it has been given you from above." (John 19: 11) He could have called down Angelic warriors, but he did not. He could have mobilised his followers to defend him, but he did not. With his power, he could have defended and freed any other person so falsely accused and condemned as he found himself, but rather he put all his strength in obeying for the sake of the trust in the faith that his lot was God's will.

This obedience in faith reaches its apex in the garden of Gethsemane (Mt.26: 38): "My soul is sorrowful to the point of death; if it is possible let this cup pass me by." But he knows he has to obey so he immediately adds: "nevertheless, let it be as you not I would have it."

So, our Lord sacrifices his own will, "not my will, but your will." Whenever obedience becomes difficult, remember our Lord's words: "let it be as you, not I would have it." In other words, "not my will but your will be done."

Authorities may not necessarily demand such a heroic obedience as death, I believe. But there are and there will be, little unpleasant tasks, for the good of the community, for the good of the Church, for the good of the society. In each case it is in deciding to obey God or human being in trust, in faith, that you can say: "I have done it" for the sake of my vocation. Thus through your obedience, many more will be saved as your participation in our Lord's Mission of obedience, as an act of faith, commitment to authenticity.

After this reflection on vows or solemn promises as an act of faith, we shall reflect on hope as Challenge of Authenticity, the next topic for reflection. Before that let us close this reflection with 2 Cor.3: 4-5:

Such is the confidence that we have through Christ toward God. Not that we are competent of ourselves to claim anything as coming from us; our competence is from God…

Reflection IX

Hope as Challenge of Authenticity

Introduction Verse: John 11: 26:

"I am the resurrection. If anyone believes in me, even though he dies he will live, and whoever lives and believes in me will never die. Do you believe this "?

In our previous reflection we reflected on faith as trust that what we hope for will actually come to pass. Now we shall reflect on this hope itself.

What sustains the African, or rather black peoples of African heritage, anywhere, and in spite of all the natural and human catastrophes, is the authenticity of spirit. This is expressed in spontaneous enthusiasm of joy - music and dance, to rejoice or to mourn, to celebrate a new life or to celebrate the departure of one of the "family" to the ancestors. Some foreign scholars and their indigenous African followers regard this spontaneous, omnipresent enthusiasm, usually expressed in music and dance, as simplistic emotionalism. These scholars claim indigenous African spontaneity is a sign that indigenous Africans cannot be serious about anything and are naïve. They claim this indigenous enthusiasm shows indigenous Africans or black peoples lack will power, drive, self-assertion and a sense of achievement. But is that true?

If the indigenous instantaneous expression of enthusiasm is a sign or symptom of the lack of will power or lack of drive, then there is an important question to answer. How come indigenous Africans, or black peoples of African heritage have survived centuries of exploitation, slavery, and colonialism, neo-colonialism, imperialism and mercenary dictatorships till now? What has sustained our ancestors on the cotton fields and sugar cane plantations in the Wild West, uprooted from their ancestral lands? How come slaves, who were meant to lose their will power through the most humiliating acts of physical and spiritual torture, suddenly explode with the force of the same inherent, almost natural, indomitable spirit of spontaneous joy of music and dance, which has conquered the hearts of their very oppressors, and in fact has become the most popular musical revolution of the century? The Afro-rhythms have become the most powerful exhilarating force, especially for the youths of the "global village."

Is this sincerity of spirit, authenticity through spontaneity of reaction, and the almost unrestrained enthusiasm for life, not in fact an irruption of deep-seated reservoir of hope? Is this enthusiasm, this spirit of hope, which has sustained the indigenous black peoples of African heritage everywhere, surviving the most gruesome forms of oppression, abject dehumanisation?

My answer is: this spontaneous, omnipresent expression of joy through for example music and dance, is in fact one of the most precious spiritual endowments of the indigenous African heritage. This is an instantaneous expression of inner freedom, expressed in the almost irresistible outburst of joy. It is the loudest expression of authenticity, the outward overflowing of inner sincerity of spirit, conformity of external life with the inner life of freedom, to express oneself, which no external form of indignity, domination or manipulation can suppress. In fact there is a certain intrinsic element of primal innocence about it. This is the expression of hope so deep that it conquers the most helpless situation.

Let us remember the outburst of our brothers and sisters: "We shall overcome!" This is a prophetic outburst almost from nowhere, an outburst of hope without any grounds, of those whose history is most depressing even to recollect. This "groundless hope" is personified by the prophet-martyr, Martin Luther King, with his famous prophecy: "I have a dream!" In fact such prophetic voices go beyond living memory and geographical boundary as the ongoing African renaissance history demonstrates. In effect the explosion of this indigenous spirit of authenticity on the global scene in the form of Afro-music and dance is in itself prophetic.

There is some form of fulfilling interrelationship between this dream and the global outburst of the Afro-music and dance. Let us reflect on the import of the achievements of our brother, James Brown. He is acknowledged as the pioneer of the "Afro-music" revolution. We can even say he is the "inventor" of the Afro-beat. For, he is said to have changed and revolutionised the sound of music itself. His initial eruption was the prophetic: "I am black and proud!"

With this eruptive music James Brown transformed being black, which had been regarded as a symbol of humiliation and hopelessness, into a symbol of pride and hope. Thus with his musical prophesy James Brown has, in a sense, fulfilled the "dream", or rather "our dream", that, one day, humankind shall walk "hand in hand" as one family, irrespective of the skin pigmentation. All humankind shall shine with the dignity of the adopted "first born" children of the Almighty Father.

Where does this spirit of Martin Luther King come from? Where does this spirit of James Brown come from? Is this not the instantaneous outburst of the same deep-seated reservoir of hope of the indigenous African? In indigenous African languages, this deep-seated hope is often expressed in relation to the attributes of the Almighty. This may appear coincidental, but the expression of this indigenous African hope in relation to the Almighty gives further insight into indigenous African religion. This demonstrates the fact that instead of being the religion of defeatism or nihilism, the indigenous African religion is in fact the religion of hope.

This hope is expressed in paradoxical senses- courage in spite of apparent weakness, forward looking in spite of apparent backwardness, joy in spite of sadness, health in spite of disease, and life in spite of death, in short, hope in spite of hopelessness. I once experience this indigenous paradoxical sense of hope, expressed by an old man, forced to live outside Africa for political reasons. After trying to trace his whereabouts for quite some years, I happened to get him at last. When I enquired about his health he said rather instantaneously: "The end in this world has come. I am now preparing to go home finally to prepare for my death."

Before I could express my sympathy, I heard some strange sound at the other end of the telephone contact. So I was also about to remark instantaneously: "Don't worry...". But he immediately sensed my feeling, and remarked: "No! I am not sobbing! I am only laughing because, at last, now I know, I am on my way to meet the ancestors, especially those whom I have never met in this life. I am looking forward to that moment with joy!"

Could a Christian express his hope in life after physical death so instantaneously on the deathbed? Certainly some could, and in fact do express their Christian hope in that type of a dramatic moment. But how many Christians could sincerely express their hope in that way, in such a situation, when life, physical life in this world, is at the point of no return?

That was the last contact I ever had with that elder brother. That was certainly a most inspiring parting word. Or, rather, should we say, a most inspiring spiritual gift of hope, life after death, or, so to say, life in spite of death. This fact that indigenous African religion is a belief in the Almighty Creator, who is a source of indomitable hope, is the great challenge of authenticity for Christianity as the religion of hope, based on a belief in the resurrection.

This unconquerable hope is heard so often in times of trial, especially in the indigenous African languages: Nyame woho (An expression of the Akan in West Africa, literally meaning: "God is there"), or Enso Nyame yɛ! (This is also Akan expression meaning literally: "In spite of all, God is good"), or Mawu li (An expression of the Ewe in West Africa meaning, literally: "There is God!"), Mawuko (This is also an Ewe expression literally meaning: "God alone", but in fact expresses the idea: "As long as there is God, there is hope", Mawu awoe (This is also an expression of the Ewe, literally meaning: "God will do it"); Mbu sieh (An expression of the Bamileke in West Africa, meaning literally: "God is there"), Chukwu noya (An expression of the Igbo in West Africa, meaning literally: "There is God"); Nzambe Aliza (An expression in Lingala, West Central Africa, meaning "God help me!"); Mungu Wangu (An expression in Kiswahili, East Africa, meaning "My God {help}!"). All these indigenous African expressions actually stress the idea that as long as there is the Almighty (God), there is hope.

This indigenous African zeal for life and joy in the face of death is the greatest spiritual gift to express the Christian hope and joy of the resurrection. It is interesting that what those, who are not given to understand it, are saying of this indigenous African spirit of authenticity, is the same thing that was said about the expression of spontaneous joy by the first Christians after Pentecost. Those who could not comprehend the new authenticity of spirit of hope and joy at Pentecost regarded the new Christians, the first Pentecostal church, as drunk.

Thus, this tenacious spirit is a great challenge of the authenticity of the Christian faith, as the faith of the resurrection. It is a challenge to live our faith in hope, the faith in the Son of God turned a brother human being, who refuses to succumb to constraining situations of life. But how do we face this challenge of authenticity of the Christian hope posed by this indigenous spirit of authenticity, of tenacious hope and joy?

We can face this challenge by reflecting on the words of our Lord and his whole life, and their implications for our faith.

In the last meditation we meditated on faith as trust in divine providence, in the Spirit of Christ, that whatever we do is for our good. This kind of belief is comfortable. But to carry this belief further, to commit yourself to authenticity in this belief, to believe not only in the good, but also in a new life of joy, of satisfaction, of peace in the world today, all that sounds absurd, even unwise. To commit yourself to authenticity of joy, satisfaction, the more so personal fulfilment in this world of impending doom, this world of impending nuclear holocaust, injustice, political, social, economic, may be also ecclesiastical confusion and hopelessness, to find a place for joy and personal fulfilment in our world of hunger, utter poverty, it seems or rather sounds absurd. It sounds absurd because things never seem to become better. It seems unwise because it may arouse false hopes to tell human beings today to look for a better future.

Even relating our reflection to the Christian Churches or Confessions, to say we should find a place for sincere hope and joy in conflicting faiths, conflicting proclamations of the Word of God, conflicting principles and styles of ministry, in a life of broken vows, broken relationships, scandals and misunderstandings, all that sounds absurd. In short, to try to find some personal ground for commitment to authenticity of hope and joy demanded by our indigenous spirit of authenticity, hope for something better, when everything seems, in fact, getting worse every day, it sounds absurd and most naïve.

As indigenous Africans, when we have become the laughing stock everywhere, as blacks, as visible ethnicity, as "Niggers" or "Neger", Third World citizens, or whatever the euphemism may be, to commit yourself to authenticity of hope and joy, that sounds most naive. It sounds most unwise when our governments and leaders continue preaching hopelessness to us: We do not have the technology, we do not have the know-how; we do not have the experience, we are only qualified for begging, so they tell us. Therefore we need experts, experts in farming, experts in sanitation, experts in the family, experts in carrying babies and experts in feeding them. I guess soon our concerned leaders will have to import foreign experts to teach us how to put food in our mouths! In fact our leaders seem to tell us we do not have any grounds for any development, no intelligence, no technology, nothing!

What actually has The Almighty God, the Creator, endowed us with as black peoples, or indigenous Africans, at our creation, as fellow human beings in this world? One would wonder! Our situation appears to be like the time of the prophet in exile: We have no King; we have no prophets to tell us how long it will last.

Then priest and prophet forage in a land they do not know (Jer. 14: 18ff.). Wherever you go, wherever you look, placards, magazines, newspapers and leaflets trumpet it aloud: You are a beggar! You are the most needy! You are the poorest of the poor! You belong to a continent full of wars, full of hunger, full of natural catastrophes, full of disease. In short it is everywhere, you are a people without hope.

It is in this situation today, it is in this situation of seeming utter confusion, that our Lord puts it to us point-blank "I am the resurrection! Do you believe this?" Who asks this question at all? It is Jesus of Nazareth, a carpenter's son (in the earthly sense), tortured and crucified. The young man, who suffered and died on the cross, and that was the most humiliating execution at that time. The one who puts this question to you to answer as commitment to authenticity, to answer in sincerity, is in fact, a saviour who, it appeared, could not save himself from the cross. The human being who is in fact the son of the Almighty God is asking this question: "I am the resurrection. Do you believe this?"

This sounds still more absurd.

But, we have to answer. If you are a Christian, of whatever confession or denomination, we have to answer because you and I have been baptised in His name, as his followers, in fact, his workers, who carry on his mission. We have to answer because we professed to follow him, to share in his mission to save the world. He is asking us, in this world, in this Church (whatever Church you belong to), in this seminary, in this novitiate, at this workplace, in this society, in this world: "I am the resurrection! Do you believe this?" Well, brothers and sisters, we have to answer. But, how?

"No" or "Yes"? We could say No! We do not believe this. We do not believe that he is the resurrection. But then if we don't believe in his resurrection, or rather that he is the resurrection, we have to know that our belief, our baptism, our vocation, our ministry, or suffering, is all in vein. As St. Paul says: "If Christ has not been raised then our preaching is useless..." (1 Cor.15: 14). "If our hope in Christ has been for this life only, we are the most unfortunate of all" (1 Cor.15: 19).

Well, are we? Are we the most unfortunate of all? To this latter question I believe, No! We are not the most unfortunate of all! This answer to the latter question means, "yes", to the former. That is, if we believe Christ has risen, it means our faith has been vindicated. If we participate in the mission, therefore also in his lot, we participate also in his resurrection.

Now if we share or participate in the mission therefore also in the lot of his earthly life, we share or participate also in his resurrection. We know our Lord came to save this world! He converted sinners, healed the sick and preached justice, love and peace. Yet, we know, even before his death, there was still sin, there was still sickness, there was still death (even his own death), injustice, hatred and violence, which caused his own crucifixion.

And yet, he could say: "I am the resurrection", that is, before his death, he could proclaim he was the sign of hope, a new life in the face of corruption and death. He is confident to utter: "I am the resurrection." Mark the words. He says: "I am the resurrection" and not "I am resurrected." Thus he has not only realised his hope but he has also become this hope, this salvation as his personal fulfilment through commitment to authenticity, truly divine, truly human. Accordingly, despite the hopeless situation, in fact, we can say, because of the hopeless situation of his time - his own impending death and the Roman imperialism, our Lord becomes a sign of hope by realising his purpose of life on earth. He fulfils this purpose through the realisation of human values, or rather virtues, of love and mercy. In a seemingly inhuman world, our Lord Jesus Christ has become a sign of new life, even in the face of corruption and death.

This was the source of the outburst of joy and hope at Pentecost. Was that naivety? No doubt those who were not filled with the Spirit of Jesus Christ could not believe the original Pentecostal community was sane. Why should they believe, when, according to them as outsiders, this group had no grounds for such hope, for such joy?

Which group was the Pentecostal community at all? This was a motley group of people, without common language, without common origin and without common profession. They were even without common aim in life, before the Pentecostal event of the outpouring of the Spirit. But suddenly this motley group bursts out with uncontrollable joy, beside themselves! Certainly this group should be a group of drunks, who might have been drinking some wine the whole nightlong, so the on-lookers thought.

After all who were they, these individuals, who happened to become members of this group? Or rather who were members of this group of drunks as those who saw them considered them? As far as we know, the outstanding ones among them were some fishermen. Even then one could not regard them as professional fishermen any more. They had, a long time ago, left their nets and boats to follow a preacher, a foot preacher, too poor to own even a horse. They still fished from time to time, but only as sort of a hobby, just for a change, so to say. In deed that master proved to be a wonder worker. More than that, for his followers, he had been in fact the long awaited messiah, the saviour. At least that was the faith professed by Peter. But then that was it. Towards the end many followers deserted him. Except, of course, the tenacious women companions, including his devoted mother. Why?

The disciples had not realised that being a disciple was far more than going about healing, eating and drinking. They forgot, being a disciple meant, especially, accepting and doing the word of the master, however hard, and that meant sometimes very hard indeed! Loving thy neighbour was hard enough. But that was not enough to be a disciple. It meant also loving your enemy. Forgiving the one, who wronged you, was acceptable, if it was once, twice or thrice, or even seven times. But that was not enough to be a disciple. You needed to forgive seventy times seven times!

All these teachings were hard enough. But the hardest was yet to come, especially for those who could not understand:
I am the living bread, which has come down from heaven.
Anyone who eats this bread will live forever
And the bread that I shall give
Is my flesh, for the life of the world (Joh 6: 51).

This was the hard one! They were to be willing to eat the flesh and drink the blood of the master: "For this one", they might have thought, "The master goes beyond ordinary decency. This master of ours is no longer normal. He must be mad!"

"This is intolerable language." They might have thought. "How could anyone accept it?" The response of the master to this "panic reaction" of the disciples did not help much to allay their fears.

"Does this upset you", he said (John 6: 60). "My God", some might have thought, "does that mean the worse was to come! "They began to go away.

Maybe some disciples had gone away because they had not understood what the master actually meant. Their minds were still working with human, worldly, thought patterns of interpretation. They might have thought Jesus wanted to turn them into cannibals. They thought he would kill himself for them to eat, to put it in a brut, banal way.

Or it is possible some went away because they understood the Lord too well: They understood that his body would be tortured and crucified, and his blood would flow, on the cross for the salvation of all humankind. If they truly understood it in this true sense, what made it too hard was that, if they continued following him, then they would have to accept his fate too. That is, as disciples they would have to offer their bodies to be tortured and pour their blood one day for the faith. And that was certainly too hard for the weak ones.

The worst was still to come. One of the followers betrayed where he was hiding from so many enemies. The chief priests, the Pharisees and their followers got the long awaited chance to "finish" off this troublesome young man, who pricked their consciences right from the age of twelve. That was just after returning from his refuge in Egypt. Or, was he not in fact, with his black African brothers and sisters? Anyway, that did not matter then. These religious leaders at that time had the master arrested, tortured and crucified on the cross with a lot of derision. He had actually been buried dead. But for the enemies, their joy of getting rid of him at last seemed to be short-lived indeed! He did not seem to remain in the grave too long. Suddenly the followers began to spread the rumour, so they put it, that he had risen. Certainly the enemies could not bear that type of a return of the young man, actually executed and buried dead. So they seized upon the weapon they were experts at: persecution! Thus the followers, those who still had the courage to admit they remained his followers, had to hide behind closed doors.

Then it happened! Tongues of fire fell on each. There was suddenly a burst of uncontrollable joy. But given the background of this group as we have just described, observers could not believe the members were sincerely so full of joy and excitement. They should be drunk. That was the only explanation.

Given this history of the Pentecostal community, it is understandable that on-lookers could not believe they were sane. In the same way, given the history of oppression, enslavement, suffering, hunger and death of indigenous Africans, or black peoples of African heritage, till today (2003), external observers of the spirit of joy and hope could only conclude: these people must be out of their minds, possessed by irrational emotionalism. According to these observers, just as the Pentecostal group, there are no reasonable grounds for such exhilaration, excitement of joy and hope.

So then, the apparent hopelessness of the world, instead of being a discouragement for us, has to become the opportunity for commitment to authenticity, that is, becoming what we have to become because of what we are: the image of God. We are called to be signs of hope in a hopeless world. As indigenous African Christians this challenge of authenticity of hope is our God-given gift to the Christian faith and in fact to all humankind.

Our Lord becomes a sign of hope because, instead of being discouraged by the hopeless situation, the hypocritical Pharisees, the greedy women of Jerusalem, the corrupt tax collectors in the colonial government, and his own worldly disappointments and impending death (considering all in worldly, human sense), he was rather encouraged to go about doing good, going about his apparently insignificant things: healing the sick, converting corrupted officials, preaching the gospel of peace, justice and love, forgiving sins and attending banquets, failures, temptations, and dangers notwithstanding.

Our Lord was a human being of hope, or rather the hope of human beings. That is, a human being who refuses to succumb to constraining situations of life. A human being of hope discovers not disappointments, but opportunities in even the most hopeless situations to actualise virtues. A human being of hope, who, in the midst of apparent futility, can sigh with satisfaction and say: "I have done my best. I have committed myself to authenticity"; just as our Lord, amid confusion and hatred, can proclaim: "I am the Resurrection," a sign of hope in a seemingly hopeless world; a sign of salvation in a seemingly doomed world.

Instead of allowing difficulties to overcome him, he overcomes them. This reminds me of one comic strip I saw some time ago. There was a big gutter across a road. Before it, stood a big signboard: "Stop! Danger!"

Many people wanted to cross over to the other side of the road. But as soon as they saw the danger sign they turned away. Then came a small child. He looked up at the signboard. He put his finger to his forehead in a reflexive mood. Then he pulled the danger signboard down and put it across the gutter. So he created a bridge. He could now cross to the other side. For many others, for adult passers-by, that sign was a sign of danger. But for that child, that same signboard became an instrument for overcoming the danger, a bridge over the gutter.

Reflecting on this image further, the adult wayfarers got frightened by the danger sign. They either went back to their past, or remained standing before it and bemoaned the danger sign in their present. These adults saw their future progress effectively blocked by the danger sign. They neither had any hope any longer of further progress in their journey, nor of arriving at their destination. But the innocent child, without any complicated rationalisations of adults, acted on instant inspiration to transform hopelessness into an instrument to overcome that, which blocked future progress. For a human being of hope, no situation is hopeless. It is all opportunity!

Thus we can find fulfilment in our lives through commitment to authenticity in spite of, or even because of the hopeless situation we find ourselves in. Just as our Lord Jesus Christ, we have to bring hope to the hopeless world: consoling the sorrowful, praying over and for the sick and the emotionally troubled, visiting the lonely, the imprisoned, encouraging academically and spiritually weak, in short giving hope to the hopeless. There are many ways to create hope. When people, almost everybody, gives up hope for Africa, cannot we, Christians, the more so Pastors to be or Pastors, have anything positive to say instead of joining the chorus of lamentation? When everybody condemns, or rather bemoans the indigenous African system of doing things: the laziness, the lack of the sense of time, the lack of will power, the lack of drive, the lack of rationality, the lack of administrative talent, the lack of business acumen, the lack of orderliness, in short, the indigenous African lack of all that is positive and right in a human being, is there no indigenous African to reply with something positive? Is there no one to remark at least that the indigenous system has produced some leaders in the Church and State: bishops, moderators, priests, pastors, scientists, technologists, lecturers, politicians, diplomats and administrators, educationists, businessmen and businesswomen, of international standing, who defy all the stereotyping of the indigenous African, or black peoples of African heritage? Even if they are not in positions of authority are they not all the same indigenous Africans, who make it against all odds?

What about our brother, Kofi Annan, the Secretary General of the United Nations Organisation, in most trying times as these, in 2003. Is he not a most capable diplomat? Is he not an indigenous African, or a black man of African heritage? When politicians, administrators and other leaders in the society, including our indigenous leaders, are made to blame the political and social incompetence on our tradition, our culture, our religion, even our indigenous languages, as doomed to failure and backwardness, is there no one to remark that there are at least some positive developments? Is there no one to remark that our indigenous, pre-colonial, socio-economic systems had survived, and are surviving, millennia before the introduction of the so-called modern or even post-modern systems?

Is there no one to point to the fact that, in fact in Africa today, it is only the traditional, indigenous systems, which have kept African societies still in existence at all! If others blame all our woes on our susceptibility to religion, including Christianity, is there no one to remark that it is our indigenous spirit of commitment to authenticity in the tenacity of faith, which still keeps our social structure viable at all, as the so-called modern political ideologies simply emerge, destroy and vanish only to be replaced by another more destructive than the previous one?

If prophets of doom proclaim African economy as hopeless, is there no one to point at the fact that at least the "Makorla" system has survived all destructive modern political economic systems at least in West Africa? May someone not point to the fact that it is religion which has kept the spirit of our grandmothers, mothers, aunts and sisters alive in the face of destructive economic policies of successive governments and their host of "foreign advisors", "foreign consultants", "foreign experts" etc.? How else could our tenacious women revive their drooping spirits after the hard day or days under the heat of the sun or in the wet rain, without spiritual nourishment at the end of the day or at the end of the week? In short, is the situation of our continent; is the situation of our people, as indigenous Africans, or black peoples of African heritage actually so hopeless? Or, committing ourselves to the authenticity of hope of our people in the Almighty God, in the resurrection of the saviour of all humankind, in spite of all troubles, don't we have enough grounds to believe and confirm that there is certainly hope for the future?

Then, for ourselves, however bad our frustrations, disappointments, embarrassments, weaknesses, failures and fears are, are we not capable, can we not always overcome the situation by accepting facts as opportunities to realise values or virtues of endurance, courage, fortitude, and humility as personal challenge of the authenticity of our Christian hope? If we, Christians, accept our role as prophetic voices among our people, as indigenous Africans, are we called to be only prophets of doom?

Let us remember, authentic prophets were and are no prophets of doom. They were and are prophets of the truth. They were and are prophets of warning. True prophets see the future and proclaim it to fellow human beings. They prophesy dire consequences for the people of God and humankind, if the people, especially their leaders, do not convert and turn from their evil ways. It is true, there were and there are dooms-day scenarios resulting from the hardheartedness of the people of God. We can readily recollect the destruction of Sodom and Gomorrah (Gen 19: 24 – 28), the destruction of Jerusalem, the first and second world wars and others still to come.

However, in spite of dooms-day scenarios as a result of the refusal to heed the warnings of prophets, every true prophet is always also a prophet of hope. This is because the merciful love of God always wins the day. In spite of human failures, God's love endures forever (Psalm 117: 1). For instance, in the end of his prophecy, one of the most bitter and most scathing prophets of all time, Amos, still had some words of consolation, of future glory, for the people:

"Behold, the days are coming", says the Lord, "when the ploughman shall overtake the reaper, and the trader of grapes him who sows the seed; the mountains shall drip sweet wine, and all the hills shall flow with it.
I will restore the fortunes of my people Israel,
And they shall rebuild the ruined cities and inhabit them;
They shall plant vineyards and drink their wine
And they shall make gardens and eat their fruit.
I will plant them upon their land
And they shall never again be plucked up
Out of the land which I have given them,
Says the Lord your God (Amos 9: 13- 15).

Thus every true prophet seems to announce a happy end. That is also the Christian hope, the hope born out of the resurrection. Hope is simply self-transcendence, transcending even the most intractable situation here and now, living in, or rather living out, the resurrection. Hope is using misfortunes as resources of strength to overcome these very misfortunes.

Often, as Pastors or ministers in the field, as seminarians or novices on pastoral assignment, committed Christians or fellow human beings of good will committed to the welfare of others, we ask people to accept difficulties but we ourselves refuse to accept our own difficulties. Often we encourage but we refuse encouragement. Often we console but we refuse consolation.

This was the remark of the women on the mummy truck about the unfortunate pastor, which I cited in the introduction.

But how do we minister to this hope as pastors and fellow Christians? This brings us to hope as poverty in spirit, ministry to hope in word and life, the humility to accept the inevitable and the unchangeable, the courage to avoid the evitable and change the changeable.

That means as ministers of hope to other human beings and to the world, we ourselves have to be this living hope in our own hopeless situations. This could be sickness of any kind, failures, misfortunes and other humiliating and disappointing situations. Our fortitude in depressing situations, like the fortitude of our indefatigable indigenous cultural enthusiasm for life, will inspire those we minister to in their own depressing moments to cling on to hope. The ministers of hope need be a sort of a light at the end of the tunnel, which guides people out of their own darkest situations and problems of life. In fact, just as our indigenous hope, this ministry of hope would be a constant source of health, not only psychological and spiritual, but also physical health.

I believe our problems truly give us the opportunity to put into practice the promise of poverty in spirit. As I often told students or seminarians in class, poverty does not necessarily mean asceticism, living without material goods like cars, radios and other luxuries. The commitment to authenticity of the spirit of poverty means disinterestedness in worldly standards, or striving for earthly success, by accepting the fact that one is also human, instead of playing "supermen."

This physical, psychological or even spiritual "superman" obsession, if we may term it so, could afflict any person convinced of being a model for others. One psychotherapist, Klaus Thomas, terms it "ecclesiogenic neurosis." This refers to the inability or anxiety to accept failures or weaknesses. The said author relates this "neurosis" to ecclesiastics, those whom the structure of the Church, endows with some status in the church or society (See Klaus Thomas, *Lebensmüdenbetreuung als Behandlung* "ekklsiogener Neurose". In: Handbuch der Selbsmörderverhütung, Stuttgart: Ferdinand Enke Verl. 1964: 299- 331) Thus poverty in spirit could help us accept and overcome feelings of hopelessness, conscious or unconscious. This could relate to any problem or weakness: illness, physical, mental or spiritual, temptations, failures and misfortunes. For instance, let us say, as a pastor or committed Christian, you are acknowledged as a person of a strong character, a model of Christian faith and hope. Then suddenly everything seems to unravel. You struggle not to admit there is any trouble. At the back of your mind you are aware, maybe too much aware, that others are looking up to you for inspiration. But at last you have to admit you have a problem. May be you are forced to seek help yourself. The diagnosis of the specialist is depression.

This may become a real crisis, which could lead to real illness, even physical illness, if you take for granted "that is the end of me", or "there is no hope" for me anymore. Somehow you may begin to hide away from others, who, you may now believe, may be disappointed in you. If you do not arrest this situation it may deteriorate very fast with more complications, such as alcohol or general backsliding. Instead of running away from the problem, the only way to arrest the situation is to accept it in humility. This acceptance strengthens your resolve to hope for solution. The way you keep up hope in your tribulation is in itself a loud sign of hope for those in similar situations. In fact you strengthen your being a role model, as a model of hope.

Such situations of real trial could be multiplied for any state of life and any individual Christian, regarded as a model of faith. For instance you may be a well-known spiritual healer, or rather a person through whom Jesus Christ heals others. Then suddenly you yourself are afflicted by an illness. Prayers of your own church members do not seem to help. Then things may get complicated when you overhear others, or you think you overhear them, whispering behind you back: "He has been a powerful man or woman of God. His (or her) prayers have healed others. Why is he himself (or herself) so afflicted incurably?" You may then begin to lose hope of any cure. In a worse case scenario, given the indigenous African society, you may be pressured to lose your Christian faith, and fall on the indigenous African religion for healing. If things do not improve you may lose hope altogether.

However there is always a way out of the cul de sac. Pluck up new courage and retrace your steps. Your status as a prodigal son will indeed improve your illness, and even improve upon your image as a role model of hope. This could happen in any relationship or any state of life.

Your family may be a model Christian family. You are a wonderful wife or husband. You are a model of honesty and love as far as marriage relationship is concerned. Suddenly you are irresistibly caught up in an affair with another woman, or man, whatever the case may be. You begin to lose your interest in your church. Probably you do not see any hope any more left to regain your status in your church community as a true Christian husband or wife. Your marriage itself may be threatened. The matter may even get most complicated. Your partner too may, for the meantime, also find his or her own way with another relationship. You then lose hope of ever making it together any more.

Even in this apparently hopeless situation you can still regain your status as a symbol of tenacious hope if you retrace your steps back to one another. That both of you have achieved the humanly impossible, by keeping up hope till the end, certainly improves your image as a true Christian, ready to accept faults in humility, and revive the marital bond of love.

You may be in the same type of situation. You can reflect now on your particular case: It may be the problem of mistrust by parents or children, pastor's scandalous relationship with members of the church, mismanagement of church finance, unjust treatment of others or even apostasy altogether. In each case, remember St. Peter had denied his Master, Jesus Christ, but still remains St. Peter the apostle, a symbol of faith. This is because he never lost hope of regaining his faith. He was not kept back by the sense of shame, that he who had been proclaimed the rock foundation of the faith could fall so low.

As he writes to his fellow Christians:
Blessed be the God and Father of our Lord Jesus Christ! By his great mercy we have been born anew to a living hope through the resurrection of Jesus Christ from the dead (I Pet 1:3).

You as a Christian share in this "living" hope of being born anew. Hardly is anybody born a saint. The greatest saints, therefore the greatest models of the Christian faith, are those who had kept up the hope through greatest temptations and trials. Saul, the persecutor of Christians, became Saint Paul, one of the greatest "Apostles" of all time. St. Augustine has his own "Confessions"; St. Magdalene has her own past history. Till our time we have "born again" Christians, who make it to become "born again" Saints.

Sometimes there is real anxiety about the remarks others might make, real or only suspected. This is because those whom you inspire, or you believe you inspire, by your pious ways, would be disappointed by your weakness, in spite of your constant prayers and struggle to be a good Christian. You may fear to lose the status of a "role model". But to discard your inward commitment to authenticity, simply in order to present an image pleasing to admirers, you become in a sense, an artificial "role model". This external appearance without the inner conviction would make you only a double personality. In truth, being consciously or unconsciously a double personality is self-deception. You may continue to appeal to superficial admirers. But the true indigenous African admirer in the village, with a keen "native" sense of observation and character assessment, would make you out as non-authentic, a fake. For you yourself this "role playing" type of life would backfire in the long run. Then begins the psychological problem of dual identity. This will keep you constantly running and hiding away from yourself. For it calls for a lot of energy to struggle constantly to be what you are not. This is coupled with constant anxiety of being "detected", being "found out". Certainly that would not take long in a typically indigenous African society. The grey-haired wise man (or wise woman) would only observe you from head to toe and shake the head. He or she could tell you exactly what you are, and has his or her own way of making you understand that he or she knows your true self.

However it would also be positive commitment to authenticity if you discover that you are in fact a role model for many admirers, and then struggle to develop the inner coupling, as I may put it. It is understandable, like any type of "fitness" exercise; you require strenuous efforts to achieve positive results of authentic role model. Gradually with the "inner coupling" your role model personality will become effectively your true personality, the external expression of truly what you are within, your authentic self.

One other aspect of the fear of losing your status as a role model is the anxiety relating to the typically cultural phenomenon. Studying the legends and myths of various peoples, of various cultural groups, one could say that in different ways and in different degrees, it is a universal cultural phenomenon to attribute misfortunes of any type, personal or collective, to some spiritual or supernatural agent. A classical case of this cultural phenomenon, which I may term "ethical aetiology", in human history, is witch hunting. This moral judgment on misfortunes is still something to reckon with especially in our indigenous African society, because of the close-knit relationship in communities, where everybody is known by and to everybody, and in a sense concerned with the welfare of the other.

Even though, as a Christian, you may not believe in any such connection between your state of life and the action of others, you are affected. Any type of misfortune is interpreted as the result of conscious or unconscious fault of oneself, one's family or the doing of others. This anxiety is real. But we need not condemn ourselves to guilt complex because of our embarrassing illness or weakness.

Let us reflect on St. Paul's journey of faith and hope. He was not only a converted persecutor of the Christian faith, as we have already referred to. In spite of the power of his prayers to effect healing and even raising the dead to life (Acts 20: 9-12), he also suffered from a most embarrassing illness, a thorn in the flesh (2 Cor. 12: 7), which, some say, was epilepsy.

There could be several types of embarrassing physical, mental or even spiritual handicaps or misfortunes. For instance I know a pastor whose voice diminishes according to the number of people around. During sermon no one hears anything even when the microphone is close to his lips. In spite of his constant search for cure in health centres, he has still not found the cure for his voice. Yet he accepts his role as a Pastor, and still hopes to overcome his problem.

Some of us suffer from forgetfulness, confusion or even total blackout even during the celebration of the Eucharist or other religious services. We need not continue worrying. Worrying too much can actually make the condition worse. The best medicine for such embarrassing conditions is to put a bold face on it. We need not hide it until it becomes too late to cure. We need keep up hope, that even if we cannot be relieved from it, at least we can bear it in humility. Just like St. Paul, we can even discover a spiritual meaning in our weakness, a spiritual fortune in misfortune. As he puts it:

I besought the Lord about this, that it should leave me; but he said to me; 'My grace is sufficient for you, for my power is made perfect in weakness.'
I will all the more gladly boast of my weaknesses, that the power of Christ may rest upon me. For the sake of Christ, then, I am content with weaknesses, insults, hardships, persecutions, and calamities; for when I am weak, then I am strong (2 Cor. 12: 8-10)

Often we have to temper humility with courage, the courage to be yourself, provided you conform to what is good, the will of God. This does not mean you should always insist on doing your will. You have to grant that those who have authority over you, the staff members, Novice Master or Mistress, your teacher or director, have the responsibility to form or train you in such a way that you grow into a responsible pastor, religious or good Christian. Those placed over you have to account for the trust the higher authority has reposed in them.

All the same you need courage to accept responsibility for your own decisions. An important aspect of this hope as poverty of spirit is the humility to hope, that the other person who might have wronged you would one day reconcile, and improve his or her behaviour towards you. This humble hoping that the other would change for the better could be a real trial in certain bitter experiences in relationship such as betrayal.

The most destructive thing that could ever happen to any human being is betrayal. The writer, Klaus Thomas, whom I have referred to above, refers to this experience of betrayal as "Uriah's Syndrome". You remember Uriah, whose wife David coveted and plotted his death by having him betrayed at the battlefront, as his fellow fighters suddenly fell back and left him alone in the hands of the enemy (2 Samuel 11-12). Many a time, you may feel liked, even loved, by everybody. Suddenly you realise everybody has deserted you. Your own friends, even your dearest and closest friend, seem to relate your most intimate conversation to others. You feel bitter, angered, or even saddened. You may even curse and swear never to have any friend any more. You are hopeless, even desperate.

But remember that kiss, the kiss of Judas Iscariot. Judas, who had been a disciple and even an Apostle, and had eaten at the same table, was the one who betrayed his own teacher and Lord. So the Son of God was betrayed. What about you and me? Should we not bear our cross after Christ by accepting betrayals?

In the case of Pastors or marriage Counsellors, such betrayals teach us what happens to married couples, who come to us with betrayed married love, betrayed confidence and betrayed trust. Remember, if you convince betrayed couple to forgive and forget as a sign of love, what about you, what about us. Should we not also forgive betrayals as a sign of love?

With patience, we should still hope that such betrayals would help strengthen our wills, our faith, our hope and love, one for the other. But especially in this case, we who preach hope to the hopeless; we who impress upon broken marriage partners to trust even when they are grabbing one another's throats; we who tell drug addicts, thieves and drop-outs to hope and trust in a better future; we who preach endurance and humility to those, who suffer from incurable diseases or persistent misfortunes, should also learn to accept ourselves as we are. After all what are we? We are also ordinary human beings, the product of "humus", the earth. I do not think God demands super-human qualities of us - physical, intellectual, psychical, moral, or spiritual. We need not accept defeat before we are defeated. I think God accepts us according to what we can become, because of what we are, not what we are not.

We who take after Christ need not fear failures. Let us now reflect on this. Imagine you were Jesus Christ himself, as Karl Rahner dramatically describes it in his Meditations on Priestly Life: Jesus Christ, the Son of God, also experienced this futility. There he was, the Son of God, preaching, healing, feeding and converting, but in the last moment only desertion, betrayal, disgrace, torture and painful death. He was crucified with brigands and buried. As the author puts it: "He perished in the fate of the world."

He also experienced weakness, sadness and desperation. In the last moment, when he met suffering face to face, he had had to cry: "Remove this from me." It is too much; it is impossible! It is morally impossible; it is sheer horror, sheer death, sheer void, sheer disaster. This was, or rather is, God's son's absolute impotence, utterly inconceivable darkness. Three times he fled to his disciples. Probably he needed encouragement. But he never got any encouragement. The Son of God got no support, no consolation from His most trusted human friends on earth at the moment of his dire need. In fact they were sleeping, or may be only dozing! Yet, this Son of God had courage: "Rise, let us be going!"

So is God's love experienced in the most abysmal state of life. And God himself descends into the lowest depths of our Gethsemane existence, so that there is no abyss in which God, his love, his mercy, were never yet borne at the deepest level.

Well, do not throw broken vows away. As an indigenous African proverb expresses it: "You don't throw away the baby with the dirty water." To use a "native image", see whether you cannot use carpenter's glue to mend, and make the broken spot of your life your strongest point, through prayers, meditations and serious spiritual exercises. If you are empty, feeling a hole within you, see whether you cannot use a wood-carver's paste to fill it, once more with prayers, meditations, spiritual exercises, good works and the like. So also if your vocation is in shreds, relationship broken into pieces, see whether you cannot try spiritual "carpenter's glue". It is often said the spot where two broken pieces of wood have been glued together with carpenter's paste becomes the strongest part of the wood. You may never know. Your weakness may turn out to become your strongest instrument of the apostolate. Suffering is often the most effective school of wisdom.

It is also often said if a swimmer begins to go down in a swimming pool, he or she can spring up only when he or she touches the bottom. However deep you might have fallen, you can rise. Whatever our position, as human beings called to help other human beings in their spiritual life, we have to accept that we are also weak, sinful human beings. We have to accept we are not super-men (or super-women), but wounded healers.

In this connection we can consider the Uriah's syndrome as giving a second lesson in spirituality or moral courage and humility. This relates to David himself. David remained and remains undoubtedly a great king, and certainly also a great personality in history. But he was and he is also certainly a human being like you and me, like any person else. We may regard him morally and spiritually as a person who springs up, and keeps afloat, even after touching the bottom.

Let us consider his case. Here he is in his palace as a great king. That period is certainly a very tense period of his reign. War is raging around him. He or rather his country is at war with an enemy. He is looking desperately out through the window of his palace. Then he climbs the steps onto the flat rooftop. Certainly we can grant that at first he is not searching for just something to satisfy his male senses, simply to satisfy his luscious desires. He has enough in his harem for that, if he wants to. We can grant he is on the rooftop anxiously waiting for news from the front, a soldier running with a parchment from the General conducting the war. But then inadvertently, maybe by chance, his eyes fall on the low-lying apartments or barracks of his army officers just below his palace. At that very moment, through a window of what happens to be a bathroom, or just in the open, something strikes his eyes. There is an extremely beautiful, young woman taking her bath, unaware that the eyes of the greatest person in her country, the King of Israel, are upon her. First maybe it is only a glance, but then human weakness turns it into a real "observation". This great king at the sight of female beauty suddenly becomes just a normal, weak human being, incapable of controlling his feelings. He just cannot resist it. So he falls into a moral quagmire, sinking helplessly. He goes back to reflect on things that matter. But then the sight of that beauty continues to impress upon his thoughts. He has to act. So he takes the most immoral, in a sense also inhuman, decision. He sends for the beautiful lady he has seen taking her bath. Certainly he may have known who she is. She may have accompanied her husband, Uriah, an officer in the army, to pay their respects to the great king. She may also have been really sad all the time, not knowing what may happen to the husband at the front. So she may have taken the summon to the king's palace in an ambivalent way. Is she asked to come to hear the worst news about her husband?

With this uncertainty she hurriedly makes herself presentable, innocently, to appear before the great king. But some embarrassing and incredible thing happens. The king smiles and embraces her in a luscious way. She as an ordinary citizen could not have the moral courage to refuse. So the morally unthinkable happens.

What makes the plot, if we may term it so, so ethically despicable, "evil in God's sight" (2 Samuel 12: 9) is that the great King does not stop at simply enjoying stolen love of an irresistible beauty. But he actually desires her company permanently. This is really an extreme type of greed, covetousness. As the Prophet confronts David later, why take the only human companion in love of a person, who has only one, while you already have so many, and could still acquire more if you wish?

So it comes to pass that King David commits the worst type of crime, indirectly arranging the husband's death by betrayal, and so possessing the beauty, which should belong to his own army officer. Uriah has to die so that the beautiful wife may become the wife of the great King David! So deep a great personality could fall!

But the positive lesson is that this great King, in fact the greatest of all kings of Israel, becomes so humble when confronted by the Prophet, to acknowledge his sin and accept to do penance: "I have sinned against the Lord", he admits (2 Samuel 12: 13). The lesson is, if such a great personality in history can fall so morally deep, but still be so humble to accept the punishment for his actions and do penance, what about you and me?

Certainly if God forgives murder by a king believed to be His own chosen servant, should we not then be consoled with the belief that the same God would forgive our sins too? Our faith in God, our faith in Jesus Christ his only Son, should teach us that no sin is beyond His (God's) mercy. However deep we may have fallen we can rise. That is the loudest message of the resurrection.

If someone comes to me to say he is leaving the seminary or the novitiate because he or she has become so useless and hopeless that he or she cannot bear it any more, I have two suggestions for him or her:

The suggestions would be: Take a piece of paper and draw a line, dividing it into two. On the right, list the good things you have done. The number of fellow Seminarians or Novices who are inspired by your example, those who have received the faith through your catechism instructions, those whose marriages you have mended, and all the positive things you might have done for others or in the interest of others. Then on the left, list the negative things you might have done: maybe being drunk, making the Bishop or Rector angry, putting a fellow Seminarian in trouble and all the sins by commission or omission.

Now, balance your accounts. Let us say you have helped one hundred and wronged fifty. Then you have fifty percent more reason to keep on making more effort. That means you have more chances of becoming a pastor or Religious. If you help more people than you wrong, if you will be able to satisfy the needs of hundreds or even thousands as a Pastor, is that not worth suffering for?

If you willingly suffer in the Seminary or the novitiate for the thousands of children and adults to be baptised or instructed, marriages to be restored, sorrows to be taken away by your consolation or smiles brought back on faces, do you not then fulfil the purpose of life, being Christ for others? Is the painful road to change itself not the challenge of authenticity and personally fulfilling?

So, you see, your balance sheet shows you need to struggle, why leave? This spiritual or moral "balance-sheet" could be made by anybody for any state of life relationship- friendship, marriage relationship, professional relationship etc. Then my other suggestion would be: Take a week or two weeks off during the long vacation, or even request one full year of spiritual stock-taking; take your spiritual life seriously; pray at every prayer hour and at odd times as the need may be, do your spiritual exercises sincerely; you may even ask permission to go to a monastery or a spiritual renewal centre somewhere near if you can afford it. I would say if after all these efforts you still decide to leave, then I say your decision is a mature decision. You could go. But not until you have taken your Seminary or your novitiate life seriously, making your pastoral or religious vocation personally fulfilling! That is facing the challenge of hope, the challenge of authenticity,

Sometimes by restoring hope to the hopeless, you restore your own hope too. For those who are already pastors, counsellors, or ministers in any type of the apostolate as devoted Christians, or simply as men and women of good will, let us reflect on the following scenario. Let us say you have had really a serious trouble. You try to get it off your mind and heart, but without success. You sit in your room reflecting on the mess you are in. You begin to feel there is no way out. You are reflecting on how to end it all, because you think you have the worst side of life. You have even begun to think about writing your will. This must be the end at last. May be you are even shedding tears, aloud in your room. Suddenly you hear a knock at the door. You jump up, struggling to dry your tears. You try to clear your voice so that you do not betray your tearful mood. You quickly mop up the remaining tears on your cheeks, may be even with your bare palms. Who could that be? You rise, put on the appearance of being "normal". You go to open the door. Someone standing at the door delivers the message: "Someone would like to see you."

"Tell the person to wait for me at the office." You struggle to reply in the normal pastoral way. Then you go back to your room. Maybe you look into the mirror to see whether all your appearance is in order. You come out walking to the office, pretending everything is in order with you. You stretch your hand to greet in a most affable manner, may be even putting on a welcoming smile. You sit down with the person in the normal pastoral position.

Then you realise the person can hardly talk. He or she may struggle to wipe away his or her tears; no words are possible, only sobbing. The situation may be ironical. But you have to play your official role. After all you are a trained pastoral counsellor. What do you do? You make some encouraging remarks. But acting according to the counselling rule, you do not interfere too much. You allow the person to sob on and continue wiping his or her tears. You look on consolingly in silence.

Then after some silence the person begins slowly at first, but suddenly bursting out in tears, may be putting all the blame on himself or herself for the mess he or she is in. Allowing the person to pour out his or her problem from the heart, you find yourself only making consoling, empathetic remarks: "Sorry-Sorry…that is really hard…" Finally the message is clear. The person has also had the thought to end it once and for all. But he or she has thought it worthwhile coming to you for your final blessing.

As you listen and observe the painful way the person may have narrated his or her case, he or she makes you understand you are even lucky. In comparison your case might have appeared, now, no longer so catastrophic at all in comparison with the pathetic case of the person before you. What would be your reaction?

Suddenly it occurs to you, here is a person needing your consolation. Suddenly you are awake as if from a very deep sleep. You cannot pretend anymore to be what you are not. Certainly, if you happen to be a disciple of Viktor Frankl, as logotherapists would suggest, you can say to the person: "Go ahead and end it all!"

I guess the person would retort: "You don't mean it!"

Then both of you would be shaken with a surprise. That may suddenly change the moods of both of you. This logo therapeutic solution of your problems is the most dramatic way to achieve the fastest results. Anyway, if you do not happen to belong to the school of Logo therapists, whose principles are sound but practically recommended only to those who are experts, well-versed in the techniques, since Logo therapy can be dangerous and risky in the hands of amateurs, you may have to take the long way of counselling. But certainly, at least in a normal case, at the end of comforting and consoling the other, you end up solving your own problem too.

So then when you are challenged to find words of consolation for that pathetic fellow human being, you gradually understand that your own words were meant more for yourself than for the fellow human being before you. This is because it would be extremely insincere on your part as a pastor, a counsellor or a fellow Christian, to convince someone else that life is worth struggling through, while you are resolute in ending it all. That would be the height of insincerity, an exercise in self-deception. This is because you cannot believe you can convince someone else if you yourself are not convinced at all. In normal cases you would be forced, or rather motivated, to go along with your own positive motivation. That is certainly a challenge of authenticity!

So in the apostolate someone's problems may help find solution to your own. Angels are still real and active! So in the moment you are down under, the Lord sends an Angel to your rescue. This Angel happens to be your fellow human being in trouble and in need of your help. This demonstrates Dody Donnelly's affirmation in her Team and Team Ministry: We are all people needers and people feeders. Also, as she expresses it somewhere else in the same book: We are all chipped edges. From time to time we need fitting together one and the other to make a whole.

By giving hope to the hopeless, we receive hope in return. Probably our exhilarating Afro-rhythms are the loudest fulfilment of this ministry of hope to humankind. This is our ministry to the world. This is our indigenous contribution to the desire for justice, peace and happiness. I should think we could all say, individually: "I believe!" Even more than that, we can also say "we are the resurrection!" Rise, let us be going!

Let us end this meditation with Rm.8: 18-21.

I consider that the sufferings of this present time are not worth comparing with the glory that is to be revealed to us. For the creation waits with eager longing for the revealing of the sons (and daughters) of God; for the creation was subject to futility, not of its own will but by the will of him who subjected it in hope; because the creation itself will be set free from its bondage to decay, and obtain the glorious liberty of the children of God.

After this rather long reflection on hope as the loudest message of the resurrection we shall now reflect on the greatest value, the greatest virtue of our faith: Love.

Reflection X

Celibate Love as Challenge of Authenticity

Introduction Verse: Jn.15: 12
"This is my commandments: Love one another, as I have loved you "

In every Christian community the commonest word is "love". But in practice, in any Christian community, the least practised virtue is often "love". As one young Bishop once said when preaching at a religious profession, he did not know why the Church had not demanded the vow of love. This is because, according to him, "love" would have been the most difficult religious vow in a community. This remark sounds so striking because it is so true in any Christian, religious or ecclesiastical community.

As I remarked at the beginning, the reflections were originally for those preparing for ordination, the religious and the clergy in the Catholic Church. Thus instead reflecting on "love" in general, we shall be reflecting on love in the context of celibacy as the inner freedom to minister to love. Before we begin this reflection, it is appropriate to make readers aware that this reflection is not a sort of "advertisement" for celibacy. Since it is still being observed, I deem it a service to reflect now how we can make it relevant to our indigenous African culture.

The vow of celibacy, especially in the Catholic Church, has always been plagued with scandals till our day, year 2003. Every Christian denomination, irrespective of whether the ministers or pastors could marry and do marry, or not, has its own spate of scandals relating to "intimacy". The explosion of such scandals is no longer the respecter of official positions. Thus scandals run through all the structure of the Christian churches or congregations. Even if we may not talk about celibacy problem among other Christian groups, the problem exists in one form or another. We may term them problems of continence, problems of modesty or moderation, problems of courtesy, problems of chastity, problems of indiscretion, problems of marital dishonesty, or simply problems of immorality.

Whatever be the term applicable in each case, the problem does exist and affect the moral integrity of Christians and their leaders. Therefore it is appropriate for each Christian to reflect on his or her own life, relationships, vows or marital promises, attitudes toward employers or employees, clients, patients and other persons under one's authority. It is a challenge of authenticity of our Christian faith as religious faith with a moral code of behaviour, within the context of our indigenous African culture.

As we have already seen concerning the "sacred" in indigenous African culture, certain spheres of life are regarded sacred, therefore secret. One of these sacred, therefore secret spheres of life is the human body, especially intimate organs of the male and female. Their sacredness is protected by secrecy. Elders instruct the young ones about the importance and use of these organs. Since they are held as sacred, the instructions are in secret. Then the sacredness is also protected by various rituals, tabus (or taboos), other rules and regulations such as those concerning incest and adultery. The breaking of those sanctions incurs, often, ritual pacification.

It is therefore obvious that the vow of celibacy exists in the indigenous African religion in one form or another, temporal or permanent, as a sign of total consecration to the deity or spirit. Dire consequences follow, or are believed to follow, if devotees disregard the vow. Even for indigenous cultic officials who do marry, there are rules of abstention preceding official duties in the shrine.

This is the great challenge for the Christian celibate "devotee" to prove the authenticity of his or her self-consecration to God in Christ. It is a challenge to live celibate love as the authentic spirit of inner freedom to consecrate one's total life to self-giving love for all, at all times.

But what is love?

In any community, in one form or another, love is the greatest human force, the greatest human value or virtue ever. But in practice, even sometimes in theory, love is also the most abused; the most neglected, in fact, the most misunderstood human virtue or value.

Often it is not only the so-called die-hard conservatives, but also normal Christians like some of us, you and me, who are tempted to explain love away. Sometimes we have strange ways of interpreting love in practice, when we find ourselves challenged by the authenticity of love. This challenge becomes really demanding, when love in such a situation would demand a difficult decision to make real sacrifices. To face the challenge of love in that type of critical situation we are often called upon to accept to reconcile with a person who might have betrayed our offer of love in a real difficult situation; or when we are confronted with the need to practice merciful love as a person in authority. In such situations, suddenly we get mixed up with arguments like: "If I give in I am only encouraging him or her"; or "Order is order, Law is law!" Or "The principle must be upheld" Or, "We should not encourage evil.". Or, sometimes a cleric may put forward officious arguments such as: "This is against my ecclesiastical dignity." There are endless such arguments available for anyone who needs them, in and out of season.

In such situations, when we are challenged to show authentic love, which affects our human pride, real or presumed, the human mind is never short of tricks to avoid the practice of love. Especially when it is a case demanding true self-giving, true self-sacrificing love. Often when we talk of "dignity", if we are true to ourselves, we mean rather "pride". Often when use "principle", "law", or "rule", we are doing nothing but depersonalising, reifying, what is actually concerning the relationship between persons with blood and bones, with desires and feelings, with needs and preferences. Love is in fact the greatest challenge of authenticity.

Certainly, the love, which we are meditating upon now, is the great gift of the Spirit. As St. Paul describes it in 1Cor.12: 31-13: 1

"Set your hearts then on the more important gifts. Best of all, however, is the following way. I may be able to speak the languages of men and even of angels, but if I have no love, my speech is no more than a noisy gong or a clanging bell"

In this sense "love" is the total, unconditional, self-giving to any and everybody. One can say "love" is certainly the greatest commandment; in fact it is the basic interior drive towards authenticity, towards self-realisation. Permit me to be little bit theoretical, or let us say philosophical, here. For instance, the urge to fulfil the value of justice is not primarily out of the appreciation of justice as such, which may be only theoretical, but the impulse of love for the human victim of injustice. Now, authenticity, which leads to personal fulfilment, implies the conformity of a person's total self with the interior drive. Accordingly we can say that the realisation of love is the most basic act of personal fulfilment. Since the Christian faith is based on Jesus Christ as the love of God revealed to humankind, for the Christian, the realization of the virtue or value of love is the most basic challenge of authenticity, therefore personal fulfilment. So also it was said of the early Christians: "See how they love one another." This love is the most powerful force uniting Christians, at least in principle, the bond of unity.

Accordingly, anyone in a typical indigenous African community, let alone a Christian, who does not love, can hardly find any fulfilment in his/her life, let alone his/her pastoral vocation, his/her ministry. This is because in the indigenous African cultural milieu, without love, there is no Christian commitment to authenticity. This is because, as I have already mentioned, in the indigenous African culture, it is believed that the conscious or unconscious disregard of the principles, norms or rules of your religious confession, incurs misfortune, personal, communitarian or social, or even natural catastrophe. Any religious commitment is believed binding, under the pain of punishment in one form or another. Therefore for the Christian faith, only authentic love in concrete situations, in the seminary or novitiate, in the Parish, in the

Diocese, in the congregation, in the community or in the society, can make individuals truly experience self-fulfilment.

As Archbishop Peter Sarpong of the Diocese of Kumasi, Ghana, West Africa, usually affirms, indigenous Africans are concrete thinkers. This does not imply in any way that indigenous Africans do not think theoretically or logically. The truth is far from that. This is demonstrated by discoveries of original indigenous African scientific scripts. To affirm that indigenous Africans are concrete thinkers is simply to affirm that the truth is not just a concept, ideals or ideas separable from the concrete expressions in words, acts or actions.

In this context one has to acknowledge that even in this indigenous African system of concrete thinking, there is allowance for the element of human weakness, or rebellion. There may be indigenous Africans who just do want to believe in or practise certain indigenous values or virtues. But in a typical African way, such cases are ritually "neutralised", as we may put it, through the sacrifice of appeasement of the guardian spirits, believed to be the custodians of these rules, virtues or values in the interest of the community and the people, or simply the appeasement of the spiritual bond of solidarity.

For instance, among indigenous Ewes of West Africa, it is said: "Wo te ga de edzi": literally, "They have sounded the gong on it" (the word, act or action). This expression derives from the expression: "ga", the indigenous Ewe word for "iron". This is because the "Gong" is often made up of two or more hollow conically shaped casts of iron, which are struck at each mention of the act, action or behaviour to be neutralised. The belief is that from then on such a word, action or behaviour would no longer incur any respective punishment for the individual or the community. Of the person who persistently indulges in acts, actions or behaviour against principles, norms or values is said in Ewe: "Edu ka tso". This means, literally, "One has snapped the rope attaching him or her to the community, which is regarded a communion". We may express it in English: he or she has outlawed himself or herself. It is also said: "Edze anyi le amitowo do me." This means literally: "One has fallen among (palm) oil sellers". This expresses the idea that the one is acknowledged as effectively disgraced, or dissocialised. This is because palm oil has a deep red colour which makes the one who falls into it well besmeared with deep red oil colour, difficult to remove. Any person who meets the one would know why the one's appearance is so despicable. This expression also denotes being outlawed with a sort of a stamp of humiliation. Some other expression is: "Haho di asi de dzi" This literally means: "The crowd has constituted a market on the one." This implies all the people know what one is, and regard one so. This means the one's action or behaviour does no longer look strange to the community, therefore does not incur any respective misfortune any more. Still another expression is: "Wodee de kpese me". This literally means: "One has been outlawed."

All these expressions point to the fact that there are, and there will be, individuals going against the norm. But there is a communitarian way of neutralising the effect of their disregard of what is regarded the norm.

One other general communitarian means to render these misdeeds or misconduct spiritually ineffective is the periodic ritual cleansing or purification of individuals or the community.

I hope I am not getting too theoretical here. I believe it will be of interest to those interested in certain basic theoretic foundation for the practice of religion, or the way of life among indigenous Africans.

Thus as I may put it, in the life of the indigenous African, at least generally speaking, there are no concepts, ideals or ideas as simply, so to say "logical-existential misfits". The indigenous Africans are also interested in theoretical arguments, but such arguments are not considered valid, unless they are practicable or practised in one form or another.

This is not to say this type of logic is only applicable in the indigenous African society. In fact the words of Our Lord Jesus Christ insist on the practice of virtues in the life of his followers as the only way to express authentic belief. As it is often said, even

Satan believes; the only thing that makes Satan truly Satan is that it refuses to practice or act in conformity with this belief.

Even generally speaking, in the most practical way, in any society rules or laws are made to be observed in one way or the other. For instance the police would arrest you if you drive without a license in any society. The police would not leave you free simply because you are capable of arguing that you know the rule or the law well, or that you are well versed in all theoretical and practical techniques of driving

In conformity with this indigenous practical logic, there are no confessional rules, norms, values or laws per se, unless they are meant to be practiced by the respective followers of the particular religious confession. Therefore in this indigenous cultural context your Christian faith is authentic only if Christian principles, such as love, are seen to be practised by those who profess to be Christians. It is only this practice of love, which makes the Christian faith authentic. And it is only when you, as a Christian, live this faith sincerely through the practice of love, that you find personal fulfilment, just as the lack of love can destroy individual lives and relationships.

If the Church is the sacrament of the love of God for human beings then we, Christians, future pastors or pastors in the field, Religious and committed Christians in general are to mediate this love of God to humankind. We fulfil this mission of mediation by participating in the mission of Christ, the love of God made flesh, thus completing his saving work in the world and in the universe.

Thus, sacramentally, our concrete practice of acts of love in our human society, as the disciples or the apostles of Christ, is the outward expression of the inward grace of love of God at work in the universe. In this sense every concrete act of love anywhere in the world is the local realisation, or the actualisation of divine love for humankind, in fact for all the creation. For whatever has been created by God has been created as an act of love. So in a sense, we can say the whole creation is the sacrament of divine love. Thus, in the whole or in part, creation manifests this divine love.

But as we know, sacraments are the external expressions of internal or invisible grace in visible, palpable and audible signs. Since these signs are perceptible representations of imperceptible realities they are called symbols. And since love denotes a relationship between two persons, or among a group of persons, the most relevant and dynamic symbolic or sacramental expression of this divine love is binding relationship between two individuals, entailing reciprocal acts of love as self-giving. This living and dynamic symbol of divine love then is marriage. Thus the history of this reciprocal loving relationship between human beings and God is represented by marriage relationship between man (male) and woman (female), bridegroom and bride.

Thus right from the time of the prophets in the Old Testament to the time of our Lord Jesus Christ himself in the New Testament, the scriptures express this love of God for his people by conjugal love. This conjugal love involves all the dynamics of love or virtue of love, namely bitterness and sweetness, sorrow and joy, trust and betrayal, fear and courage, anxiety and hope. Thus the relationship between creature and the Creator has come to be expressed in human terms of emotion, desire, offence and forgiveness, anger and compassion, hate and mercy. These creaturely expressions of divine love make it truly sacramental, as the visible, human expression of invisible divine grace. But the mediation of this love to humankind is not a married person. According to our faith, I mean here the official teaching of the Catholic Church; the mediation of God's love to humankind is through a celibate person. As far as we know, or rather as far as our official Catholic teaching is concerned, Our Lord Jesus Christ had no wife. So though as the Second Vatican Council affirms, marriage could be effective and even efficacious expression of divine love (Vat. II: The Apostolic Constitution of the Church in the Modern World, Nos 48-50), our Lord's life, and the life of the Apostles, reveal that a person mediating this love of God can be so consumed by the preaching of this love, so preoccupied with being at the service of this love for all humankind, that he or she has no time for the expression or experience of marital love.

This is not to deny the fact that one or the other might have actually married. At least we know from the scriptures that the Apostle St. Peter had a mother-in-law. This implies he had actually married, and had had a wife. Therefore the important point here is that even if the disciples of Our Lord had married and had wives, the mission of the word of God left no time for conjugal life or the physical experience of this conjugal love.

As theologians express it, the apostles were made to offer their total existence to the discipleship, and later to their own missionary activity. Accordingly it is understandable that they had no time for anything else apart from their dedication to the Word, the mediation of the love of God to fellow human beings. Thus this "apostolic celibacy", as we may term it, can be considered as, to use the term used by spiritual writers, the "existential inability to do otherwise." That is a life of dedication to the love of God, which has no room for human or earthly marital love.

Thus considered, celibacy could be an opportunity to express and to experience, symbolically, this divine love in its pure form. This pure expression and experience of divine love can become a true sacramental expression of this divine conjugal love, namely God as husband of all humankind. This is in fact the imagery used often to describe the relationship between God, Yahweh, and Israel, his chosen people. Since the church or, by extension, all humankind redeemed, is new Israel, chosen as heirs of this biblical love relationship, this imagery of marital love relationship between God and humankind is valid.

In this connection may readers who are not members of the Catholic Church, or are Catholics but do not share this belief excuse me for being so exclusive here. This applies to other members of other religions or cultural groups who may have heard or learnt a different history of Jesus Christ. It is understood our Muslim brothers and sisters have a different history of Jesus. So also Hindus or Buddhists may also have a different history. But this particularly Catholic theological digression, as I may term it, is on account of the fact that the original reflections were meant for Catholics.

Now let us be back on track with our theme of celibate love. Just as any type of divine grace, this sacramental love is a gift. The more so because, as Pope John Paul II expresses it, the original creation is of man and woman joined together. But our Lord confirms that in spite of this original plan by God for man and woman, leaving their own respective families to become one flesh, some have a special gift of pure love at the service of this divine, prophetic conjugal love. In fact, self-dedication of this celibate love as a sacramental sign is also at the service of human conjugal love. This is clear from the pastor's role of witnessing to, and confirming, the marriage bond at weddings, of blessing the couple in marriage, and later attending to their family problems. Thus the ideal of the practicability of celibate love is that it frees and motivates the celibate to dedicate his/her whole life to the service of the kingdom, the nuptial banquet of love. In this sense, carrying the imagery further, the celibate could be considered a sort of God's best man. In the service of marital love, celibate love should be spiritually sound. As a life of commitment to authenticity of love, celibate love needs be faithful love. So also like any gift of the Spirit, celibate love needs be fruitful; it needs bring forth many children of God through tirelessly preaching of the Word of God by word and deed. In fact the challenge of authenticity of celibate love demands that the whole person be devoted to the realisation of this divine love in the world.

This fruitful love of a celibate, mediating divine love as a sacramental love, is a sign of Christ's love for his Church. Just as Christ's love is faithful, total and sincere, celibate love has also to be fruitful, total and sincere.

Once more, to be fair to those who may not be Catholics, or are Catholics but do not share this official Catholic stand on the need of what we may term actual physical celibacy or being single as a pastoral minister, the point here is not to claim that only celibate clerics or religious could or are worthy of mediating divine love to humankind. That would be unjust to many married pastors of other Christian confessions, or even of other religions, men and women of good will, who are totally devoted to the course of the love of God among humankind.

As I have already mentioned, since these reflections were originally meant for prospective celibates or those who had already professed or promised to lead a single life of celibacy, "for the sake of the Kingdom", the thoughts being expressed here are to help them find meaning in their choice of life, in their particular vocation. For the latter, celibate love is a challenge of authenticity indeed! This is because if we sincerely accept that the lives of others can also be valid mediation of the love of God without opting for a single life of dedication, without conjugal love, then our lives as celibate mediators of divine love are at best superfluous, at worst self-deception, the abuse of the grace of God. This is not to affirm that celibate life is null and void by any act that betrays it. But the point is that human weakness needs not be the excuse for unfaithfulness. The challenge of authenticity demands that at least there needs be a sincere effort to keep one's solemn promise or vow.

However, making room for human weakness should not overlook the fact that religion in indigenous African culture heightens the challenge of authenticity for indigenous Africans, who are celibates or profess to be celibates. That is, those who profess or solemnly promise to dedicate their lives to the Word of God, to be in the service of fellow human beings by leading single lives, need struggle in honesty to keep to the promise. But this single life has to be considered and accepted "in toto", as we used to say when learning Latin those days. That is, if you choose to dedicate yourself absolutely to the service of the Word of God, then it implies, or should imply the acceptance of life as a single person, without any relationship with another person as if you were leading a life together, being "one flesh."

It is true that many priests and priestesses of the indigenous African religion or religions do marry. But, as we have already seen, we have to bear in mind that there is celibacy in the indigenous African religion too, for life, for certain periods such as the period of formation within an enclosure or when the priest or priestess has to render himself or herself worthy for official duties in the shrine.

This vow of celibacy in the indigenous religion is so strict that one risks losing his or her life through insincerity. Unlike Christian religion, the guardian spirits or mystical forces or powers do not make room for human weakness. According to the indigenous African belief the consequences follow whether the person who commits an act or action against the rule of celibacy or spiritual purity has done it consciously or unconsciously. The indigenous Africans, at least in the general sense, as I have already remarked, believe the guardian spirits would afflict you with some illness or even strike you dead if you are unfaithful to vows made to them. For the Guardian spirits also guard against dishonesty and carelessness in matters relating to the observance of religious vows or what is often termed tabus (taboos) by Anthropologists and Ethnologists.

This is not to frighten readers who may be in this position. We believe God would not afflict any one with a disease or strike anyone dead for committing any act against celibacy. We believe God's merciful love is greater than our sins. He is a loving Father ready to forgive us, his recalcitrant children, provided we are ready to accept our weaknesses in humility, and convert. However, we need to be aware of how people feel about the way we live out our solemn promises or vows, on account of the indigenous cultural background. We need to respect the indigenous African religious sensitivity, not to weaken the trust usually reposed in religious leaders or spiritual authority. We need strive to maintain the spiritual trust of the people in our effectiveness as mediators of the divine, worthy of the title: "Men of God" or "Women of God." Thus faithfulness in the matter of celibacy is a great challenge of authenticity as regards our vocation in the indigenous African cultural milieu.

We know if God could cease loving us we would cease to be. Despite human unfaithfulness through hatred, even against prophets sent to warn, correct, and lead humankind back to the right path, God's love is ever faithful. So also is Christ's love for the Church, ever faithful despite Christians' unfaithfulness. As St. Paul puts it:

"If we have died with him, then we shall live with him. If we endure, then we shall also reign with him. If we disown him, then he will disown us. We may be unfaithful, but he is always faithful, for he cannot disown his own self" (2 Tim.2: 11-13).

Thus, celibate love is unconditional, not even dependent on reciprocity. If we expect reward or thanks for the least service we render to people, for sick-calls (which requires petrol fee) or for counselling a couple, we shall always be disappointed. We shall not find fulfilment in the pastoral work. What should satisfy us is that we have been able to be at the service of others. Our satisfaction should be in the fact that someone has been healed through our help or that a marriage bond has been restored. If you are to help only those who pay us, if we visit and pray for only those who pay their dues or come to Church, then we are not faithful loving pastors revealing Christ's love.

As one retreat leader once remarked, to reserve our love for those who pay is spiritual prostitution, love for sale. Let us remember, no amount of money can buy God's love, which you accept to mediate for humankind. That is why I find it embarrassing when I hear about rules forcing relatives to pay up before burial. I mean the rule at certain places enforcing "no pay, no burial" policy. I think, that is a typical form of spiritual prostitution. For, if even our primary school catechism teaches that burial is a corporal work of mercy, I wonder who can pay for the mercy of God, or for the love of God mediated to the fellow human being.

I should think if pastoral activity or spiritual service should be personally fulfilling then every pastoral service should be a free self-donation. Any physical reward should only be the beneficiary's spontaneous gratitude to God, an offer (not demanded) through the pastor.

This is not to imply that pastors among indigenous Africans do not deserve sustenance from the people. Even St. Paul approves of it. As he puts it those who preach the Word deserve to have the minimum to survive while preaching the word. But we need also take seriously what our Lord demands of his disciples. They are to depend totally on the generous response of those who benefit from their mission of love (Luk 10: 4). In this connection I believe it is beneficial that in indigenous Africa, generally, Catholic pastors are not officially paid, but are given allowances. Moreover, indigenous Africans are generous enough to care for their pastors, if they have the means.

For those of us who had been baptised before the age of the so called "development aid", we could remember that indigenous parishes were capable of feeding, housing, and even paying for holidays of missionaries, as well as buying vehicles for them. Why is it no longer possible for indigenous Africans to look after their pastors? We have already mentioned that in relation to our reflection on the society today and the challenge of authenticity. The truth is that we, the pastors, prefer begging from the exploiters of our people rather than doing our work for which we have been commissioned: namely to be a prophetic voice in the society, the voice of the voiceless. Thus we have to blame ourselves too, not only the politicians. As I have already stated above, politicians and their foreign allies and so called experts are in need of our spiritual care too. They are in need of our call to conversion, and not only our appeals for funds.

Moreover the members of indigenous African Christian churches also suffer from the problems brought about by development aid and the accompanying economic restructuring measures and privatisation programme. But they are capable of looking after their pastors. And that is without foreign aid. Does that not indicate that missionary churches do not fully support their pastors because, somehow, our readiness to go begging for them makes them take it for granted that they have to wait for foreign money to look after their pastors, as well as finance their so called development projects, including the building of churches and schools? Concurrently, does that not indicate that we are neglecting one of our prime functions in the society as Christians? That is the neglect of our function as prophetic voice of the society, as I have already mentioned above.

Accordingly, as indigenous African Christians we have to reconsider our role in the society. That is, our role as prophetic voice in our society. In addition to being the prophetic voice of the society, we have to consider seriously our commitment to the option for the poor. These two cardinal functions of the Christian faith in our African society are a great challenge of authenticity for Christian leaders in indigenous Africa today. To continue preaching love and care for the neighbour while you are living a life of the rich in the society puts doubt on the authenticity of your preaching.

In this connection another particularity of the pastoral demand in indigenous African cultural milieu even today is that the apostolate is twenty-four hours, without opening hours or closing hours. For among indigenous Africans, spiritual care takes precedence over social, medical or legal care. This is because indigenous Africans believe the spiritual care can take care of the social, medical and legal care. Often when someone is suddenly ill or involved in an accident, the first person on the lips of the person involved is the pastor. So also in any type of need or with any type of trouble the spiritual authority is the first to provide help or counsel.

Moreover, as I have already mentioned, the indigenous Africans request prayers, not only at any time, but also anywhere, on the street, on the bus, in the market, at school or even in the office.

Thus in the indigenous African cultural milieu, to be ready to offer spiritual services around the clock is not simply a principle, or exaggeration. It is a challenge of authenticity, called upon as a single celibate pastor to be ready to be called at any time and at any place to mediate divine love unconditionally. So also a celibate love, in fact, a Christian's love, should be available to all including "enemies" who return evil for the good you do for them.

It would be destructive for the community if the pastor takes sides one against the other among the faithful. The catechist or teacher who reports you to the bishop or moderator, and backbites you also deserves your love. Already in the seminary, the staff member who sees nothing good in you also deserves your love. As our Lord remarks: "For if you love those who love you, what right have you to claim any credit? Even the tax collectors do as much, do they not?" (Mat 5: 46).

The way to destroy your personality, and, therefore, the way to obstruct the authenticity of your faith, your personal fulfilment, is to return hatred for hatred, an eye for an eye. Conversely the only way to take up the challenge of authenticity and find fulfilment in loving your fellow human being is to love unconditionally. To love unconditionally means to love with a free heart. And freehearted love is the love without making distinctions. This is love for anybody at any time: for the unapproachable Bishop or Parish Priest, for the unreliable staff - the Rector, unfriendly fellow Seminarians, or even unpleasant kitchen staff, or for the drunken husband or drunken wife, for the overbearing parent, for the runaway child, for the insulting employer or disrespectful employee, for the "unbearable" fellow worker, in short love for anybody at any time and in any situation, all who need your unpretended love.

A celibate love has to be total. Physical, psychological and spiritual strength should all be geared towards the love of fellow human beings without distinction, even if love in a specific case would amount to the literal participation in the death of Christ on the cross. Most of the time it may not mean being crucified in the literal sense. But it would mean being available at all times at all places, being everything to everybody, as St. Paul would put it. You have to be available to all, all day and all night. You need offer yourself as the Kingdom at hand, doing the business of your heavenly Father.

Celibate love as total self-consecration means offering our human, physiological self: our senses, our feelings, our loneliness, our pains and anxieties for the ministry of love. Since you are not married, there is no fear of embarrassing questions when you stay out late into the night. If your celibate life is not total, your love cannot be total either. This is because you have reserved part of your heart for the special lover. Often that special lover would be jealous of any other person taking too much of your attention, and before you realise it you can be a bone of contention for two "wild dogs" which may explode in a scandal. So be truly free to love, face the challenge of authenticity of celibate love. Taking up the challenge of the authenticity of celibate love would mean being pure in mind and heart.

Sometimes, you may read one or the other writer condemning celibacy altogether. After reading such a book, you may begin to rationalise your celibate life. After all, celibacy is not important at all, you may begin to tell yourself. However, in spite of your rationalisation, it hangs around your neck as you pretend you are escaping from it. Even when people call you "Father," "Brother", "Sister" or "Man of God" you feel so flattered because you realise you are not so "Fatherly", "Brotherly", "Sisterly" or "Godly" inside that externally immaculate cassock, habit or "clergyman".

I believe we are aware that this rigorous application of the rules of spiritual purity is applied to non-clerical and nonreligious persons as well. In many communities today young women and men openly relating one to the other without marriage are de facto excommunicated. This is because, fellow Christians often say, such people cause scandal to the people. And I, myself, have heard such comments from the remnant few believers in the indigenous African religion. They often say: "Christians are destroying the morals of our society." This is because, as they put it, Christians are taught to disobey the guardian spirits, the ancestors and the elders, who are believed to be the guardians of moral norms and rules. Some even accuse Christians: "They do not know God!" In the indigenous language it means by their attitude or behaviour Christians show they do not keep to moral principles. These days what makes people make such comments may not have anything to do with indigenous African Christians at all. Some times it is just a news item from some other continent. But since the people of that continent send missionaries to Christianise us, as indigenous Christians we get the blame. Sometimes we say, "but that is the general problem in the world". Or some of us retort to such arguments by saying, but we are better here in Africa than those elsewhere. Some of us even try to make our consciences comfortable by saying: "After all our people need also think and act according to the modern trends". Some of us even accuse our people of being "backward". We talk about human rights and democracy, women or feminine liberation. For our people such arguments do not hold water. We are indigenous Africans, therefore we are judged by indigenous cultural standards. That is our challenge of authenticity in our indigenous African cultural milieu.

Thus, in the kingdom of the Mighty Eros, or rather during the reign of the Mighty Eros, we have been called, or rather, we have been challenged, to witness to pure love, or as theologians would term it: "integrated affectivity". As a participation in the saving act of our Lord Jesus Christ, our celibate love, pure affection, is to save humankind from the clutches of the proselytisers of the religion of Eroticism. Our pure love is to be a sacramental sign of hope, that despite today's society's smoochy sounds, peep-ins, adult shows of "X" rated films, a young man or a young woman can still lead a morally pure life without frustration. By taking up this challenge of authenticity on our part as spiritual leaders, as true symbols of moral and spiritual purity, we challenge in turn our youth, who are often deprived of the indigenous African cultural and religious formation, and are tempted to go along with anything regarded "modern" or "civilised". In facing the challenge of authenticity we show to our youth today that it is still worthwhile keeping our "old" indigenous religious and moral principles.

Our clerical chastity bears witness, or better put, ought to bear witness to the validity and the great value of premarital chastity, which is still tested the first night after wedding among certain indigenous African peoples even in our "modern" or "post-modern" times. All this requires that a Pastor or a Religious, or even any confessed Christian be, not a sign of contradiction for the other faithful and other indigenous people, but a sign of consistency. People lose hope if they hear that "they also do it." As they say, if those who spend thirteen years in training cannot help it, how could they who have been born into it, are living in it and have not made any solemn promises?

It is a challenge to be able to relate with others as male or female, as human beings, distinct but with the same dignity, in need of love from fellow human beings, which we can provide unconditionally, with love unblemished. With this reflection we can say, after all, celibacy has meaning, not only for those who happen to be celibates, but also for married couples. From our reflections so far our celibate love is also sacramental love, at the service of conjugal sacramental love.

All said and done, Our Lord Jesus Christ himself is, or rather should be our model of celibate love. He accepts the human, female expression of love, even from those regarded by the society as immoral and great sinners. One may even say, to show love to, and accept love from those avoided by others as "sinners" is itself a healing touch. This is the challenge of authenticity of love, love as unconditional gift of the self to or for the sake of another person or other persons.

Let us end this meditation with Joh.3: 16.
For God so loved the world that he gave his only Son, that whoever believes in him should not perish but have eternal life.

Reflection XI

Fruits of Love as Challenge Of Authenticity

Introduction Verse: 1Cor.13: 4-7

> *"Love is always patient and kind; it is never jealous; love is never boastful or conceited; it is never rude or selfish; it does not take offence, and is not resentful. Love takes no pleasure in other people's sins but delights in the truth; it is always ready to excuse, to trust, to hope, and to endure whatever comes."*

In the last meditation we meditated on celibate love in general. This means unconditional self-giving, self-sacrificing and selfless relationship with the others. This reflection makes us reflect positively on our role in the society in relation to the Vow of Celibacy. This is to help us find positive meaning in our celibate life as a life of total offer for love.

In the meditation that follows we shall meditate on the Fruits of Love as Challenge of Authenticity in concrete situations. Thus, we shall meditate on how the demands of the mystical bond of solidarity in the indigenous African community as mystical (spiritual) union poses a challenge of authenticity for the fruits of love in practice in the Christian community as the spiritual bond of love, the body of Christ. We shall reflect on how various types and situations of relationship pose the challenge of commitment to authenticity and personal fulfilment in the community, when considered on the background of indigenous principles and practices.

The indigenous community as mystical (spiritual) communion makes an offence against solidarity such as hatred, jealousy, rudeness, and destructive insults an offence against the spirit of the individual and the spirit of the communal solidarity, in a sense a sacrilege.

Offence against a member of the indigenous communion is sacrilege, because, as the etymology of the word: "sacrilege" implies, it is an act that harms the sacred character of the bond.

The bond is the relationship between the supernatural and human beings on one hand, and between human beings on the other. The supernatural include the Almighty God, the spirits and the Ancestors. However obligations or responsibilities arising out of supernatural and human relationship involves human relationship with the universe or cosmos- vegetation and fauna.

The microcosm, or the sacred symbol of this solidarity is the throne, stool or skin. This makes the individual person selected to occupy the throne, stool or skin also sacred. This sacred interrelationship of solidarity implies the sacredness of certain relationships, such as King, Chief or Queen mother and other members, kin and kin, child and parent, husband and wife, friend and friend, host and guest etc.

The sacred character of each relationship is protected by rules and regulations, taboos (taboos), which sanction the respective moral code of behaviour. Thus any person initiated into the communion is bound by the sacred code of behaviour.

In different forms the contents of the sacred code of behaviour resembles what I term "the fruits of love".

It is the responsibility of each member as well as the co-responsibility of the communion or community to keep out "bad spirit", which destroys individuals as well as the bond of solidarity of the communion, such as boastfulness, conceit, jealousy, resentfulness, rudeness, selfishness, pleasure in other people's sins and other negative types of behaviour. So also it is collective and individual responsibility to cultivate virtues, which build up a secure bond of solidarity and the welfare of each individual, such as endurance, hope, kindness, patience, readiness to excuse, trust and truthfulness.

This is a challenge to prove the authenticity of Christian communal solidarity as Eucharistic communion, covenant of love, the body of Christ (1 Cor 12: 27). This is a divine-human communion, as sacred bond, with implications. As we read from 1 Cor 10: 16-21

The cup of blessing, which we bless, is it not a participation in the blood of Christ? The bread which we break, is it not a participation in the body of Christ? Because there is one bread, we who are many are one body, for we all partake of the one bread.

Thus, just as in the indigenous communion, an offence against the spirit of the Christian bond of love can also incur dire consequences (1 Cor 11: 27-32).

Whoever, therefore, eats the bread or drinks the cup of the Lord in an unworthy manner will be guilty of profaning the body and blood of the Lord. Let a man (or woman) examine himself (or herself), and so eat of the bread and drink of the cup. For anyone who eats and drinks without discerning the body eats and drinks judgment upon himself (or herself).

Thus this challenge calls for inner conviction and external commitment to the fruits of love stated in 1Cor.13: 4-7:

"Love is always patient and kind; it is never jealous; love is never boastful or conceited; it is never rude or selfish; it does not take offence, and is not resentful. Love takes no pleasure in other people's sins but delights in the truth; it is always ready to excuse, to trust, to hope, and to endure whatever comes."

I regard this text as one of the greatest texts in the bible. This text describes all the dynamic elements. I guess it is this text which justifies St. Augustine when he states: "If you love you can do what you will", and you will be right, a true Christian. If any human being can master all the implications of this text on love, or rather the hymn on love, in word and deed, then he or she is already perfect.

I recommend this text to you: lovers, suitors and fiancés, those already married, as well anybody in any type of relationship. This text needs be committed to memory, recited and reflected on each day and whenever there is crisis in the relationship. To forestall destructive crisis in the relationship each person concerned with any type of human relationship needs reflect persistently on how his or her life reflects the elements or the fruits of love mentioned in this text. This text balances the emotional and the realistic elements of love. Each element or fruit of love presents a challenge. This text presents what we term as the "crux" of the matter of love. This is also a text, which could be used as a sort of a Christian anthem of love. It deals with all the dynamics, the dialectics and the radical demands of love.

Each person, each occasion, each occurrence puts its own twist to each of the elements mentioned. To be patient with someone, who responds to your love is something else as to be patient until your wayward husband or wife comes back from his or her escapades or adventures. So also being kind to your own kin or relative does not involve all the risks and anxieties of being kind to an unknown foreigner. So also being kind to a friend is not the same as being kind to a foe.

As I have already mentioned, the text for reflection contains what could be considered "elements" of love. This expression, "elements", suggests that the various attitudes or virtues mentioned in the text are interpreted as that which constitutes, or that which makes what love is. As matter of fact this expression, "elements" of love is correct. For instance it is correct to say: "patience" is an element of, or one of the values or virtues constituting or making what love is. But since we have already reflected on love in relation to the solemn promise or vow of celibacy, I deem it appropriate to dwell on that which results from truly loving someone. The question in this reflection is: What does true love produce in the heart, mind and spirit? Or, What do I gain from truly loving? In other words, what vices am I freed from, and what virtues do I acquire, by truly loving God or Jesus Christ, some other human being or even some other creature? The virtues we acquire from truly loving strengthen us to fight and stand against respective vices within society and ourselves.

It is true, for instance, to love truly you have to be patient, to love truly you have to be kind. In this sense, as it were, patience or kindness is what you invest in loving someone. But to invest in love is only one aspect of love, we may say the altruistic aspect of love. But love is also, as we may say, a school, where you learn something really significant for life. For instance by learning to be patient as an act of love you also, as it were, become a master of patience. And if you are master of patience you enhance your personality and capabilities for achieving great things in life also for yourself. So also by learning to be kind as an act of love, you become a master of kindness. And being a master of kindness enhances your personality and capabilities for achieving great things in life such as being a leader, a head of state, a minister of state, or even the director or a manager of a business concern. This second aspect of love may sound utilitarian. But that does not diminish the challenge it poses. These are the reasons for which I choose to title this reflection: The Fruits of Love.

Love is always patient

One of the greatest indigenous African values or virtues is patience. Patience is a divine attribute, which especially every person of authority or in leadership position, an elderly person or a truly responsible person must possess. In fact patience is a mark of wisdom. For patience is the expression of inner peace. Therefore it means calm or serenity, undisturbed by the external world of noise and commotion. Among Ewes of West Africa patience is represented by a thick leaf of a plant usually used in cultic activities, called in the indigenous language: "ma". One says often, "Efa abe ma ene", meaning he or she is as calm as "ma". Thus the image of this patience or calm is often an old man with a long beard, sitting down, surrounded by young people pulling his beard. As the expression of patience, as inner calm or serenity, such an old man, who is also a wise man, does not show any feeling of being disturbed or being angry at all. Often nothing can make him angry. He just sits there as young people tug at his beard. He may continue being deep in thought, and delivering his words of wisdom.

This quality of indigenous African patience as serenity and calm is a great challenge for Christian leaders, or those in authority. This quality of wisdom is demanded especially by the contemporary world of noise and commotion. Normally a person in authority or an elderly person loses respect if he is disturbed, angered by the least irritation.

Thus patience is a challenge if we truly minister to love to people of our time (2003). We all know this is a time of confusion. This is a time of confused morals, confused beliefs and therefore confused personalities. People tend to be aggressive, sometimes unconsciously because of their own confusion, as a result of the lack of inner peace. There is always a lot of irritation from those to whom we need show love. It is in this time of confusion that we, you and I, are challenged to be true to ourselves and all that we stand for, to be authentic. We need to hold our ground, come what may, not to be pulled into the fray, as it is often said. It is in this period of confused personalities that you and I are challenged to be what we are, to be sincere to ourselves. We need commit ourselves to authenticity in order to experience personal peace through patience. In this time of confusion, a person, especially the Pastor, in training or in the field, needs patience, and that a lot of it. One needs a lot of patience in dealing with different people. Otherwise, he or she would find his or her life always irritating, always full of anxiety, even bitterness. In the seminary or the novitiate, it is always good to listen to the other person patiently. This other person may be the rector or the Novice master or novice mistress, a staff member, or fellow Seminarian or Novice. You need listen patiently before replying to unpleasant questions. Instead of giving immediate reply to such irritating questions you need reflect for a moment, or even excuse yourself and leave the person or the place for a moment. If and when you are a pastor, or a spiritual leader in any capacity, it is good to listen patiently to any one who comes with a complaint, until the person exhausts whatever he or she has to say. It is always helpful to avoid angry interruptions while the complainant is still emptying his or her chest. If you interrupt, the person may become only more agitated, even aggressive and violent.

However it all depends on whether the complainant is a fellow Cleric, a fellow Religious, a worker (employee), a student, a seminarian, a Novice, a husband or wife. If the complainant is only a well-known person such as a fellow Cleric or Religious, impatience may not be so disastrous. But if the person is a wife or a husband, you better be careful not to lose your patience. Otherwise, without patient listening, even to what you may regard as trivial, your impatience may lead the next moment to a human tragedy, a catastrophe in some people's life or relationship. Without a ready ear of patient listening out of love for a fellow human being, a husband may flare up; rush to confront a partner, and the consequences of your careless listening may be regrettable. A marriage may be destroyed. Not only that, if you are not lucky, a wife may incur a bruised nose from an impatient husband. According to our indigenous culture, as you know, a man bruising his wife! That is an abomination! So on account of your impatience to listen through the complaint, the poor man will have to pay for the ritual pacification of the spirit of the wife. Or a wife may pack up on the way to her parents in the village. Then you have a bigger problem trying to bring them together once more.

Love that brings forth patience needs apply, not only to those whom you minister to, but also to those who have authority over you or those over whom you have authority. This applies to the Bishop or Moderator as well as the catechist or teacher. It may be that you are just from the out stations, full of dirt and really tired. Just as you enter the sitting room or veranda there stands the Bishop or Moderator, bombarding you with angry questions even before you put down your mass kit or service kit. What do you do in such a situation? It is most certain, without a breath or two before answering you are also going to reply angrily.

The Bishop's or Moderator's reaction to such an angry reaction from you, his priest or pastor, may differ from case to case, depending on why the Bishop or Moderator is there at all, or what he might have gone through before coming there. If you are lucky, the Bishop or Moderator himself might have been frustrated, and looking for some one on whom to release his tension. Sometimes such uncalled for confrontation from the side of a superior authority may be a way of seeking counselling from you. Or it may even be an indirect way of asking you to listen to his confession. If the superior authority is a Sister Superior, it may be she only wants someone to release her tension and stress by using you as a sort of scapegoat, but in a good sense.

In any such situation, which threatens to explode, recall the image of the old wise man in a village square, surrounded by noisy youth tugging at his beard, just so calm and serene, almost immovable. Thus patience, which is born out of love, means also the capacity for waiting for others or yourself. That means also waiting for God's own time. In these so-called post-modern times, the catchword is punctuality, rush, "time is money", hectic. Sometimes we even forget that with God there is no time. So if we expect something from God we want it immediately. If God does not "deliver the goods" in time, to use a modern slang, we are disheartened, sometimes we flare up against God. The result is often stress, depression or even complete dejection. Then instead of doing things faster we become paralysed, confused where to go next with our lives.

Accordingly, be it the Bishop, Moderator, teacher or the catechist we need listen patiently. Give some time before reacting to unpleasant requests or comments or before reacting to even unwarranted insults. As a Religious Sister it is good to listen to the Superior or the lady teacher patiently. Allow some breathing space before making a reply to irritating questions, comments, remarks or insults.

Without patient listening, you may miss the opportunity to inform yourself through the suggestions, criticisms and requests of others. But when you listen patiently before making decisions, you will always experience satisfaction about the decision as something out of conscious and conscientious mind, not just emotion. In facing the challenge of patience, which can help us tone down our emotions of anger and unnecessary tension, stress and even depression, it is only patient listening to others which can make helping others truly personally fulfilling. For true personal fulfilment demands that a person in authority, a pastor, any spiritual leader or even any person in leadership position in any profession, such as a director or a manager, as well as a wife or husband, a parent or a teacher, one needs seek conviction rather than obedience from subordinates where and whenever possible.

In this case we can take St. Peter the Apostle as our paradigm of a leader who is full of patience born out of love for his fellow disciples. For instance, when he was confronted by Judaisers for partaking the meal of the uncircumcised, he did not command obedience by his apostolic authority, but, on the contrary, he respected their right to question his change of attitude and patiently "gave them details point by point..." (Acts 11:4).

With the monarchical development of church authority over the centuries, especially the role of St. Peter the Apostle, as the Prince of Princes of the Roman Catholic Church, I guess some would be surprised by this attitude of his in relation to this question. His patient listening should be a guide to every person in authority and in training for leadership. Love for his fellow disciples teaches him to bear with their slow understanding. Probably he was aware that he had also been a slow learner, and the Lord has had to bear with him too. The Apostle Peter knows the command he has got from the Lord is to "feed the sheep", which implies leading to pasture and waiting till each has enough water.

I wonder how many of us could go to such pains in explaining things even to our head Christians, or to use the modern term, our church presidents. Could a seminarian accept criticism of discriminating attitudes from the seminary staff or fellow seminarians so patiently? Could a Reverend Sister Superior accept the criticism of her discriminating attitude from fellow sisters, let alone from lady teachers or the faithful so patiently?

Having made these reflections on love-born patience, as we may term it, it is a great challenge, especially in our indigenous African society, where you cannot ask people to come for counselling according to the hour. People approach you spontaneously when something happens to them. However, talking about patience we need not support one of the problems caused by economic dislocation and imposed working habits. This is the so-called "African time", implying inability to keep time or appointment.

It is true, for our indigenous people, when there is a feast, then it is a real feast day. The elderly or the "royals" exercise patience, take time in coming out with regal steps. It is a sort of unwritten code that those in authority come only when all are already assembled. It is also said the intentional patient delay in arriving on the festival grounds is to confuse those who may be plotting something against their persons.

Certainly our people in the villages know and cultivate punctuality. It is interesting to see the aged, with their lanterns, converging on the king's palace or any place for meeting at dawn. Most do not have watches. Yet all are gathered at cockcrow, almost at the same time. It is true some may be late, but those arriving late apologise the first thing they arrive at the meeting place. They have to rise before sunrise to go onto the fields, or to the market. Moreover our people have no holidays, weekends, or pension. Some in our villages continue working on the farm even when they are eighty or even hundred years old. In short being patient is not the same as being lazy or wasting time.

In this context, I would like to narrate an incident, to explain this misunderstanding of indigenous African culture. I remember at one time I was to celebrate the holy Mass with some children somewhere outside Africa. Probably with this prejudice in mind, the parish priest came to the sacristy to tell me to change the readings for the day. Why? I asked. He replied: "We are not in

Africa. Here children have to learn to do things according to time and be aggressive!"

This parish Priest wanted the readings changed because the theme was patient waiting and humility. So his remark implied it was only black Africans who needed to be patient and humble. Others needed to be in haste and be aggressive.

Well. How do you react, confronted with such prejudice, just as you are supposed to compose yourself and prepare to celebrate the sacrament of love with children? Understandably I had to exercise patience. I thanked the parish priest for his instructions. But I insisted that we could not twist or avoid the word of God simply because it did not fit into the cultural perspective. We have to let the word of God into our hearts so that we can convert. That is the challenge of the Word of God. Anyway I told him the spirit would talk to the hearts of the children. So I had the readings read as in the liturgy of the day. The pastor sat through the celebration.

Among other things I told the children, if you love somebody, you need be patient with the person: your teacher, your parents, your brothers and sisters, your classmates and of course yourself. I explained to them that patience meant, if you were the most intelligent pupil, you needed to be calm if others still asked questions, which you might have thought were unnecessary, or when the teacher had to explain something over and over again for others to understand. "Put yourself in the position of the weak pupils", I told them. Then I asked: "If you fail an examination once. What would you do?" Each replied: "I shall learn harder in order to pass the next time". Then I asked: "Why? Wouldn't you leave school and stay at home?" They all replied: "No!" So I said, "children, as you see, you need to be patient, with others and with yourselves too".

In the end I asked: "Let us say you commit a sin. You tell God you repent, and you will never do it any more. But you still do it over and over again. Would you like it if God says He cannot be patient with you any more, and therefore He will no longer forgive you? Or would you be angry with yourself and stop praying?" They replied: "No!"

Then I said: "Children. As you see, if you are not patient, you will become sad, depressed and hopeless. Then you will begin to fail more examinations, you will have headache, and you will make everybody unhappy. So you need be patient with God, with your parents, with your teachers, with your friends or classmates, and you need to be patient with yourself. With patience, in spite of all problems, you will be healthy and happy"

Then the parish Priest nodded his head.

It is true we need budget our time to be effective as leaders. But patience is something far different from simply waiting or wasting time. Patience born out of love is the state of self-composure, self-control, a state without emotional reaction, or rather un-reflected action or aggression, which wreaks havoc with the nerves. Impatience causes so called "civilisation sickness", stress, nervous breakdown and other health problems. Patience as the fruit of love is an inner attitude of calm, peace, serenity and reflexive action or reaction. And this inner peace is a recipe for psychological and even physical health.

Loving patience is worth cultivating for inner peace, serenity and calm. This is also important for being kind-hearted as one of the fruits of love.

Love is always kind

In our indigenous society, being kind-hearted is also one of the virtues of an elderly person, a person in authority or a leader. Kindness implies being generous in spirit as well as in attitude and behaviour. In our indigenous culture being kind, in the sense of being generous in spirit, means being considerate, accepting even those who may look repulsive. This is an important virtue because elders are supposed to be able to relate to all, as the king, the head of the family or simply an elder brother or sister. Everyone needs feel free to present and discuss any problem with an elder.

The other meaning of being kind is to be outwardly generous with goods. Often in the village, when there is scarcity, the elderly are ready to deny themselves in order that the younger and weaker ones may have enough. Though begging is discouraged right from childhood, anybody in need can approach an elder of the family for help. To protect the image of the family, the elder who has not enough means takes it upon himself to approach those who have the means for help. The wealthy are obliged by the bond of solidarity to support the needy, by being kind towards the needy. Anybody visiting the king or family elder is sure to get something, be it a calabash of palm wine or even food. In fact to refuse to give water to the thirsty or food to the hungry is an offence to the bond of solidarity, and requires pacification ritual.

According to indigenous custom it is regarded an insult or even a bad omen to thank a host for food. It is often said: "The hen does not thank the waste heap." It would have to come back for more anyway. Thus to thank your host for food, it means you do not appreciate his or her hospitality enough to wish to come back on a visit another time. If your host is a woman, she may reply to your thanks: "Do you want me to become (or remain) a spinster?"

In certain communities funeral court hearing is often held after the death of a member. If it is found that the family members or neighbours have neglected the person, these are made to pay for ritual pacification of the offended spirit of the dead.

Strange enough, in the case of strangers, when people have to be careful of dangerous people, our indigenous culture rather calls for extra kindness. This is the spirit of hospitality. Anybody that arrives at mealtime is supposed to at least taste something of the meal. It is regarded even impolite to announce your visit beforehand. That would mean you do not trust the capability of the host to express his or her kindness with a surprise visit.

This sacred kind-heartedness is transformed into sacred magnanimity towards enemies during the time of conflict. According to this right to hospitality during war, people from the enemy side, who happen to be sojourning among people of the enemy, become automatically the guests of the king. They are not prisoners of war. They remain guests, and no one has the right to touch any of them until hostilities are over. According to indigenous code of conduct during war, to touch such a special guest of the king would be a "war crime".

The understanding is that the guardian spirits or the ancestors themselves may visit as unknown wayfarers. That is why there is almost something sacred about a guest or a foreigner among indigenous Africans.

Just as patience, this indigenous spirit of kindness is a great challenge of authenticity to Christians, especially the leaders. This is because just as the indigenous African culture, the Old and New Testaments similarly proclaim the sacredness of the bond of communal solidarity, with similar code of behaviour for members in relation to other members and foreigners. In the Old Testament the "people of God" implies similar co-responsibility for the community and individuals (Exodus 20 - 23), as covenantal communion (Ex 24: 3-8). It demands similar hospitality to foreigners (Ex 22: 21-24), with similar belief that the divine being and angels could visit as foreigners (Gen 18: 1-8).

Moreover, our Lord makes it clear that an act of kindness to a fellow human being, is in fact an act done to him (Mat 25: 34-36 and 40):

Come, O Blessed of my Father, inherit the kingdom prepared for you from the foundation of the world; for I was hungry and you gave me food, I was thirsty and you gave me drink, I was a stranger and you welcomed me, I was naked and you clothed me, I was sick and you visited me, I was in prison and you came to me. ...Truly, I say to you, as you did it to one of the least of these my brethren, you did it to me.

Christian community too is considered Eucharistic communion, the body of Christ, the covenant of love, with the sacred duty of unconditional kindness to members and fellow human beings (I Cor. 11-12). The gospel demands similar brotherly or sisterly solidarity of reciprocal kindness (Joh 13: 1-17), which extends even to enemies (Mat 5: 44).

Thus in the light of the Christian message itself indigenous cultural demand for kindness is a great challenge of authenticity to the Christian. A pastor or parish priest, especially in our indigenous society, needs be kind-hearted to all. The indigenous spirit of kindness especially to strangers, who are not members of one's congregation or church, or who are not even known by anybody, is a challenge, especially in the modern social set-up.

It is true that every parish or Christian community makes provision for emergency help for those who may approach the church for help, even if they are foreigners. It is also internationally accepted that the church or church leaders may play host to asylum seekers, even if the government rejects them. But is the pastor or parish priest ready to share that which actually belongs to him, by denying himself something? Would he or she be ready, for instance, to give his or her bedroom to a stranger? Are Christians ready to lodge needy members in their own homes?

Often people are referred to social welfare office or other institutions and organisations. However, especially for missionary churches, are care institutions or organisations a sort of excuse for personal commitment to kindness according to the demands of the gospel?

It is understandable, that given really serious cases of visitors turning out to be real armed robbers, our indigenous spirit of kindness is a real challenge. For the story of the "Good Samaritan" (Luk 10: 29-37) teaches that there is no true loving kindness without a risk. Therefore the indigenous openheartedness to unknown foreigners is a real challenge in a modern society full of really dangerous characters.

Many readers might have had the experience or expression of love themselves. A person who is truly in love becomes extraordinarily kind-hearted, often without counting the cost. Kindness has many aspects. As the fruit of love, kindness in turn issues from a generous heart. It is this generous heart, a heart open to the others, which is sensitive to others' needs, with a spirit of sharing. This makes the individual unhappy to have for himself or herself alone, but happy to give generously. This spirit of giving, this spirit of sharing, creates a happy environment for living like brothers and sisters, supporting one another through patient endurance. This would be conducive to the spiritual growth one of the other. It is very important to learn to share or even to sacrifice.

As pastors, as religious, as Christians, or simply as fellow human beings, are we sincerely imbued with this fruit of love? Are we ready and happy to have to share with the others? What is often the state of affairs among pastors or priests in a parish house or rectory? What is the state of affairs of two or more Religious Brothers or Sisters living in a convent or in a monastery? What is the state of affairs of a husband and wife living in a house? We can continue mentioning many more possible situations in which two or more fellow Christians have to live together and show kindness one towards the other. The reader himself or herself can fill in other possible situations from experience or observation.

Lack of kindness in living together may be an occasion for temptation to seek comfort elsewhere outside. Every human being by nature requires a modicum of kindness for healthy living. If one is deprived of this kindness where he or she needs it most, one may have to find somewhere else to get the kindness and intimate warmth which every human being needs. Unkindness can drive a fellow pastor, a fellow Religious, the new or old colleague, a fellow Christian, or a partner in marriage into the hands of emotional trouble. For, then, without kind-hearted love we destroy the spiritual bond of unity.

If two human beings keep together, it is because their love produces kindness, or rather kind-heartedness. Each being considerate, watching out for what the other needs, material, intellectual, psychological or spiritual. This demands inner spirit of self-giving. Sometimes even if you do not have the means to satisfy the needs of the other, inner readiness to give, to serve, and to understand another's needs before he or she requests it, already makes the other satisfied, at least psychologically and spiritually. For even if you have nothing material or otherwise to express your kindness, being concerned is in itself a great gift, the gift of the heart.

This is the service of kindness, which pastors, parish priests, other Christian leaders and all concerned are to promote and exemplify by their lives. As I have already remarked, to forestall the humiliation of begging by needy members of indigenous communities, the elders take it upon themselves to search for ways and means to get what others need from the wealthy members of the communion. In a sense, since only elders are involved in the search, the image of the needy individual is protected. So also since the wealthy person regards it simply his or her sacred duty to support others as personal contribution to the survival of the sacred communion, the "donors" often remain anonymous. Sometimes this kindness is kept so secret that someone may study up to the doctorate level without knowing where the money and other resources come from. This is one important indigenous African value that needs cultivating, preserving and inculcating into each new generation, protection and promotion of human dignity and human rights of the needy.

This is a reminder to all indigenous Africans concerned with this indigenous respect for privacy and the utmost preservation of individual dignity, irrespective of the material, intellectual and spiritual state of the individual. Thus the "pornographic" destruction of this sacred value of indigenous African culture through aggressive advertising of the needy is an aberration of the sacredness of human identity. According to the indigenous virtue of kindness, which protects the rights of the needy, this is indeed a great challenge of authenticity for Christian self-giving love. For in this indigenous logic of human dignity and human rights as sacred endowments, their preservation is more treasured than the material kindness, which deprives the needy of their right to them.

Here too I would like to narrate a personal experience. At one time we were requested as students to collect material goods, including food, for some other people outside Africa, suffering from a catastrophe. Unaware of the indigenous respect for the identity of the needy as sacred, I took the placards home to display in the local church for donations. Immediately the elders in the church stopped me. According to them, the pictures of the suffering were an insult to their willingness to help. Some one, who was not a Christian, even told me later, I could have been made to pay a fine for pacification ritual.

It is clear that the old man considered it the desecration of the sacred domain of fellow human beings, their right to dignity, even though they were not members of our immediate communion. For the Christian leader and Christian "charitative" organisations or institutions, this is a great challenge of authenticity within the indigenous African cultural milieu. This is because the gospel also demands that kindness or generosity be sacred and therefore secret (Mat 6: 3-4).

When you give alms, do not let your left hand know what your right hand is doing, so that your alms may be in secret; and your Father who sees in secret will reward you.

Moreover, if every needy person is, in a sense, our Lord Jesus Christ himself (Mat 25: 40), then Christian charity needs respect the identity of each needy person as it would respect the identity of Our Lord Jesus Christ himself.

If human rights demand that the identity of criminals be sometimes protected, is it not understandable that generosity or kindness preserve the right of the innocent needy and the weak, to privacy, which is an important element of human dignity? Thus, the indigenous African understanding of kindness or generosity as sacred duty of those giving, and sacred right of those in need, as a demand of the sacred bond of solidarity of the spiritual communion is a great challenge of authenticity.

Understandably, directly or indirectly, modern social structure seeks to displace indigenous socio-cultural networks. Therefore it is a great challenge for Christian leaders to show that the Christian communion, the bond of the covenant of love, the new "people of God", or even one family of one heavenly Father, the sacred body of Christ, is capable of replacing indigenous sacred networks of kindness, the generosity of the spirit. For instance, just as the spirit of kindness demands that elders seek to support the needy, by taking it upon themselves to seek support from the wealthy, so also Christian leaders need accept the responsibility to seek support from wealthy Christians for their needy brothers and sisters in faith. In addition this Christian sacred network of kindness would be a most effective way for Christian leaders to motivate individuals to accept the sacred duty of kindness as Christian co-responsibility.

This Christian "school of kindness" would teach individuals to learn to sense the needs of others and offer to satisfy them before the persons in need even request for help. This sensitivity preserves the dignity of the needy while at the same time satisfying the needs. This kind-hearted sensitivity is to be translated into the "code" for life - together in various forms of relationship: husband and wife, parents and children, in-laws and marriage partners, friend and friend, brother and brother, sister and sister, teacher and pupil etc.

In the same way this Christian sensitivity is to note that what makes a person needy, is also varied. It could be various types and degrees of illness or handicap, weaknesses and other misfortunes, which require kind-heartedness from fellow human beings.

Once more, for indigenous Africans, what is sacred needs also be kept secret. Human dignity is sacred, therefore must be kept secret. This sacredness of human dignity, irrespective of one's condition or state of life, is one of the greatest endowments of the indigenous African culture, and therefore one of the greatest spiritual gifts of the indigenous African culture to humankind, especially as contribution to the search for human rights, the right to dignity and freedom. This is therefore a challenge to individual Christians, who have enough of worldly goods, to regard their kindness or generosity as the expression of divine generosity, a participation in the beneficence of our heavenly Father.

It is true, however, humanly speaking, kindness or kind-heartedness brings joy to both the giver and the beneficiary, especially when it is acknowledged, sometimes with thanks. That is, to cast one's "bread upon the waters" upstream, as an act of faith, that one would finally come upon it downstream, when one is hungry, and needs it most in one's turn. But it becomes a true Christian challenge of authenticity when one becomes so spiritually mature that the capacity to give alone gives great pleasure, a sense of fulfilment. That is when kindness is a complete, disinterested self offer, without expecting any reciprocal reward, except the joy that one can say one meets the challenge of being a true Christian, being true to one's faith.

This is because in some cases, it is not only that one's kindness remains materially unacknowledged and unrewarded, but also that one's kindness reaps only "insult", mistreatment in return. This can be bitter if one's kindness is not fully and truly out of disinterested love. So also, as I have remarked above about indigenous African spirit of protecting the dignity of the beneficiary of kindness, it demands great sensitivity not to "impose" one's kindness. That is, one needs avoid turning kindness into paternalism. This is in fact a callous type of oppression. For such kindness may actually have the motive of forcing the beneficiary to remain permanently needy. Thus, to put it in a modern spiritual language, true kindness should be "empowerment". It needs have the purpose of motivating the beneficiary to become self-reliant in spirit. This requires great sensitivity towards the person benefiting from the act of kindness. Thus true Christian kindness, born out of love, is the gift of the heart. Accordingly, through kind-heartedness Christians become "Christ to the others", "alter Christus" "another Christ", as old Priests used to say?

This kind-heartedness born out of love is the safeguard against jealousy.

Love is never jealous

Patience and kindness, as sacred demands of the indigenous African communion, neutralises, or at least minimises the evil spirit of jealousy. In the indigenous communities, it is believed that when two persons share a meal, while being jealous of each other as rivals, the result would be some misfortune, illness or some disaster, unless those concerned confess and undergo rites, which expiate the abomination. When there is general cleansing of the community, one of the evils mentioned by name to be rid of to keep the sacredness of the communal bond is jealousy. So also public prayers, the pouring of libation, involves the supplication, that the supernatural guardians change the minds of those who may be jealous.

On account of the destructiveness of jealousy, it is a great challenge to render the Christian community free of it. This is because jealousy is one of the evils, abomination, the work of the flesh, desecrating the body of Christ, which is the bond of the spirit. As we read from Gal 5: 19-21

Now the works of the flesh are plain; ...idolatry, sorcery, enmity, strife, jealousy, anger, selfishness, dissension, party spirit, ... and the like; I warn you, as I have warned you before, that those who do such things shall not inherit the kingdom of God.

Moreover, as we read from the citation from 1 Cor 13: 4, at the beginning of this reflection, jealousy is one of the vices which desecrate the spiritual bond of love. Though jealousy in the Christian community may not incur immediate sickness or death, the Gospels and the Epistles regard it destructive to the individual and the community all the same, and dire consequences may follow for those guilty of it, if they persist, and partake in the table of the Lord, the Eucharist, without repentance.

If your love bears fruits of patience and kindness, then you would not be jealous. Jealousy stems from the inordinate desire to possess that which someone else possesses. It could be natural endowment, such as physical beauty, strength, intelligence, or even moral integrity, which makes the individual outstanding in the society. Or it could also be friends or material possession such as wealth. Since you do not possess this or the other, you are angry with the person who happens to possess it. If this anger is not held in check, it could boil over into violence, even murderous aggression. Love that bears fruit in kindness neutralises, or at least minimises the tendency toward jealousy. This is because kindness borne out of love is the outward expression of the inner spirit of sharing. This makes everybody aware that what the other may have is for the benefit of all.

This awareness of the spirit of sharing deprives jealousy of its basic cause, the feeling of deprivation, which triggers the desire to possess it as well. Thus the spirit of sharing is the best bulwark against jealousy, or rather the temptation of jealousy. Although as long as human beings remain human beings there would always be some degree of jealousy in relationships.

As Christians, what we are called upon to share is not only material goods, but also intellectual and spiritual goods. In this way, through the spirit of generosity, the spirit of kindness, we human beings make up for what may be lacking in one or the other person. This spirit of generous love helps us supplement the needs one of the other. The spirit of reciprocal satisfaction of the needs of one or the other is the main element of the principle of solidarity. If this spirit of solidarity were at work in relationships, or in living together, then no one would be in dire need of anything that others might have. This is the spirit of the so-called "primitive communism" or "biblical communism" of the first Christians as reported in the Acts of the Apostles:

Now the company of those who believed were of one heart and soul, and no one said that any of the things, which he possessed was his own, but they had everything in common...there was not a needy person among them (Acts 4: 32-35)

This radical ideal of sharing among the first Christians seems to have been lost somewhere during the historical development of the Christian faith and its social teaching over the centuries. As the Church assumed worldly power, she also accumulated worldly possessions. Gradually the material possessions of the Church came to be separated from the material possessions of her members. This historical spirit of possessiveness of the Church, or rather leaders of the Church, to be exact, has influenced her social and political leanings and affiliations. This gradually blunts the original gospel spirit of sharing, possessing everything in common. In fact, gradually private possession of property in the exclusive sense came to be regarded the will of God. Any talk of possessing goods in common has come to be regarded as even something against the will of God. That is regarded often as communism or socialism, which is practically synonymous with atheism.

Even during the apostolic times there was problem with this ideal of possessing things in common through the spirit of sharing. At least from the Acts of the Apostles itself (Acts 4: 36 to 4: 1-11) we know there was this problem. Human nature being what it is, even some of the first Christians began to cheat the system. They withheld part of the proceeds from the sale of their property. So one can understand that temptations of human weakness set in selfishness and dishonesty. This shows that right from the beginning, right from its inception, this principle of Christian "communism" did not have much chance of being maintained throughout history.

Still later in the historical development of the Christian movement, if we may term it so, there were further complaints against the system of sharing as it was practiced. This time it was not individuals trying to "cheat the system", but rather the system of sharing itself was fraught with racial discrimination and favouritism. The Hellenists began to complain that their needy fellows, especially the widows, were overlooked in the distribution of goods (Acts 6: 1-6). This resulted in further development of one of the most important structures of Church leadership, the deaconate.

In spite of these historical lapses the intrinsic principle itself is still valid for the Christian spirit of love. The crux of the "primitive" or "biblical" communism was: "There was not a needy person among them" (Acts 4:35). This means through the spirit of sharing everybody had what he or she needed to live. This echoes God's injunction on the Israelites: "There should be no poor person among you". Throughout the history of Christianity, some groups or communities have aspired after this apostolic ideal. One such community is the Putney community of the United States of America. In the pursuit of this "Bible Communism" this Community possessed everything in common. The only aspect of this community of sharing, which was not all that Christian, was that just as material goods, women were also common possession of the men (Gerald R Leslie and Sheila K. Korman, The Family in Social Context, Oxford: Oxford University Press 1985: 110-114).

In Africa today (but also in America and other countries) some indigenous African Christian Churches subscribe to the letter of this "Christian communism", at least in principle. Those who become members of these churches leave their families or towns to settle together. Often this settlement is around the house of the founding prophet or prophetess.

However, in spite of these sporadic attempts at following the apostolic example of possessing everything in common in the spirit of sharing, it never became a universal practice of the Christian churches. Given the historical development of Christianity in Western Europe, with vast possessions of its own, it might be impossible even to propose such a radical principle for any Christian community. Moreover in this age of the so-called "turbo – capitalism" of privatisation and globalisation, it may be an impossible expectation to practise this Christian communism to the letter. But all the same the spirit of kindness may make us strive after the spirit of sharing in such a way that no one is in a dire need.

One would wish that at least our parish houses and religious communities would strive after this principle of sharing as the response to, or rather the fulfilment of, the vow or solemn promise of poverty. This would then be a prophetic sign of disinterestedness in material possessions. That would be an antidote to the inordinate greed for material possessions, which in turn tempts people to be jealous.

This is a great challenge of authenticity especially in our indigenous African cultural milieu. The affluent lifestyles of leaders may trigger off jealousy. This jealousy may be destructive in two ways. In the negative sense jealousy may lead to deadly plots of Christians, one against the other. Thus those who may be naturally endowed by God, to be capable of helping others generously, would be frustrated. Those who could help by putting their material, intellectual and spiritual gifts at the disposal of others or the whole community would be frightened to keep them to themselves. In the end the whole community loses. Or jealousy may trigger unhealthy competition. Those who could not afford certain things would be tempted by jealousy to possess them by any means. This may lead to unfaithfulness.

If the evil of jealousy is among Christian leaders themselves, pastors, parish priests, other pastoral ministers and Christian community leaders, it destroys their spiritual effectiveness, puts doubts on the authenticity of the word they proclaim. Thus in any sense jealousy destroys the spiritual bond, and tarnishes the image of the Christian faith. This destructive spirit damages the authenticity of the Christian faith, especially among the indigenous people, who are not Christians.

The spirit of sharing, which neutralises or at least minimises the temptation to be jealous, also removes the grounds for selfishness, at least to a large extent. Thus true love that bears fruit in kindness, with the spirit of sharing, makes everyone have enough. Or at least it makes everyone benefit from whatever another may have, in one way or another. This makes jealousy unnecessary. This is because each one knows whatever the other may have is for one's interest also. Of course this presupposes good will on each side. That is, those who have need a sincere heart to share with those who may lack something. So also those who lack something need to accept sharing, instead of wishing by all means to have for themselves what others may have.

For those, who may be gifted, there is extra responsibility to be humble. That is, those who have need be humble enough not to show all the time that they are the only generous ones, and the others only beggars. This means those who have need be sensitive enough not to make others feel left out. Jealousy sets in when those who have begin to show they are the generous ones, who have to move others acknowledge their generosity.

For instance others may feel humiliated when those, who have, seek to give even when it is not necessary, or those to receive do not actually need what is being offered. That is to seek to help even where help is not called for. In a sense this is paternalism. And paternalism is the most crude and subtle form of oppression. In a sense, in projecting yourself as the only person capable of giving, with all that it implies, you make the other feel he or she is nobody, and has to depend on you for livelihood. You reduce the other to a beggar. This is a sort of selfishness in disguise of generosity. For by imposing gifts on others, you want to keep the praise and glory for yourself alone. In the spirit of sharing we need give the chance to others too to feel proud as givers sometimes. We need motivate others to discover their own gifts too. We need make others too aware that they also have something important to share. We have to give the chance to others too to know that others need them and their talents for the welfare of all. As it is often said, no one is too poor to offer gifts, and no one is too rich to accept or even need gifts. Others also have to show how generous the Almighty is to them too in the abundance of gifts. Others as human beings also need to be happy to receive and acknowledge thanks and praise sometimes. It is psychologically, even spiritually, healthy to receive appreciation as well as to offer appreciation from time to time. In this way we all learn to appreciate God's gifts to each person, and offer Him thanks and praise. This is the challenge of authenticity to avoid jealousy by balancing pride with humility.

This challenge of authenticity is most demanded by the typical indigenous African social etiquette. This is shown in the solidarity in sorrow and joy. If for instance a wealthy person is ill, even the poorest in the village never goes to visit without something in hand. It could be fruits or one or the other foodstuff. Often it is money, however little. By giving the money to the sick person or the relative taking care of him or her, the person adds often, literally in English: "This is my little something for bread or porridge." Then the person receiving the gift in turn says to those around: "Thank him (or her) for me. He (or she) has given us a lot for bread (or whatever the case may be)"

So also on a joyous occasion like blessing a new car, a corn mill or whatever it may be, even the poorest, who could not afford a bicycle, let alone a Mercedes Benz car, would be proud to offer something, often according to one's capability, in money or services:

A local fitter may say: "I offer to make the first repairs, if the car breaks down." Even an old lady may come, drudging on her stick, and announce: "I am very happy and proud that our son (or daughter, whatever the case may be) has acquired this beautiful car. This is my little something for petrol."

Thus instead of arousing jealousy in those who could not afford a Mercedes Benz car, the occasion rather arouses pride even in the poorest, as if he or she shares somehow in the success of the wealthy person. Of course this solidarity demands reciprocity. The person riding in the new Mercedes Benz car has also the responsibility to take the old lady to the hospital, if she is ill. The children who mill around the new car are also sure to get a lift on the way to or from school.

Just as the whole community rejoices and celebrates in solidarity, so also the whole community regrets and mourns in solidarity. When there is misfortune, such as death, each person in the community immediately knows the part to play, what to contribute or what to procure, often according to family (or lineage) relationships. Some prepare the corpse; others make the shed or procure foodstuffs or drinks. Some, especially the women, constitute themselves into a dirge choir, and some men sing heroic songs. No one comes to the funeral empty-handed. On such occasions, contributions in such cases are not so much according to means or status, but rather according to family or lineage relationships. Of course, it is understandable that those who have more may donate something separate in addition to what is due according to family or lineage relationships.

Although some would say this indigenous solidarity is now dying out, it still poses a great challenge of authenticity to Christians who openly proclaim their religion as the religion of solidarity in love. Since indigenous solidarity does not remain a mere principle but practice in the lives of individuals, which mitigates the excesses of jealousy, the Christian principle or value of solidarity against jealousy is a challenge if the Christian faith is to be accepted as authentic among indigenous Africans. It is true, just as in any society; it is not to deny the fact that there is jealousy in the indigenous African society also, even within the family. But what is important here is that there are visible and practical structures and social attitudes of relationship and customs, which minimise the negative factors as well as effects of jealousy. All these strategies, as we may call them, borrowing from the social sciences, can be summed up as solidarity in sharing and participation in one another's fortune and misfortune. For the Christian belief and practice in this indigenous society, this is certainly a challenge of authenticity.

Just as jealousy feeds on the desire to show off that one has more than the other, instead of the will to acknowledge the endowments of the others and to share, so also jealousy detracts you from your own dignity. In a sense by being jealous of the other you become preoccupied with the other's dignity. You begin to believe you have dignity only if you are like him or her. Thus gradually you are unaware of your own dignity. You begin to invest your dignity in the other person, in what he or she is or in what he or she has achieved or can achieve. When jealousy becomes a real complex your whole preoccupation would be the worthless struggle to be like the other person, or to have what the other person has. Thus instead of struggling to improve upon your own endowments, you are rather struggling to make what someone else has achieved your own. Gradually you even become blind to your own talents, your own endowments. When jealousy becomes a deadly complex you become almost incapable of living your own life. Your only desire is now to get rid of the other person. This deadly logic is, that since I cannot become what the other person is, or to have what the other person has, the only solution is to get rid of the other person. According to this logic by getting rid of the person of whom you are jealous, you deceive yourself into believing both of you are now equal. But that is only deception. On one hand the other person goes away with all that you wish to have. On the other hand you become poorer because in a sense you come out empty-handed. You lose both ways.

This deadly logic of jealousy is possible in any type of human relationship, or state of life. A seminarian or novice, who feels authorities favour the other; a pastor who feels a colleague is favoured with wealthy communities; a friend, who feels the friend has got his or her beautiful girl friend or handsome boy friend; a marriage partner who feels another has some dealings with the partner; a professional who feels another has "stolen" his or her promotion or success. These could be multiplied. So for whole nights you cannot sleep. You begin to hate yourself. You are no longer satisfied with anything that you are or you have. Your only growing preoccupation is to become like the other person. Your growing desire is only to have whatever the other person may have, to have the same opportunity. So gradually you are no longer in your own world. You are living in the world of the other person whom you are jealous of. In a sense you have even lost your bearing in life.

In this state of utter blindness to your own self-esteem you cannot discover your own talents any more. To become yourself once more, you need radical reversal of your attitude. You can discover your own self-esteem, your own dignity and your own talents only when you free yourself from the debilitating stranglehold of jealousy. That is, you can realise your own strengths and talents only when you liberate yourself from the fixation on another's achievements. You can be happy only if you face the challenge of your own life. You can find fulfilment in your vocation only when you are satisfied with your own physical, spiritual and intellectual endowments, potentialities, talents and opportunities.

In a sense you are in a better position to observe your fellow human being of whom you are jealous objectively only when you are finally free from the blinding and debilitating force of jealousy. For instance when you are jealous of someone, you only view the one in positive and superior light. Everything would seem to be going extremely well with the one. But in reality this conception of the state in which the other person is may be false. You may not be aware of the actual state in which the person is. The other person's life may not be so glorious as jealousy frames him or her. The truth may be that the glorious image of the other person of whom you are jealous of is all the creation of the jealousy itself. An objective assessment of the other person's purported "luckier than me" life may discover a state of life even worse than your own state of life. For it is even possible that your friend's or partner's apparent better luck or even cheating is actually bad luck for him or her, and good luck for you.

Let us remember the verse of the Letter to the Romans 8: 28: "We know that in everything God works for good with those who love him"

Love is never Selfish

Being kind, the spirit of sharing, obviously minimises the temptation to be selfish. It is true, that in the indigenous African society there are cases of selfishness, even greed. But the strong bond of solidarity of communal spirit, everybody being concerned with the other, discourages individualism, which could be a fertile ground for selfishness and greed. Thus, as already mentioned, the indigenous African society has certain cultural instruments, customs, and norms in the form of tabus (taboos) and sanctions to discourage selfishness. For instance the "death courts" still held after the death of a person serves also as instrument against selfishness. During the session, the elders request from the family and neighbours to give evidence of their efforts to prevent illness and the eventual death. If the sitting is dissatisfied with the efforts of those around, these are made to offer something for pacification rites for the spirit of the dead. In a sense the rite is the pacification of the bond of the communion, desecrated by selfish acts of commission or omission. This ritual restores the sacredness of the bond. Thus individuals tempted to be selfish and greedy are made to reflect on the effects of their way of life on others and on the community as a whole, since they are aware that in the long run, they would face public rebuke, if their selfishness or greed withholds what is needed to sustain another person's life.

So also it is against the evil of selfishness that children are taught from early childhood to eat together from one dish, to learn to be considerate, avoiding selfishness and greed. To refuse to share food or water with a fellow human being, even if that person is a stranger passing by, is a grave offence against the spirit of human solidarity. Such hardheartedness displeases the guardian spirits and the Ancestors. So the person involved has to offer something for ritual pacification, the restoration of the spiritual bond of solidarity.

This indigenous African solidarity against selfishness is a great challenge of the authenticity of the Christian faith, which was founded on self-sacrificing love, the offer of the Son of God. Thus hardheartedness among those regarded as Christian leaders does a great damage to the faith of our people. This is a great challenge of authenticity of Christian faith as faith based on self-giving love. This is because selfishness destroys not only the Eucharistic communal bond, but also individual relationships, such as marital bond, kinship (family bond), friendship, collegiality among officials or workers and other bonds.

The whole Christian community suffers if leaders are selfish and keep common resources for themselves or for their families alone. If it is granted that most of the suffering in African is caused by selfishness, directly or indirectly, then Christian leaders must accept most of the blame, if their own selfishness is a source of a negative example for leaders in the society. Selfishness of Christian leaders themselves compromises their prophetic role in the society.

Thus selfishness is a great challenge of authenticity to Christians in the indigenous African cultural context. For if the Christian community is a communion of love, a covenantal relationship sustained by self-giving love, and true love bears fruit in kindness, the spirit of sharing, then selfishness in the Christian community negates its validity.

In the indigenous African societies personal wealth is accepted and even cultivated as a sign of blessing. But our indigenous people distinguish wealth from evil source, which is usually "quick money", from wealth acquired from genuine source of industriousness. It is believed wealth arising from inordinate greed or cheating becomes a curse for the possessor. This curse is believed to bring catastrophes to the family or lineage. Normally in the indigenous community individuals or the community would not accept gifts from such a person. For gifts from such a person, who might have acquired wealth by immoral means, is believed to be unclean, impure

There are other customs discouraging selfishness or egoism. For instance, if certain types of mushrooms suddenly abound on your own farm, you are supposed to shout and sing aloud for neighbours to come and share in the harvest: "Ame deka mewua o, wudzaxee lo!" (A song in Ewe meaning: "No individual alone should harvest it, it is 'wudzaxe'!"). "Wudzaxee" is a type of mushroom, which suddenly abounds

This is how in different ways our indigenous African culture holds the temptation of inordinate greed in check. All this may sound out of date. But this indigenous spirit or principles of sharing and respective beliefs still linger on in certain communities. Therefore it poses a great challenge of authenticity of our Christian faith. As I have already remarked, it is acceptable that pastors are "beggars" from the wealthy for the needy. But if the pastor keeps what he gets to become a wealthy "beggar-benefactor" of the people then the public proclamation of the vow or solemn promise of poverty does not seem authentic, just a formality. It is not authentically evident in the lives of "poor" for Christ.

As I have already noted, the spirit of sharing is not limited to only material goods, but also, and especially, spiritual gifts. As St. Paul counsels Corinthians 12: 7-11:

To each is given the manifestation of the Spirit for the common good. To one is given through the Spirit the utterance of wisdom, to another the utterance of knowledge according to the same Spirit, to another faith by the same Spirit, to another gift of healing by the one Spirit, to another the working of miracles, to another prophecy, to another the ability to distinguish between spirits, to another various kinds of tongues, to another the interpretation of tongues. All these are inspired by one and the same Spirit, who apportions to each one individually as he wills...

Love is never boastful

As I have already remarked the indigenous arrangements are such that everyone has in a sense a role to play, especially in a typical African village, irrespective of one's status. A rich person who gives generously may remain anonymous. Therefore there is no temptation to boast of his affluence. It is true some boast of their wealth. But the others may not respect such persons. Moreover the materially wealthy also knows he or she may need support when in trouble. This could be illness, marriage breakdown, bereavement or problems with law enforcers. As it is often said, money cannot run errands for you. Someone may be materially poor. But such person may greatly be respected because of his or her wisdom. Others seek his or her advice when they have problems. In the second place titles do not matter in a typical African village. You may be a Professor at the university, but in the village you are only a daughter or a son, an uncle or an aunt.

This indigenous system, making everyone a king, so to say, is a great challenge to the Christian claim to humility, based on the Son of the Almighty God. As a Christian, is it necessary to boast to the hearing of all that you have paid someone's hospital fees, or that you are the most intelligent in your community, which humiliates others? Boasting makes others reluctant to approach you for anything. For a pastor, pastoral minister or any Christian leader, boasting compromises his or her role as a representative of Jesus Christ, who came to serve and not to be served. Moreover, there are no grounds to boast of your services to others. This is because whatever you do or give, is only the fulfilment of your responsibility towards individuals or the communion of love. In fact, boasting is one of the vices reprehensible to our Lord. Apart from hypocrisy, our Lord reserves the sharpest condemnations for those who boast of their piety, wealth or their power. So he says: "Beware of practising your piety before men, in order to be seen by them; For then you will have no reward from your Father who is in heaven" (6: 1) The parable of the rich fool (Luk 12: 16-21) shows the futility of boasting because of one's wealth. So also he says of

Pharisees and scribes: "Everyone who exalts himself will be humbled; every one who humbles himself will be exalted" (Luk 18. 14).

To minimise the causes of jealousy, especially in a clerical or religious community, I think everybody has to learn not to boast of talents or extras to tease or look down on others. If your new acquisition is rather conspicuous, I think one can just declare its source to the other, be it a new car or new furniture. So also in a pastoral context, it is human that you, a new colleague, have got some new Vatican II insights as regards your theology, liturgy and other aspects of the pastoral practice. In such a case it is a demand of loving relationship to be considerate. For the sake of healthy relationship it is appropriate to avoid making the older colleague feel out of date, or non-knowledgeable. To make him or her preserve his or her own human dignity it is appropriate to discuss new ideas with him or her, granting him or her the respect of an older colleague. It is worthwhile noting that the older colleague may not have the new theological concepts for theological disputation in the academic sense. But he or she may have more wisdom borne out of long years of experience. For successful implementation of new ideas, you also need your older colleague's practical wisdom. It is boastful, to refer to an older colleague as simply a "museum piece".

It may be true that some may be even "allergic" to Vatican II, but I still believe that any human being is capable of changing for the better. It is hard for anyone of us to change old ways. An older one may be a bit uncomfortable to ask a younger one always about new trends. So it is left to the younger one to share new ideas in a respectful way. We have to be lovingly considerate. As St. Paul puts it (Gal.6: 2): "Help to carry one another's burden"

To accept, and give due honour to the aged as the seat of wisdom, is a great challenge of the Christian in indigenous African cultural context. This is because, in spite of the fact that the aged lack modern knowledge about new ideas, their practical wisdom is still revered in the society. The youth gain more respect if the aged realise that they do not boast of their new knowledge, but rather that the new knowledge makes them humble to seek more.

Boasting destroys not only the communal bond of love, but any type of loving relationship, because boasting humiliates others who may not be so gifted in one's particular area of excellence. For instance a pastor who boasts of his intellectual achievements may scare away those who have never been to school, or only up to secondary level. Is it necessary to display your certificates for show in the parish office? Or is it necessary to turn every discussion into theological academic disputation? This type of boasting causes discouragement among the faithful. It may gradually give rise to pharisaic factions, boasting and looking down upon the others, which may cause tension, and gradually destroy the spirit of solidarity. Boasting can even destroy the faith of fellow Christians, who may begin to feel they are "nothing", "cheated" or even "accursed" by God.

Boasting can also destroy relational bonds, such as marriage and even friendship. A husband or wife can hardly endure a relationship in which the partner makes him or her understand that he or she has no talents, and has to endure constant humiliation. Or, who could endure a husband or wife, who should always be adored on account of his handsomeness or her beauty? So also a friend who constantly has to accept an overbearing relationship of un-equals would soon break off the relationship, because there could be no reciprocity, which is the basis of true loving friendship.

Boasting of only one's talents suppresses other talents of the spiritual communion. Thus the Christian leader is challenged to demonstrate God's loving beneficence by motivating each one to discover one's own special gift or gifts of the Spirit, for the building-up of fellow Christians, and the communion of love. Thus boasting destroys the essence, therefore the authenticity of the Christian covenant of love, as spiritual bond, entrusted with diverse gifts. As Dody Dolly would put it (Donnelly, Dody, 1977. Team: Theory and Practice of Team Ministry, New York: Paulist Press), Christian leadership has to show that all are "chipped edges", which need to fit together, as "people needers" and "people givers". As we read from I Cor 12-14, as a body with different members, no particular member can boast of being more important than the other. For one member alone cannot survive as a body. Thus the Christian is challenged by the indigenous spirit of role sharing to examine his or her attitude towards fellow Christians and fellow human beings

Love is never conceited

The indigenous system of role sharing tones down the temptation to boast of one's endowments, even if these endowments are acclaimed to be true. Therefore conceit is most despicable, and diminishes one's dignity as a human being. This is because whereas boasting implies that one's endowments are real, being conceited implies overvaluation of one's endowments, or even claiming endowments, which one may not have at all. That is vainglory. Since being conceited makes the individual pretend to be what he or she is not, in reality, it is a vice against authenticity itself, being untrue to you yourself. For instance, does it improve the image of the Christian faith if the Christian leader always boasts of the gift of miracles, which he or she knows never occur? Is it Christian to use conceited advertising tactic of wilful exaggeration of the superiority of the Christian faith over and above other religious beliefs simply to impress upon members or win converts?

This challenge of authenticity demands that Christian leaders avoid being conceited and keep to their humble ways of being at service through the simplest acts of love, which any Christian, irrespective of endowments could bring to fulfilment. Being conceited could lure a non-suspecting lover into a relationship. But sooner or later the relationship could break up as the partner comes to realise that all one's glorious achievements are false. Love then becomes a deceit. Only simple but sincere acts of love win hearts and souls for Christ.

Love is never rude

Being boastful and conceited leads to being rude, being impolite to people. In the indigenous African culture, being rude, being impolite to any individual is an abomination. This is because the people believe being rude is a sort of "insult", not only to the individual human being, but also to the spiritual bond itself. Thus to be rude to the king, the queen or elder is desecration of the sacredness of the throne, the stool, the skin, or the dignity of the individual. Such rudeness incurs a fine for ritual pacification.

So also since the sacred bond of the communion sacralises other bonds of relationship, being rude to one's husband or wife, one's father or mother, or other relations is also an abomination. Among certain peoples for instance, to be rude to a mother incurs a fine for pacification ritual. Generally, among certain indigenous African peoples, even to point a finger at your mother, or even towards the direction of her hometown or village is abomination. These sanctions against being rude, once more, protect and uphold the dignity of individual human beings.

This is a challenge to Christians, especially relating to the way they behave towards fellow Christians, leaders or ordinary persons in or outside the community. For instance does a Christian husband realise that each time he insults his wife, he in fact insults, not the wife as a human being, but the sacred bond of marriage, or even the Lord himself?

As I have already mentioned in the introduction and in relation to patience, Christian leaders need be aware that with their indigenous background, our indigenous people still believe that rudeness by or to spiritual leaders such as insults, curses or even scolding is potent with disastrous effects. It is believed, whether anyone hears the destructive words or not they would come to pass unless the person involved reveals the matter to the community and the words are ritually retracted or neutralised.

Given this cultural background self-restraint in the choice of words is a great challenge indeed! Especially as a pastor, a Religious or even any Christian in a leading position, your harsh words may destroy someone's faith and life. So as a pastor or any spiritual leader in the community or society at large, one should avoid harsh words. Cursing should not be contemplated. For among certain indigenous Africans even today, the effects of harsh words linger on in the memory of the people. The plight of certain communities or families is still traced to the harsh words of one or the other pastor or parish priest even a century ago. So be aware of this if ever as a pastor you are tempted to become angry. Cursing can destroy a family or even a whole community. So we need strong nerves. We need patient and kind hearts to find fulfilment in our vocation and apostolate among our people. Remember, the tongue is not for cursing or insults. The tongue needs be controlled. The tongue is for words of encouragement and blessing. That is a great challenge of authenticity.

If we face the challenge of this indigenous abhorrence of being rude, we shall win more respect for ourselves as individuals and for the Christian faith itself. Moreover being polite wins reciprocal estimation and respect, especially in a relationship, thus saving individuals from painful separations, with resultant problems, such as frustrated children of divorced mothers and other forms of desertion and loneliness.

Thus efforts to avoid being rude, which is born out of loving patience and respect for one another's dignity is a sure way to psychological and spiritual health of individuals and relationships. It is a mark of holiness. As our Lord warns: Mt 5: 1-48, the practice of the Christian code of behaviour should be the only and loudest proof of the validity and superiority of the Christian faith, therefore its authenticity.

You have heard that it was said to the men of old, you shall not kill; and whoever kills shall be liable to judgment. But I say to you that every one, who is angry with his brother shall be liable to judgement; whoever insults his brother shall be liable to the council, and whoever says 'You fool!' shall be liable to the hell fire (Mat 5:21).

Then about swearing, he warns:

Again you have heard that it was said to the men of old, 'You shall not swear falsely, but shall perform to the Lord what you have sworn. But I say to you, Do not swear at all, either by heaven, for it is the throne of God, or by the earth, for it is his footstool, or by Jerusalem, for its is the city of the great King. And do not swear by your head, for you cannot make one hair white or black. Let what you say be simply 'Yes' or 'No'; anything more than this comes from evil. (Mat 5: 33-37).

Love does not take offence

Thus authentic Christian love demands that one avoid taking offence. This calm, avoidance of taking offence is an important factor of not only spiritual but also especially psychological and physical health. This calm, serenity or peace is the best way to keep nerves healthy. And healthy nerves save us from a lot of other physiological and psychological complications. Thus calm, serenity or peace, in other words, the avoidance of taking offence, improves the quality of life. That is a way to happy living.

The experience of the parish priest and my own experience cited in the introduction above show that the faithful could rebuke their pastors for taking an offence. As a pastor, you should be calm if, for instance, the Catechist scolds you for being late. In this situation you really need strong nerves at times. This could be challenging especially if you have arrived late because of a rough drive through the mud, or drudging under the load of Mass kit and personal belongings. The same applies if you are a Rector of the seminary or Novice Master or Mistress of the novitiate. Sometimes seminarians or novices intentionally try to "pull your legs a little bit" to see how far your nerves could take it. They may try your nerves especially when they are aware that you have weak nerves, or in situations they know your nerves usually break down. As a person of authority you need limitless patience. Otherwise, apart from ruining your health, you may lose your self-respect, or even your authority.

The need to avoid taking offence is an important factor for keeping the bond of relationship. For in marriage your partner may be hot-tempered, while you make the effort to be calm, or it could be vice versa. Vindictiveness destroys an individual and community. Especially among pastors anger can make a station a hell for all and a scandal to the faithful. It is good to take things calmly; let your friends use you as a "chewing stick" sometimes, just as you may also do about others. It is part of our ministry.

Love is not resentful

In the indigenous African society there are cases of people resenting others for one reason or another. But as I have mentioned above, the sacredness of the bond of solidarity makes it obligatory that the one resenting the other take the trouble to clear the cause of resentment. For lasting resentment is regarded an abomination, desecration of the bond. Just as in the case of jealousy, if the person shares a meal with the person he or she resents, it is believed dire consequences would follow such as illness or even death. That is why before general cleansing of the community, the ritual master warns anybody who resents the others to reconcile before the final ritual offer.

The fact that a Christian community is a covenant of love implies resentment against a particular person is in a sense a resentment of the sacred bond, even indirectly against Christ himself, since the community is his body. So also Our Lord makes it clear that resentment against someone may render an offer to God null and void. So we read in Mat 5: 23-24.

So if you are offering your gift at the altar, and there remember that your brother has something against you, leave your gift there before the altar and go; first be reconciled to your brother; and then come and offer your gift.

The resentment of a leader against a particular member of the group diminishes pastoral effectiveness. Love cannot be selective. This is because it is a free gift, unconditionally given, and needs be unconditionally shared.

How would you feel if you were giving Holy Communion to the person you resent? Or how would you feel if a person you resent comes to you for counselling. Resentment is psychologically unhealthy. Your love for the person would always be pretence. Since resentment is a form of allergy, you need to work it out. It is only when you are comfortable in the company of every member of your group that you could maintain your patience in dealing with all and every one. This need to avoid resentment towards particular persons is a great challenge of authenticity for Christian leaders as servants and mediators of the unconditional love of God the Father of all.

Love takes no pleasure in other people's sins

As I have already remarked on the church, or Christian community, to talk loosely about the weaknesses of leaders or other Christians is desecration of the church as people consecrated to God. It tarnishes the image of the church, and your own image. Often, especially if you happen to be jealous of someone for his or her good character, you are tempted to rejoice to hear he or she has "fallen" too. Then you are happy to spread it abroad: "Aha! He thinks he is an angel. He has also done it today." Or, "she thinks she is more chaste than all of us. Now we are all equal."

If your friend is doing evil, brotherly or sisterly correction is a Christian responsibility to the sacred image. This behoves that you be brave to point it out to him or her. Do not glory in another person's sins, another person's faults. Rather make the effort to help your neighbour out of difficulties. Make him or her aware of the truth about himself or herself.

I believe the golden rule works in this case too. "So, always treat others as you would like them to treat you" (Mt. 7:12). If you are sad whenever you hear other Christians talk about your weaknesses, then it is not only an act of love, but also an act of justice, that you behave the same way towards the weaknesses of others. As our Lord tells the accusers of the sinful woman, let those who have no sin cast the first stone. The recognition that every one of us is a sinner seeking forgiveness from God should make us sensitive towards the weaknesses of others.

As the indigenous Ewe (West Africa) proverb puts it: "When it is raining, the shea butter laughs at the salt. But the shea butter forgets that sooner or later there will be sunshine."

Love delights in the Truth

One aspect of indigenous authenticity is the constant search for the truth. This is why soothsayers or diviners are still important in the indigenous society. This is because, as I have mentioned above, personal vices, such as stealing, lying or secret plots destroy the sacred communal bond, which may bring catastrophe to the individual and all the community. That is why no one is at peace until the truth is out. This is a challenge for the Christian, whose faith is based on the truth of the Word of God.

The truth, love that bears fruit in sincerity makes love truly happy for both sides. For every one would be happy to invest trust in the other, without hesitation, and say the truth about the other.

As our Lord says: "The truth shall make you free" (Joh 8: 32) The reflections on being conceited above partly hold here too.

It suffices to say: this freedom should be our ground for rejoicing.

Love is ready to excuse

In the indigenous culture, it is almost unwritten code of love that the stronger partner is required to excuse the weaker. "Forgive, because he (she) does not know" The elders say that often when holding hearings in "traditional" court. The rational is that if one were truly aware of all the implications of an offence to a loving partner, one would not have committed the offence. Some elderly persons excuse their children, their relatives, or marriage partners that way.

Psychologically this is valid in true loving relationship. The heart, mind and feeling seem to excuse the person being loved of any wrongdoing, as a condition for forgiveness and mercy. This is a challenge to Christians who believe in God, who sends His only Son to die for human kind out of His merciful love, while still sinners, as I have remarked in the reflection on hope. As our Lord prayed for those who crucified him: "Father, forgive them, they do not know what they are doing" (Luk 23)

This excusing prayer is the inspiration for any loving relationship, be it family, marriage, friendship or leadership relationship. To be ready to accuse your friend or lover of bad intentions every time he or she wrongs you, only leads to a wall of hatred and suspicion. But give him or her the benefit of the doubt as much as possible, be ready to excuse with the understanding that if circumstances had been otherwise he or she might not have wronged you. That brings peace not only between you, but also peace within yourself. That makes a truly happy loving relationship.

Love is ready to trust

Just as with God, many of us cannot read the minds of others. So there is no absolute certainty or foolproof means of knowing whether the other is telling the truth from the heart. Therefore whether he or she truly loves, or truly speaks the truth or truly repents and reconciles, it is all a matter of trust. This firm loving trust entails faith and hope.

Thus the respective reflections above hold partly here too.

If we were sincere with ourselves, many a time, at the time of giving our word, we may be sincere, speaking from the heart. But at the end of the day we find ourselves going against our own word, sometimes in spite of our inner struggle to keep our word given to another. This could happen in any type of relationship, with fellow human beings or with God. But we know, God reads our hearts. And therefore forgives, if we are sincerely making the effort to improve.

If we accept that God forgives our weaknesses, then we should in turn be willing to accept the weaknesses of others on trust- even seventy times seven times. To be able to excuse and to trust is a challenge, which can redeem our indigenous culture, which does not consider the ulterior motive or intention. Your mother could not excuse you for being rude to her while drunk. It is believed if she does not reveal it to the elders for ritual pacification some dire consequences may follow. Thus in this sense our commitment to authentic love improves upon the indigenous cultural beliefs about offence and consequences.

Trusting in spite of the lack of concrete proof makes the individual also hope that things may turn out well in the long run in loving relationship. Make the effort to trust in the goodness of others, and hope that whatever their attitude they are capable of a change, a change for the better.

Love is ready to hope

We have reflected already on indigenous hope as expression of inner freedom, inner sincerity, therefore authenticity, and the challenge it poses to Christianity as a religion based on the hope of the resurrection. This hope is more intensive in personal relationships as the fruit of love. When relationships threaten to break up, the persistent pacification or reconciliation ritual is to keep up this hope of the bond of love, be it marriage, family, friendship or even between peoples. Each side is urged on by the others to keep up hope that the relationship will work out somehow in the end.

The advice given in the indigenous language to those involved is often: "Do dzi ko!" (An Ewe expression, which literally means: "Strengthen the heart". This means, in other words. "Just keep up your hope." Parents, especially mothers have this tenacious loving hope for their children, however hopeless a child's behaviour might be. This loving hope is a challenge for Christian hope within a loving relationship. Just as the indigenous community encourages loving hope, the Christian community is called upon to sustain the loving hope of relationships in crisis. This is a great challenge, especially in cases where becoming a Christian makes the individual lose this constant source of loving hope, be it one's family or the indigenous community. Often a partner may hold on to his or her loving hope, because "the parents have talked to him (or her)", or "the elders have talked to him (or her)".

Does the Christian community support loving hope the same way? Is the love between Christian marriage partners so strong as to keep hoping to mend up however impossible the situation may, apparently have become?

Often love loses its heat very fast when it does not bear fruit in hope. Partners give up loving too soon. When love produces hope, this tenacious hope itself strengthens and urges the love further, because this innate hope of the lover expressed in various forms can easily move the person loved to have a change of heart. In this way loving hope can help heal even physical ailment, which may become hopeless.

Finally is a Christian community ready to sustain its loving hope in the change of heart of a member indefinitely or rather quick to excommunicate? This is a challenge. All the above virtues, when well mastered, lead to the inner capacity to endure whatever comes.

Love is ready to endure whatever comes

Our Lord's willingness to go all the way of love by accepting the worst humiliation on the cross is the loudest and greatest demonstration of love that is ready to endure whatever comes. Lastly, true love, which leads to personal fulfilment, is the love, which can endure insults, every malice from friends and those who always try to destroy. For the inner capacity for endurance enables the individual to accomplish what he wills to accomplish to self-satisfaction - therefore, as personal fulfilment (1 Pt.3: 8-12):

Finally, all of you have unity of spirit, sympathy, love of the brethren, a tender heart and a humble mind. Do not return evil for evil, or reviling for reviling; but on the contrary, bless, for to this you have been called that you may obtain a blessing. For "He that would love life and see good days; let him keep his tongue from evil and his lips from speaking guile; let him turn away from evil and do right; let him seek peace and pursue it. For the eyes of the Lord are upon the righteous and his eyes are open to their prayer.

This brings us to the end of our reflection on Love and fruits of love as challenge of authenticity, as well as our series of reflections on the indigenous African culture as challenge of authenticity of the Christian faith. By dwelling on love in the last reflection, I hope we shall now be able to develop and promote authentic Christian love, which requires a lot of courage to trust in a world of suspicion, to hope in a world of hopelessness, and to endure in a world of superficiality.

Thus we end our reflections, trusting that as you take further steps towards the fulfilment of your life's dreams these reflections would remain constant reference points when things become difficult, even impossible, as things certainly will become from time to time. May these reflections goad you on in facing the challenge of authenticity.

For the rest, I wish you every success and God's blessings. Now that our reflections have gone through thus far, let us thank the Lord, for his great love is without end. We close this reflection with: Eph %: 18-20

Be filled with the Spirit, addressing one another in psalms and hymns and spiritual songs, singing and making melody to the Lord with all your heart, always and for everything giving thanks in the name of our Lord Jesus Christ to God the Father.

General Conclusion

As I said at the beginning, the reflections on the various themes in this book have to maintain the original intent and form. That is a reflection on vocation, the response to the Word of God, as a challenge to authenticity in the context of the indigenous African culture.

To refresh your memory we have reflected on various aspects of our Christian faith as challenge of authenticity posed by our indigenous African culture: the Call of God in Christ (vocation), Society Today, the Church Today, Vocational Response, Pastoral Vocation, Meaning of Praying, Praying, Faith, Hope, Love and the Fruits of love.

Each reflection is against the background of the indigenous culture, especially religion, as posing a challenge.

If the reflections serve this original purpose then after reflecting through these pages you would be moved to ask yourself certain searching questions:

Has the Word as reflected upon truly challenged me to be true to myself as an indigenous African Christian?

Do I now discover certain positive elements in the indigenous African culture or religion, which challenge me to rethink my Christian faith in relation to my own life, my relationships, the society and the church or congregation? Do I now discover that certain values of the indigenous African culture, especially religion, can help discover the challenging implications of the cardinal virtues or values of the Christian faith: Faith, hope and love?

Or do you have only the usual feeling after reading through any book, even a novel: "This makes a nice reading!" However, if you sincerely experience a challenge of authenticity after reflecting on the themes on the pages above then the author is grateful that his efforts are worth it, so also your own time and energy devoted to the reflections.

If I may recommend further reflections, you could take any theme, or any text. But to strive after Christian or rather human perfection, "you must earnestly desire the higher gifts. And I will show you a still more excellent way" (I Cor12: 31), take the text or rather the hymn on love with you (1Cor.13: 4-7). With this text in your heart, in your words and actions, you are sure to be capable of enduring all things, and you are sure to be capable of facing all challenges of authenticity.

The challenge of authenticity is the challenge of being true to yourself. This is the challenge of the Gospel in the context of our indigenous African culture:

If you continue in my word, you are truly my disciples, and you will know the truth; and the truth will make you free! (John 8: 31- 32).

Suggested Further Reading

Biblical Passages
Citations are taken from: *The Holy Bible*, Revised Standard Version, Glasgow: Williams Collins Sons & Co. Ltd., 1973 Edition.

Old Testament

Genesis chapters 18 - 19

Exodus chapters 20 22

Psalms 50, 138 and 150

New Testament

Matthew: chapters 5-9 and 25
Mark: chapters 8 and 10
Luke: chapters 10- 12, and 22
John: chapters 8 and 16
Acts: Chapters 1 and 4
Romans: chapters 8-10
1Corinthians: chapters 3, 11 –15
2 Corinthians: chapters 12- 13
Ephesians: chapter 5
Galatians: chapter 5

Other Publications

Arewa, Caroline Shola 1999: Opening to the Spirit: Contacting the Healing Power of the Chakras and Honouring African Spirituality, (Aliso Viego: Thorson Publishers)

Diop; Cheikh Anta 1974: The African Origin of Civilisation: Myth or Reality, (tr. M.C., Chicago: Lawrence Hill)

DZOBO, Noah, 1972: "Moral Behaviour in Marriage Among the Anfoe-Ewes of Ghana and Togo" *(Unpublished Report), Cape Coast: University of Cape Coast)*
---------1975, "Introduction to the Indigenous Ethics of the Ewe of West Africa" in: *The Ogua Educator*, Vol. 6, No. 1: 82-97

Gyekye, Kwame 1997: *Political Corruption: A Philosophical Analysis of a Moral Problem,* (Accra: Sankofa Publishing)

Paris, Peter I. 1999: *The Spirituality of African Peoples: The Search for a Common Moral Discourse,* (Minneapolis: Fortress Press)
Ray, B. 1976: African Religions: Symbol, Ritual, and Community (Prentice   Hall: Englewood Cliffs.)

Index

African culture
  indigenous, viii, xi, xii, xiii, xiv, xviii, xix, xx, 25, 28, 35, 42, 60, 65, 66, 72, 107, 109, 111, 165, 166, 175, 193, 215, 220, 232
African way
  prayer, 107, 108, 109, 169
Africans, xiv, xv, 30, 41, 55, 64, 65, 69, 72, 73, 84, 96, 108, 109, 112, 114, 118, 120, 135, 140, 145, 147, 148, 169, 170, 175, 176, 177, 178, 179, 182, 221
Almighty, 29, 31, 58, 59, 69, 72, 98, 99, 137, 138, 139, 140, 141, 185, 216
ancestor, 28, 34
apostolate, xii, xiii, 35, 60, 61, 113, 158, 161, 163, 179, 221 153, 154, 161, 163, 166, 167, 168, 174, 175, 176, 178, 179, 180, 181, 182, 183, 184, 186, 189, 214, 215, 218, 219, 221, 224, 225, 227, 232
Authenticity, xiv, xvii, xix, xx, xxi, xxii, 23, 40, 54, 59, 62, 69, 71, 81, 82, 98, 104, 117, 134, 135, 165, 184

bond
  of love, xx, 41, 59, 152, 168, 169, 174, 177, 184, 185, 186, 213, 214, 218, 220, 223, 225, 228
Christianity, xxi, 30, 64, 138, 148

Church, xii, xiii, xiv, xv, xvi, xx, xxi, 41, 42, 52, 53, 54, 55, 56, 57, 59, 61, 62, 63, 65, 66, 67, 73, 76, 78, 83, 85, 86, 87, 88, 96, 105, 110, 118, 119, 120, 126, 127, 128, 129, 133, 134, 141, 147, 151, 165, 171, 172, 173, 174, 176, 177, 192
code
  of behaviour, 30, 34, 35, 42, 60, 70, 73, 117, 118, 166, 185, 193, 197, 202, 221, 226
commitment, viii, xi, xxi, 26, 31, 36, 37, 38, 39, 40, 41, 43, 46, 47, 52, 61, 62, 67, 77, 78, 82, 85, 87, 88, 99, 108, 109, 110, 111, 112, 113, 117, 118, 119, 120, 121, 122, 123, 126, 129, 131, 134, 140, 141, 142, 145, 146, 148, 150, 153, 154, 168, 174, 179, 184, 186, 227
communication, 23, 26, 98, 99, 100, 101, 102, 103, 104, 108
communion, xvii, xxii, 52, 56, 59, 113, 121, 169, 184, 185, 186, 213, 214, 216, 218, 220
community, xii, xvi, xviii, xxii, 25, 33, 38, 42, 52, 58, 59, 64, 76, 90, 96, 110, 111, 120, 121, 128, 129, 131, 133, 134, 142, 145, 152, 165, 167, 168, 169, 170, 179, 184, 185, 214, 215, 216, 217, 220, 221, 223, 224, 225, 228
consecration, xx, xxi, 70, 72, 73, 75, 85, 166
culture

deity, xix, xxi, 27, 28, 34, 40, 41, 72, 73, 104, 166
devotee, xx, 31, 55, 70, 166
dignity, 33, 50, 88, 90, 91, 95, 116, 137, 167, 182, 200, 201, 202, 203, 211, 212, 217, 219, 220, 221
discipleship, viii, xx, 45, 127, 173

enthusiasm, xxi, 135, 136, 150
errand-duty, 24, 26, 27, 34, 37, 69
evils, xx, 41, 42, 45, 54, 110

Faith, viii, xi, xii, xxi, 37, 116, 117, 123
family, x, xiv, 24, 28, 29, 41, 52, 64, 69, 135, 137, 140, 152, 154, 174, 213, 214, 221, 226, 228
function, xiii, xx, xxi, 24, 26, 29, 50, 85, 87, 88, 89, 90, 104, 105, 178

Holy Spirit, xi, 30, 61, 70, 86, 97, 102, 108, 128
Hope, xii, xxi, 135, 149, 150
human rights
 of the needy, 47, 48, 95, 182, 200, 201, 202
humankind, 58, 60, 69, 87, 116, 130, 137, 144, 145, 148, 149, 164, 168, 171, 172, 173, 174, 176, 177, 182

identity, 24, 26, 27, 28, 29, 30, 35, 36, 69, 84, 85, 88, 94, 104, 109, 154

image
 of the Spirit, xix, 28, 29, 34, 35, 55, 56, 57, 145, 146, 152, 153, 158, 188, 191, 219, 224
injunction, 24, 27, 42, 60, 96

James Brown, 137
joy, xi, 32, 97, 100, 124, 135, 136, 137, 138, 139, 140, 142, 144, 145, 172, 202, 209

kindness, 185, 188, 196, 197, 198, 199, 200, 201, 202, 203, 204, 205, 207, 208, 214

leader, xvi, 44, 51, 52, 57, 58, 76, 83, 84, 89, 90, 91, 92, 95, 100, 107, 109, 113, 177, 188, 190, 192, 195, 201, 216, 218, 219, 221, 224
leadership, xiii, 84, 91, 102, 120, 188, 192, 218, 226
Love, xii, xxi, xxii, 164, 165, 167, 168, 184, 188, 190, 192, 195, 213, 216, 219, 220, 222, 223, 224, 225, 226, 227, 229

marriage
 bond, 59, 73, 91, 119, 120, 152, 156, 157, 161, 172, 174, 177, 181, 183, 190, 216, 218, 220, 223, 226, 228
Martin Luther King, 74, 136, 137
martyrdom, 132
Ministry, xii, 163
music, xxi, 111, 135, 136, 137

name, 24, 27, 29, 31, 44, 48, 66, 68, 69, 99, 110, 123, 132, 141
Novices, 31, 124, 160

obedience, 49, 119, 120, 121, 128, 129, 130, 131, 132, 133, 134, 192

pastor, xv, 31, 38, 45, 50, 51, 52, 56, 58, 61, 66, 76, 80, 83, 84, 85, 86, 89, 90, 91, 92, 93, 99, 100, 104, 109, 112, 121, 126, 127, 150, 151, 152, 155, 156, 161, 163, 174, 177, 179, 190, 191, 192, 194, 198, 199, 212, 215, 216, 218, 221, 222
Pastoral, xiii, xx, 81, 82, 98
patience, 89, 156, 185, 187, 188, 189, 190, 191, 192, 193, 194, 195, 197, 204, 220, 221, 223, 224
Pentecost, xi, 36, 139, 142
possessed, 28, 30, 31, 35, 45, 55, 116, 145
possession, xix, 28, 30, 50, 79, 127
poverty
and hope, 43, 45, 46, 49, 116, 119, 120, 121, 139, 150, 151, 156, 207, 215
prayer, xix, xxi, 31, 49, 63, 86, 88, 89, 93, 97, 98, 99, 100, 101, 102, 103, 104, 105, 107, 108, 109, 110, 113, 114, 116, 132, 161, 226, 229
Priests
parish, xi, xiii, xv, 38, 87, 89, 127, 128, 133

principle, xvii, 51, 67, 92, 111, 112, 116, 120, 122, 123, 132, 167, 168, 179
Providence
divine, 123

reflection, xiii, xix, xx, xxi, xxii, 23, 31, 32, 33, 36, 37, 38, 39, 40, 41, 43, 53, 58, 59, 64, 65, 67, 69, 74, 82, 84, 89, 90, 93, 94, 96, 97, 98, 101, 103, 104, 112, 113, 116, 119, 120, 134, 135, 140, 164, 165, 178, 183, 184, 187, 188, 230, 231
relationships, xviii, 57, 59, 60, 140, 166, 171, 185, 214, 221, 227, 228
religion
African, xv, xxi, 28, 30, 34, 41, 42, 45, 56, 58, 60, 61, 65, 69, 72, 90, 99, 108, 114, 117, 122, 137, 138, 147, 148, 152, 166, 170, 175, 176, 181, 182, 227

response, viii, xiii, xiv, xviii, xx, 27, 28, 30, 32, 33, 67, 69, 71, 72, 73, 74, 75, 76, 79, 81, 82, 100, 101, 109, 112, 120, 123, 144, 178, 231
role model, 151, 152, 153, 154

sacred
as secret, 196, 197, 200, 201, 202, 203
secret, 57, 58, 59, 60, 66, 67, 72, 73, 111, 166, 185, 186, 220, 223, 224, 225
sacredness, 57, 59, 60, 166, 185, 213, 220, 223

sacrifice, xx, xxi, 67, 70, 76, 83,
  86, 98, 99, 103, 131, 169
scandals, 55, 61, 65, 140, 165
self-fulfilment, viii, xiii, xviii,
  33, 48, 64, 73, 79, 92, 122,
  169
Seminarians, ix, xiii, 31, 36,
  124, 127, 128, 129, 131, 160,
  180, 193
sharing, 38, 65, 123, 125, 127,
  131, 198, 204, 205, 206, 207,
  208, 209, 211, 213, 214, 215,
  219
sincerity
  of spirit, xi, xxi, 36, 100, 108,
    136, 141, 225, 227
solidarity, xx, xxii, 41, 169,
  184, 185, 186, 213, 214, 218,
  223
spontaneity, xi, xxi, 104, 107,
  108, 135, 136

trance, 28, 31, 42, 73, 104, 108,
  109

union
  mystical, 184

virtues, xii, 71, 80, 118, 119,
  142, 146, 148, 169, 170, 185,
  187, 188
vocation, xi, xii, xiii, xviii, xix,
  24, 26, 27, 31, 32, 33, 36, 37,
  38, 39, 41, 44, 46, 50, 51, 53,
  54, 62, 67, 72, 74, 75, 76, 77,
  78, 80, 81, 82, 85, 87, 88, 89,
  90, 92, 93, 94, 96, 97, 98, 99,
  101, 121, 122, 124, 129, 130,
  131, 134, 141, 158, 161, 168,
  175, 176, 212, 221, 231
Vocation, xii, xiii, xx, 24, 40,
  81, 82, 98
voice
  prophetic, xx, 41, 43, 45, 46,
    91, 94, 95, 96, 155, 162,
    178, 179
Voodoo, xvii, xx, 28, 31, 34,
  51, 55, 64, 70, 72
vows, xiii, 37, 71, 88, 95, 119,
  120, 128, 134, 140, 158, 166,
  176

Yewe, xvii, xx, 28, 34, 51, 55,
  70, 72

Other Books by Adonis & Abbey include:

Broken Dreams (Fiction/Town Crier Series 1)
By Jideofor Adibe

Wooden Gongs and Drumbeats
African Folktales, Proverbs and Idioms
(Fiction/Town Crier Series 2)
By Dahi Chris Onuchukwu

The Making of the Africa-Nation
Pan-Africanism and the African Renaissance
(politics/political economy/history)
Edited by Mammo Muchie

Nigeria and the Politics of Unreason
A Study of the Obasanjo Regime
Politics/Political Economy
ByVictor E.Dike

Ordering this Book

*Wholesale inquiries for this book should be directed to any of the following:

Wholesale inquiries in the UK and Europe should be directed to one of the following:

Bertram, The Book Wholesaler:

+44 1603216 666: email: orders@bertrams.com

Gardners Books Ltd

+44 1323 521777: email: custcare@gardners.com

In the USA, wholesale inquiries should be directed to one of the following:

Ingram Book Company (ordering)

+1 800 937 8000 website: www.ingrambookgroup.com

Baker & Taylor (General and sales information)

+1-800-775-3700 Email: btinfo@btol.com

*Online Retail Distribution: www.amazon.co.uk, www.amazon.com

*Shop Retail: Ask any good bookshop or contact our office:
http//: www.adonis-abbey.com
Phone: +(44) 020 7793 8893

www.ingramcontent.com/pod-product-compliance
Lightning Source LLC
Chambersburg PA
CBHW020752160426
43192CB00006B/311